CURRENTS OF ENCOUNTER

Studies on the Contact between Christianity and Other Religions, Beliefs, and Cultures

Dialogue and Syncretism

An Interdisciplinary Approach

Edited by

Jerald Gort, Hendrik Vroom,
Rein Fernhout, and Anton Wessels

WILLIAM B. EERDMANS PUBLISHING COMPANY
GRAND RAPIDS, MICHIGAN

EDITIONS RODOPI, AMSTERDAM

This edition first published jointly 1989 by Wm. B. Eerdmans Publishing Co. and Editions Rodopi, Amsterdam.

Printed in the United States of America

Library of Congress Cataloging-in-Publication Data

Dialogue and syncretism : an interdisciplinary approach /
edited by Jerald Gort . . . [et al.].
p. cm. —
(Currents of encounter : studies on the contact between Christianity
and other religions, beliefs, and cultures)
ISBN 0-8028-0501-9
1. Religions—Relations. 2. Dialogue—Religious aspects.
3. Syncretism (Religion) 4. Christianity and other religions.
I. Gort, Jerald D. II. Series: Currents of encounter.
BL410.D52 1989
261.2—dc20 89-39187
CIP

CONTENTS

FOREWORD

The publication in hand represents the inaugural volume of a new series entitled **Currents of Encounter: Studies on the Contact between Christianity and Other Religions, Beliefs, and Cultures.** The idea for the series emerged from recent discussions within an interuniversity and interdisciplinary research group which meets at regular intervals at the Theological Faculty of the Free University of Amsterdam and of which the general editors are members.

This initial volume, ***Dialogue and Syncretism: An Interdisciplinary Approach,*** consists of seventeen essays originally presented as papers by an international panel of experts at a small symposium on dialogue and syncretism held in May 1988 at the Free University under the auspices of the research group referred to above.

In an article written in 1954[1] the great Dutch missiologist Hendrik Kraemer observed that even though one could see "in the history of mankind many patterns and varieties of 'syncretism'" which "appear as an inevitable result" of "genuine 'culture-contact,'" Christians did not generally conceive of syncretism in positive terms. Particularly in Christian missionary circles the notion of syncretism had come to assume "a largely pejorative character. It became a term of abhorrence" (p. 254). In the words of the title of Kraemer's essay, 'syncretism' came to be viewed "as a religious and missionary problem." And indeed, this perception has undergone very little alteration since then.

For large numbers, probably even the majority of present-day Christians 'syncretism,' as concept, continues to have strongly negative connotations and, as potential outcome of the encounter between Christianity and other faiths, is to be rejected out of hand. Moreover, there are those who are deeply concerned about the current ecumenical emphasis on interreligious dialogue. Such dialogue, they believe, will lead ineluctably to syncretism. But what does 'syncretism' really mean? Is it always to be understood as a purely negative phenomenon? Is it possible to adduce legitimate forms, valid instances of 'syncretism'? Furthermore, is it true that dialogue must of necessity produce syncretism understood *in malam partem?* The present volume seeks to address these and similar questions.

Part One contains studies dealing with various approaches to the phenomena of dialogue and syncretism.

In the introductory essay **André Droogers** makes an attempt to clarify the meaning of 'syncretism.' After surveying the discussions that have taken place between missiologists and students of comparative religion on this matter, he offers his own definition of syncretism.

[1] Hendrik Kraemer, "Syncretism as a Religious and a Missionary Problem," *International Review of Missions*, 43 (July 1954): 253-273.

Hendrik Vroom approaches the question of syncretism from the point of view of the logic of religious conviction. Foreign beliefs and practices can be incorporated into a particular religious tradition as long as they do not threaten its continuity and logical integrity.

Jerald Gort traces the historical development of the Christian church's attitude toward other religions. From the third century until recent times Christian thinking with regard to the world around it was almost wholly informed by fears of syncretism. Today there is clear evidence of greater openness among Christians toward other forms of religiosity.

Christians have often been led to oppose syncretism by a desire to preserve the purity of the gospel message, a concern to remain true to the Word of God as contained in Holy Scripture. **Anton Wessels** points out, however, that processes of interreligious penetration were already in play at the level of biblical origins.

Rein Fernhout compares the ways in which newer religions traditions, basing themselves on their scriptures, evaluate the holy books of older traditions. He contends that application of the scientific method of analysis to holy scriptures often results in a serious relativization of their constitutive religious truth claims.

It is often assumed that the meaning of 'dialogue' is clearer than that of 'syncretism.' **Maurice Friedman** argues that the concept of dialogue requires constant careful analysis. He makes a case for a 'dialogue of touchstones' that aims at a sharing of deep religious intuitions.

Part Two consists of a number of case studies of interreligious encounter and syncretism.

Hans Daiber describes the way in which the 10th century Muslim philosopher Abū Ḥātim ar-Rāzī attempted to account for and deal with the phenomenon of religious diversity.

Harold Turner offers an analysis of new religious movements in Western cultures. He demonstrates that many of them have adopted beliefs and practices stemming from Indian religious traditions.

Matthew Schoffeleers deals with the contextualization of Christianity in Southern Africa, which has yielded two distinct types of theology with apparently contradictory aims: the one concerned with the cultivation of 'syncretistic' interrelationships with traditional African culture, the other with the realization of human liberation and social justice.

Tilmann Vetter undertakes an examination of the line of thought laid down in John B. Cobb's book, *Beyond Dialogue.* On the basis of this analysis and against the background of his study of early Buddhism and the Kyoto School Vetter breaks a lance for a dialogue of mutual transformation.

Jacques Kamstra describes the phenomenon of multiple religious participation in Japan. To many Western observers this represents a clear example of syncretism. Kamstra demurs to this negative characterization of what he avers is far more properly termed: the Japanese way of life.

Walter Strolz furnishes an explication of the main lines of R. Pannikar's theological and philosophical approach to Hinduism and poses a number of critical questions with respect to certain aspects of Pannikar's thought.

Richard De Smet makes a critical comparison between the Hindu concept of *avatāra* and the Christian notion of incarnation. In some ways these two phenomena are analogous and in others quite dissimilar.

David Krieger examines the perceptions of salvation found in Hinduism and compares them with Christian understandings of God's saving purposes and actions. Krieger attempts to formulate a preliminary answer to the question as to what Christian theology could learn from these Hindu insights.

Reender Kranenborg's essay treats of the growing interest evidenced by some Christians in the concept of reincarnation. Would incorporation of reincarnation into Christianity represent an acceptable form of syncretism or a contradiction of essential Christian beliefs?

Corstiaan van den Burg calls attention to a Western form of Indian religion: Surinamese Hinduism in the Netherlands. Van den Burg outlines the ways in which the beliefs and practices of this religion have been adapted within secularized, post-Christian Dutch culture.

In Part Three, the concluding section of this volume, **Dirk Mulder** attempts to round out the design of the symposium by recapitulating, enlarging upon, and tying together some of the main issues raised in the discussions.

It became plainly evident during the course of this symposium that the approaches to and the assessments of its theme varied considerably depending on the participants' disciplinary point of view. The presuppositions and concerns of the missiologist, it was clear, differ from those of the cultural anthropologist; the assumptions and methods of the philosopher are not identical to those of the student of comparative religion. This does not imply, however, that the reflection of this mixed workshop was doomed to failure at the outset or proved in the end to be pointless. On the contrary, one of the most important overarching conclusions that can be drawn from this collective study is that the interdisciplinary avenue provides the best means of access to a proper understanding and valuation of religious beliefs and practices. An exclusively positivist description of religious processes can in no way take account of what is really at stake in religion. A normative theological, missiological, or philosophical assessment of religious phenomena which ignores the empirical, historical, and philological facts is bound to go astray. To those who took part in the symposium the interdisciplinary approach to 'dialogue' and 'syncretism' proved eminently meaningful and worthwhile. We hope this volume will help the reader to gain insight into the complexities of its themes and to arrive at answers to some of the questions raised in it.

The editors wish to express their deep gratitude to two graduate scholars of the Free University, without whose countless hours of dedicated labor and invaluable advice and support this volume quite simply could never have appeared. **John Rebel,** student of theology, translated several of the essays from either German or Dutch into English,[2] did some initial editing of the texts and prepared a camera-ready manuscript of the present book. Only he himself and the editors are aware of the severe technical problems, relating particularly to incompatible and inadequate computer facilities, that he had to face and overcome. **John Medendorp,** student of theology, carried out the final editing of the texts. His fine eye for style and careful attention to detail have contributed conspicuously to the readability of this publication. The close reader will immediately recognize the type and number of editorial problems and complexities he had to deal with. Final responsibility for the text lies of course with the editors of the series and this volume; the efforts of Rebel and Medendorp have made it possible for them to assume this responsibility with confidence.

Finally, we would like to voice our great appreciation to the publishers of this series, Editions Rodopi in Amsterdam and Wm. B. Eerdmans in Grand Rapids, for their kind willingness to cooperate with us in this joint venture. They have given us a great deal of encouragement, generous support, and all the freedom we could wish for. For this we thank them most warmly.

The Editors

Jerald Gort
Hendrik Vroom
Rein Fernhout
Anton Wessels

---

[2] Translations of citations within the articles in this volume are the responsibility of the author involved unless otherwise indicated. In such instances the [published] source has been referred to within square brackets to indicate that it is an unpublished translation.

PART I

APPROACHES
to
Dialogue and Syncretism

Chapter 1

Syncretism: The Problem of Definition, the Definition of the Problem

André Droogers

Although syncretism is a confusing concept, this article recommends it not be abandoned, but that its many meanings be outlined. The article summarizes debate on the term, and presents an inventory of options open to the scholar who wishes to define syncretism. In order to provide fresh impulses to the debate, four suggestions are offered.
First, the distinction between subjective and objective definitions is tempered. The author discusses his own subjectivity in the epilogue.
Second, the role of power relations in the rise of syncretism and in polemics against it is emphasized.
Third, it recommends viewing syncretism as a means of transforming religious symbolic systems.
Fourth, an attempt is made at bringing unchallenged as well as controversial syncretism together into one definition.

1. Introduction

Syncretism is a tricky term. Its main difficulty is that it is used with both an objective and a subjective meaning. The basic objective meaning refers neutrally and descriptively to the mixing of religions. The subjective meaning includes an evaluation of such intermingling from the point of view of one of the religions involved. As a rule, the mixing of religions is condemned in this evaluation as violating the essence of the belief system. Yet, as we will see, a positive subjective definition also belongs to the possibilities.

This confusion of meanings has motivated scholars to propose the abolition of the term. Yet, the term is so widely used that even a scholarly consensus to do away with it would not lead to a general moratorium on its use. Its abandonment is the more improbable when one considers that the number of contacts between believers of different religions increases daily, and with that, the phenomenon referred to by the term 'syncretism,' in all senses of the word. In the discussion on interreligious dialogue the term would continue to be used in any case, particularly by those who are opposed to such an endeavour and who constantly warn against the danger of syncretism (in the negative subjective sense). Moreover, those seeking contextualization may use it in a positive and sometimes almost proud and defiant sense, especially in concrete situations in the Third World.

In this article, I will therefore suggest that it would be unwise to try to discard the term inspite of the pitfalls involved in working with the concept. Since the term is not likely to disappear, it is better to confront these problems head on. Besides, the debate on the meaning of syncretism is too interesting and promising to be tabled merely because of terminological confusion. In the second section of the paper, this debate will be summarized as it has developed to date. Next (§ 3), an inventory of available options for defining syncretism will be given.

In the remainder of the paper, four suggestions will be made with a view to providing fresh impulses to the debate on syncretism. First, it will be maintained that the distinction between the objective and subjective definitions of this concept is not that absolute. Definitions that are apparently objective will be shown to contain subjective echoes (§ 4).

In the second place, emphasis is put on the importance of relations of power to the production of religion, including syncretism and the struggle against it. In connection with this issue, an interdisciplinary approach will be followed, integrating contributions from the sociology and the anthropology of religion (§ 5).

The third suggestion points to a further contribution the social scientific approach could make to the debate on syncretism. Within anthropology, recent work has concentrated on symbolic systems. These new insights might well be applied to the matter of syncretism. Syncretism will then be viewed as a means of transforming religious symbolic systems. It would be worthwhile to examine the link between changes in symbolic systems on the one hand, and relations of power in the production of religion on the other (§ 6).

Finally, it will be argued that 'syncretism' cannot be defined in either exclusively objective ('religious intermingling') or purely subjective ('illegitimate mixing' or —less frequently— 'legitimate mixing') terms. The concept refers rather to *both* unquestioned *and* controversial interpenetration of religions. On the one hand, much syncretism goes unnoticed, specifically when the intermingling takes place in such a way that the basic insights of the religions involved are left untouched. On the other hand, the *controversy* within a religion on the acceptability of syncretism should not be left out of the definition of the concept (§ 7). In an epilogue, the author's subjectivity will be discussed (§ 8).

2. The changing meaning of the term

In the course of history, even before students of religion started to use the term, the concept of syncretism went through various changes in meaning.[1] The oldest known use of the term is found in Plutarch, and refers to the inhabitants of Crete, who, in facing a common enemy, overcame their differences of opinion and temporarily joined forces. Much later Erasmus spoke of syncretism as a positive union of seemingly disparate points of view. In the 17th century, the notion took on a negative character and came to refer to the illegitimate reconciliation of opposing theological views. Syncretism, thus, became a polemical term employed to defend true religion against heresy. The distinction between an objective and a subjective definition of the concept has obvious roots in history.

From the second half of the 19th century on, there was a tendency within the History of Religions approach to objectify the term by applying it to early Christianity as well. Syncretism was shown to be present in the earliest forms of Christianity. Nevertheless, as Rudolph (pp. 196-97) has pointed out, it retained its negative meaning, denoting a deviation from original purity, and often being used to designate sect-like groups.

The first scholar to have dealt at length with the concept of syncretism is G. van der Leeuw. At one point in his book, he confined the term syncretism to the movement from anonymous polydemonism to personal polytheism (p. 186, 636). At another point, however, he broadened this definition, considering all religions syncretic on the grounds that they all combine various forms, or *Gestalten* (p. 692, quoting J. Wach). Van der Leeuw introduced the concept of *Verschiebung*, or transposition, as basic to syncretism (p. 693). This refers to changes in meaning where the form remains constant. He explicitly maintained that missions almost inevitably lead to syncretism (p. 694ff.).

Another Dutch author who has had wide influence on the development of the debate in question is H. Kraemer.[2] Though recognizing that all religions are syncretistic (1937: 7), he located the roots of syncretism in the monistic —and therefore relativizing— religions, as opposed to the prophetic religions (1937: 18-23). Monistic belief systems —such as 'primitive' religions— are naturalistic. They are auto-soteriological in character. Kraemer allowed for a type of inevitable, unconscious syncretism,

[1] Colpe 1987: 218-19; Kamstra 1970: 8-10; 1985: 210-12; Kraemer 1938: 200-11; 1956: 392-94; 1962; Rudolph 1979: 194-96.

[2] H. Kraemer 1937; 1938; 1956; 1962.

which occurs in intercultural contact. But this kind of syncretism, to which Christianity has also been subject, and which includes the naive syncretism of popular religion, is different from the conscious syncretism of religious elites. The latter is grounded in monism and is not permitted by prophetic religion.

In the introductory chapter to a collection of studies by Scandinavian scholars on syncretism (Hartman), H. Ringgren defined syncretism simply as "any mixture of two or more religions" (p. 7), suggesting that "elements from several religions are merged and influence each other mutually" (p. 7). He also presented a number of general observations on the conditions under which syncretism occurs, on interreligious encounter, on the nature of the result of syncretism, and on the psychological factors which may influence the process of syncretism.

The third Dutch scholar who has contributed significantly to the debate is J. H. Kamstra.[3] He pointed to the theological bias in Kraemer's view (1970: 16-25), and suggested an objective approach, stressing that syncretism must be seen as a general human trait, and that it is consequently present in all religions, including Christianity (1970: 23). Religious knowledge is always partial; language and situation limit people's understanding. This leads to syncretism, which Kamstra defined as "the coexistence of elements foreign to each other within a specific religion, whether or not these elements originate in other religions or for example in social structures" (1970: 9-10; Pye's tr., 83). Interestingly, Kamstra mentioned the possibility of syncretism *within* a religion and not just in contact *between* religions (1970: 27). According to him, the criterion in both cases is alienation (*'vervreemding,'* 1970: 27). In later publications (1975; 1985), Kamstra offered a typology of syncretistic religions, and adopted the distinction between conscious and unconscious syncretism. He spoke of amalgamation and identification as extreme forms of syncretism, with assimilation and symbiosis as intermediate forms of transition between these extremes (1985: 217). In the article included in this volume, Kamstra rejects the use of the term for the Japanese situation.

The ideas put forward in his 1970 lectures (Kamstra 1970) have been summarized by M. Pye, thus making them available to readers outside the Netherlands. At the same time, he criticized Kamstra. In Pye's view, the fact that Kamstra takes Kraemer as his starting point, even though criticizing him, held him within the constraints of the theological view (Pye, 85). Kamstra, as we saw, had emphasized man's inability to know totally. Pye qualified this as a theological statement, pointing to Kamstra's citation of the apostle Paul as additional grounds. Furthermore, Pye took Kamstra to task for using alienation as a key concept. To Pye the word is reminiscent of prophetic religions. It also implicitly confirms the view that religions are threatened by syncretism, either from within or without.

[3] Jacques H. Kamstra 1970; 1975; 1984; 1985.

To Pye, however, it would also be possible to speak of syncretism "*towards* without" (Pye, 87, his italics), which excludes alienation. Another criticism Pye addresses to Kamstra is his neglect of the role of meaning in syncretism. At this point Pye suggests ambiguity, instead of alienation as a criterion for syncretism. The same element may bear two different meanings at the same time. Syncretism is defined as "the temporary ambiguous coexistence of elements from diverse religious and other contexts within a coherent religious pattern" (p. 93). To overcome this ambiguity, there are at least three possibilities (p. 92) one meaning is eliminated (assimilation), a new coherent pattern of meaning is attained (a new religion), or the two meanings drift apart (dissolution).

Like Kamstra, R. D. Baird took Kraemer as his starting point, whom he criticizes for both implying and excluding that Christianity is syncretistic (1970: 142-52). In Baird's view, the concept is too confused and lacks precise definition. According to him, it is of no use to distinguish between conscious and unconscious syncretism, because what really counts is the resulting synthesis. It is a universal phenomenon; the term is not specific enough to be used for historical research. Borrowing and blending are a normal part of history. In this context, therefore, the term syncretism is superfluous and should be dropped. Having excluded the use of the term syncretism in the sense of a new harmony, Baird nevertheless considered reserving the term for "cases where two conflicting ideas or practices are brought together and are retained without the benefit of consistency" (p. 147). In that sense, he thought the term might be used to indicate a theological phenomenon. But even that solution is problematical because the category was not coined by believers: nobody describes his own religion as syncretistic. Believers only use the word in the encounter with other religions, describing the other's religion as inconsistent.

C. Colpe (1975; 1979; 1987) has no qualms about using the term. To him there are three "structural laws" governing syncretism (1975: 17ff.): the previous autonomy of components brought together in syncretism; a balance between autonomy and integration; and a certain guarantee of historical continuity. Colpe distinguished between three kinds of links between elements thus related, symbiosis, acculturation, and identification (1975: 21-23). He also pointed to the kind of relation obtaining between the religions which are in contact. This relation may be either symmetrical or asymmetrical. Furthermore, he stressed that cultural contact does not necessarily imply syncretism, and that syncretism is possible without cultural contact (1975: 25-28). Colpe saw syncretism as an initially critical concept, which is now being transformed into a category of "historico-genetic explanation" for the antecedents of a religious situation (1987: 219).

Another German contribution to the debate comes from U. Berner (1978), who, like Ringgren, discussed the term in the first chapter of a collection of case studies on syncretistic phenomena (Wiessner 1978). His goal was to offer a heuristic model. He based this model on the concept of system, as used by N. Luhmann. Religions are systems, with a certain function, composed of elements also serving specific functions. These systems, when in contact, may threaten each other's functioning. Syncretism is one of the possible reactions to such a confrontation. It strives to diminish the insecurity by dissolving the boundaries between the systems, thus ending competition. Defined in this way, syncretism is a process. The word is not meant to be applied to only one religion, but always to religions in contact. Berner suggested that this approach allows for a study of syncretism at the level of systems as well as on that of elements. Emphasizing that he was not using religious terms, he then developed a complex terminology for each of three levels: that of systems, that of elements, and that of meta-language (the researcher's terms, as distinguished from the terms of those being researched). With this model, Berner wanted to avoid metaphorical language. According to him, the phenomenology of religion is in great need of an independent, generally applicable terminology. To him, the answer is to be found in the concept of system. Thus, he intimated, the danger of ideological bias would be avoided.

K. Rudolph has summarized —in more detail than could be done here— what previous authors have contributed to the debate on syncretism (1979). In addition, he has presented his own view on the problem. His conclusion (pp. 206-10) from a survey of the literature is that syncretism is becoming a relatively value-free concept which, however, is still in need of a clear typology, and which has not yet been defined satisfactorily, except in terms of dynamic nature. Syncretism is generally seen as mixing of religions, and it is widely accepted that no religion, except the most isolated, is free of syncretism, both in respect to its origin and to its subsequent history. Syncretism presupposes encounter and confrontation. As a first distinction, still to be refined, Rudolph accepts the contrast between unconscious and conscious syncretism. He stresses the relation between syncretism and social stratification, especially between "priests, theologians, mythologians" (p. 208) on the one hand, and the mass of believers on the other. In this context he refers to Redfield's concepts of great and little traditions. The little tradition coincides with the popular and unconscious form of syncretism. Colpe's terms are adopted by Rudolph and expanded. This leads to a series of terms: symbiosis, amalgamation, identification, metamorphosis, dissolution. The outcome of syncretism will also depend on the political constellation and on possible resistance to domination. Rudolph suggests that, instead of transposition, alienation or ambiguity, *"Verschränkung"* (crossing) is essential to syncretism (p. 210).

All the authors discussed so far had the intention of presenting an objective definition of syncretism, even though some, as we have seen, were criticized for being too theological and subjective in their approach. Christian theologians have approached syncretism in various ways, depending on their theological evaluation of other religions. I cannot do justice to all the views expressed, but want to mention three authors who have been widely read. W. A. Visser 't Hooft (1963; see also Mulder 1986) has emphatically warned against syncretism as a constructed fusion of religions. To him this was a threat to Christianity. Similar warnings have been expressed by G. Thils on the part of Catholics (1967).

W. Pannenberg (pp. 85-88, esp. note 37) has shown that syncretism is present within Christianity and has suggested that it might even be seen as a positive characteristic, because it is the way in which the universal Christian message incarnates within other cultures (see also Thomas). Christian faith may be enriched in contact with other cultures by the influence and the challenging questions which come from them. Pannenberg shows that a subjective definition of syncretism need not always be negative.

3. The options available

The preceding summary of interpretations of the term syncretism may be complemented by a thematic list of those aspects which may be included in a definition. This serves not only to foster awareness of the options one faces in defining syncretism but also to make more explicit the ambiguity of the concept.

The first option has already been mentioned. Should syncretism be an *objective,* neutral, merely descriptive term, or is it a *subjective* concept, normative in its negative or —less often so— positive evaluation of religious mixing? As was clear from Kamstra's and Baird's criticism of Kraemer, and also from Pye's comments on Kamstra, it is not easy to be objective. In the next section, I will return to this issue. On the other hand, a normative definition also has its problems, since the criterion as to what is objectionable (or acceptable) is not easily formulated.

Another option regards the question as to *what* it is that is being mixed. The simplest answer is: two religions. But other ingredients may be included in what an author calls syncretism. Thus syncretism may occur between currents of one religion, between a religion and an ideology, between religion and science, and between religion and culture.

One must also chose between syncretism as the *process* of religious interpenetration, or as the *result* of such a process, or a combination of both. When one speaks of a 'syncretistic religion,' this may mean a religion which is the result of a period of religious encounter. But the term may also refer to an extremely tolerant and permanently absorbent religion, ready to adopt and adapt whatever may present itself. One could therefore ask whether syncretism is a temporary or a permanent phenomenon. There is accordingly some confusion with regard to elements considered to be contradictory or ambiguous: are they to be called

syncretism is a process, not result.

syncretic only as long as the contradiction remains, or also if a new synthesis occurs through a change in meaning?

As we have seen, various authors have proposed a typology of syncretic phenomena, including amalgamation, symbiosis, assimilation, identification, coherence, dissolution, etc. Rudolph lists sixteen such terms (p. 207). These may refer not only to types of syncretism, but also to phases in the course of the process, as well as to the final result.

Since syncretism has often been seen as a deviation from the original purity of a religion, one option arises from the question of whether syncretism may occur at the *origin* or foundation of a religion, or whether it must be used only to indicate a *later threat* to the initial pure version. A negative subjective definition tends to stress the original purity, whereas an objective definition may show how a religion was already a merging of elements from other religions at the outset.

A topic discussed by various authors referred to above, is the question of the *symmetry* or *asymmetry* present in the relationships between religions. Are the two (or more) religions in contact being mutually influenced, or is one religion dominant? Is one to adopt the perspective of the receiving religion or of the giving religion, or both? Or are both giving and receiving? A subjective definition is obviously formulated from the standpoint of the religion which is subject to the impact of another religion. Objective definitions may be broader in perspective, but, as we shall see shortly, not necessarily so.

Finally, the distinction between *conscious* and *unconscious* syncretism should be recalled. In other words, the option is between explicit, constructed, reflected, and often intellectual syncretism on the one hand, and implicit, spontaneous, relatively unreflective, popular syncretism on the other.

I will conclude this section by pointing to a similarity between the definitions of syncretism and religion. Both objective and normative definitions of religion exist. Some definitions of religion allow for ideological, philosophical, and cultural elements to be included. Religion has been defined both as a process and as a result. It may emerge as a newly founded, explicitly constructed institution, just as it may appear in a gradual, spontaneous, anonymous, popular way. Moreover, the distinction between functional and substantial definitions of religion, stressing either what religion *does* or what it *is,* might also be applied to definitions of syncretism. What is, for example, the use of ambivalence in syncretism? Or what is characteristic of the elements brought together in a syncretic pattern?

4. The possible subjectivity of objective definitions

There are three points at which the concepts employed by students of religion when defining syncretism may be correlated with the stumbling blocks at issue in theological definitions.

The first correlation is based on the conception among students of religion that cohesion and integration are normal, and consequently that any deviation or contradiction is abnormal and even inferior. This view is comparable to that of orthodox clergy. Syncretism is then a temporal phenomenon, an ambiguity which sooner or later will lead to a new synthesis — or to dissolution. This may mean that the initial stage of the history of that religion is seen as one of purity and homogeneity, setting the norm which is afterwards threatened by syncretism. In this way the possible role of syncretism in the founding phase of that same religion is ignored.

Second, the context in which syncretism takes place may be narrowed to one religion only, even though two or more religions are involved. This also happens to coincide with clerical interest and perspective. There seems to be less interest in looking at syncretism from the point of view of the influencing religion. Syncretism "towards without" (Pye, 87) is often overlooked. Even less attention is paid to the believers positioned between religions, who, unlike the clergy, perhaps no longer identify themselves with one particular religion.

The third aspect is the emphasis on the doctrinal and the official, a point also made by Kamstra (1984). Students of religion, especially when they work with texts written by the theological elite of a religion, may develop a blind spot for the practical and the popular in a religion. Their main interest then is to systematize the cerebral side of religion, often presented as the only side or the representative side. The popular side —though majoritarian— is viewed as a less interesting deviation from it. Consequently, syncretism has often been seen as doctrinal contradiction. Here again we touch on a coincidence of clerical and academic foci. Yet, from the popular point of view the doctrinaire worries of the clergy might be seen with equal right as a deviation from the 'normal,' i.e. the practical.

If these observations are valid, one wonders if students of religion might ever have spoken of syncretism without the clergy being worried about the phenomenon, just as one may wonder whether syncretism would exist if there were no clergy.

In pointing out the subjective side to objectively intended definitions, I do not wish to criticize subjectivism. My only intention is to show that perfect objectivity is impossible. In order to make my own subjectivity more explicit, I will return to this problem in the epilogue.

5. Syncretism and power

An almost decisive factor determining the reaction of a religion to syncretism (in the objective sense), is the concept of truth prevailing in that religion. In situations of contact, exclusivist claims will give rise to accusations of syncretism (in the negative subjective sense) as their necessary complement.

The exclusive claims are often maintained by a class of religious specialists who monopolize, with more or less success, the definition of truth, and spend a lot of time eliminating possible contradictions and oppositions (Bourdieu 1971). If, as normally happens, a popular religion succeeds in maintaining itself next to the official religion, this is a symptom of the clergy's power being less effective in maintaining exclusive access to the production of religion. Of course there are also situations in which the reverse occurs: a conservative laity may frustrate any effort of progressive clergy to facilitate lay access to religious production.

The attitude of the clergy will almost always be justified 'in the name of the truth,' out of love and respect for it, treating it as a separate court of appeal, as though it were a revealed ultimate meaning. Yet this disinterested attitude of the clergy does not exclude the existence of power relations.

If power is defined as the capacity to influence other people's behaviour, syncretism has a power dimension to it. In its negative subjective form, it presupposes an asymmetrical relationship. The clergy may legitimate its own power in religious terms. In addition, it is possible that the power of secular authorities is also justified religiously. In return, the religious elite may receive secular help in the struggle against all those who produce religion in their own way, without the consent of the clergy and in contradiction to official religion. As Baird observed, syncretists rarely call themselves by that name. Syncretists are always the others. They may be lay people but can also be members of the lower clergy.

When the social context involves cultural plurality, the power struggle may be not just between clergy and laity, or higher and lower clergy, but between different cultures. Official religion, whether imported or indigenous, almost always acts as a dominant cultural factor.

Situations of contact frequently produce conflicts. In that case too, the religious debate on syncretism is not just of a religious nature. The symbols used in syncretism may represent the affliction people experience at that very moment. Syncretism, then, may be viewed as an expression of protest, against clerical *and* secular authorities for example.

It is interesting that the difficulty inherent in the concept of syncretism, viz. that it has a pejorative connotation, is also present in two other terms used by religious elites to oppose unauthorized religious production: magic and sect. Thus relations of power indirectly influence the vocabulary adopted in the study of religion. It is therefore all the more surprising that in the study of religion this power dimension often remains unnoticed. Yet labels like syncretism, magic, and sect are used in describing popular, i.e., lower class religion.

It is ironic that the Old Testament struggle against syncretism, which coincided with the propagation of a central cult and political unity, has indirectly, through Christian theology, nourished, academic interest in the phenomenon of syncretism.

It is even more ironic that phenomenologists of religion basically think like syncretists: comparing religions and emphasizing the common characteristics over and against the differences. In that sense, these students of religion are much closer to the popular masses of religious traditions than to the religious elites most of them have preferred to research.

On the other extreme, when considering the attitude of religious traditions towards truth and syncretism, we run across religions which accept that there are numerous ways to knowledge of the truth. This kind of religion will perhaps not even have a term comparable to syncretism. It may instead employ a term, absent in religions with a negative view of syncretism, whose meaning is the opposite of the negative subjective definition. Contradictions may be hailed and cultivated as paradoxes. Other religions will not be seen as competitors, but as welcome and legitimate routes to the sacred and to salvation. The opposition is not between true and false, but between good, better, and best. The lack of rigid, exclusive, doctrinaire orthodoxy may be accompanied by a practical interest, closely related to that of popular religion. Syncretism —in the negative sense— is simply not an issue.

To argue that power is a dimension of syncretism is one thing; interpreting relations of power is another. Within the social sciences various models, have been presented. Two categories of model will be discussed in this section.

Without going into much detail, we might say that a first category, consisting of functionalist models, interprets power processes as tending ultimately towards a situation of relative equilibrium. Cohesion is normal, since society cannot survive without order. If tensions arise, a complicated process of give and take will lead to a new phase of order.

A functionalist interpretation of syncretism will stress its function as a manner of overcoming ethnic or cultural contradictions, and as a new synthesis which will serve as a basis for cohesion. It should be recalled that one of the options in defining syncretism was an emphasis on cohesion as being normal. The functionalist preference is clearly for that pole. Thus, the role of syncretism as a new synthesis will be emphasized in nation-building. It guarantees a new national identity for a new social context.

In the second category, which consists of Marxist models, the story is told in a different way. Not cohesion, but conflict is viewed as normal. Syncretism is then not a useful functional mechanism in the transition to a new order, representing a new compromise between opposing powers. Instead, being a *contradiction*, it is an expression of conflicting interests, including protest against dominant religious and secular power. As a *synthesis*, syncretism is interpreted as an instrument of oppression, creating a false unity and hiding social conflicts.

6. The symbolic dimension of syncretism

Though not commenting directly on the issue of power, a third category of social scientific models is relevant to the debate on syncretism. In these models, man as a meaning-maker occupies a central place (Crick 1976). Especially within the field of symbolic anthropology, ideas have been developed which are applicable to the study of syncretism.

Syncretism may be viewed as a way in which people play, though in a serious way, with symbols and meanings, and with the patterns in which these symbols are arranged. Of course, an interest in meanings is not new in the study of syncretism, as we have seen in Van der Leeuw's concept of '*Verschiebung*' (transposition), as well as in Pye's use of the word ambiguity.

Much work inspired by this third category of models can still be done. A first application concerns speaking of syncretism as a borrowing of elements. This suggests that elements are the basic units in a process of syncretism, and that the only change which occurs is that of displacement to another religious context. Yet, one should question what people do with elements, what these elements mean to them, and whether these elements are in fact autonomous and unrelated units.

The borrowed elements in question are symbols or clusters of symbols. People may change these symbols or give other meanings to them. They may integrate them in a new context, within another pattern. Merely the new position within that pattern may already alter the meaning of the symbol and of the pattern, as happens when one changes a mosaic. Sometimes the similarity in symbols, meanings, or patterns between two religions invites changes which might be called syncretic. So in general, there is more at stake than just the borrowing of elements (Ortiz 1975).

Research on symbols may shed light on the dynamics of syncretic religious change (Droogers 1981). Since symbols, meanings, and patterns do not all need to change at the same time, an almost infinite series of possible transformations may occur. The 'multivocality' (Turner 1969a: 8) of symbols contributes to this variety. The terms several authors use when indicating phases in the syncretic process or the results of that process —the whole range from amalgamation to dissolution— may be viewed as characterizations of the symbolic patterns which emerge.

The change of meaning is almost by definition prominent in situations of contact. The recipient of a message does not necessarily understand that message in the same way as the person sending it meant to be understood. This alone can mark the start of syncretism. Since communication between cultures and religions takes place in the context of doubled sets of symbols, patterns, and meanings, reinterpretation, misunderstanding, and distortion will be the more probable.

Symbolic changes may be better understood when studied within the social context. As we have argued above, this includes relations of power. Of special interest for the study of syncretism is the approach proposed by Victor Turner (1969b). He has shown how important the margins of society may be for its renewal, particularly because hierarchical relations are experienced less prominently there. The same happens when society goes through a marginal phase. It can be shown that founders of world religions started out from such marginal situations (Droogers 1980). Because of the temporal or structural relativizing of centralized hierarchy, the founding of religions may show syncretic traits.

Other contributions have been made with regard to the relation between symbol systems and relations of power. Bourdieu (1971), amending Weber, shows how the adoption of a division of labour in the production of religion, and changes in that division, influence the nature of that religion. Bax has coined the term "religious regime" to indicate relations of dependency legitimated by a class of religious specialists (1987). In studying the syncretic candomblé religion of Brazil, Willemier Westra has shown how priests manipulate symbolic paradoxes in order to maintain relationships of power (1987).

Furthermore, we should be aware that situations of contact have their own dynamics. As we saw, they may be characterized by crises. Syncretism may then be created as a function of the needs of the people in that situation. This may lead to something completely new, which will not resemble any aspect of the religions involved. Borrowing of elements is again an insufficient appraisal of what happens.

In the light of symbolic anthropology, the distinction between conscious and unconscious syncretism does not seem correct. If all men are meaning-makers, the enquiry must pursue to what degree this capacity is used, when, and how. Even in reproducing traditional symbolic systems, people may alter meanings. The binary distinction conscious–unconscious is too simple to represent the whole gamut of possibilities. Accordingly, the distinction between great and little tradition is not helpful. It may obtain a pejorative connotation, and it reinforces the clerical perspective.

7. Conclusion

In this paper I have summarized the contributions students of religion have made to the debate on syncretism. I have explicitly listed the main options to be confronted when defining syncretism. Several of these options have returned in subsequent sections of this paper. The influence of a negative subjective approach on presumedly objective definitions has been traced. I have put syncretism in a wider social and cultural context and have argued that asymmetrical relations of power are essential to the understanding of syncretism. The advantages of a symbolic approach have been presented. I have advocated that students of religion avoid a unilateral clerical perspective. Whether the key concept for the analysis of syncretism be transposition, alienation, ambiguity, contradiction, or crossing, there is always the possibility of coinciding with clerical foci and interests. Only rarely is syncretism looked at from the point of view of the 'syncretists' themselves. Moreover, and more importantly, it has often passed unnoticed that deviation, contradiction, etc., are not the essence of syncretism, but rather the *contesting* of that deviation by an orthodox clergy, without whom syncretism would not even exist as a term. Only if relations of power are included in the analysis is this basic characteristic of syncretism uncovered.

With the possible exception of Pye (pp. 92-93) and Rudolph (p. 208), no definition of syncretism mentions this aspect. Yet, both in the origin of the term and in its present content, this is the real issue. The fact that many students of religion have not seen this is a consequence of the clerical perspective they —often implicitly— have adopted. A switch in definition from negative subjective syncretism (an illegitimate mixture of religions) to objective syncretism (e.g. the coexistence of elements foreign to each other) has not been sufficient to grasp the essence of syncretism. Throughout, the clergy's role in the phenomenon has remained invisible. Yet theological and clerical views are part of the field under study. Only when the power dimension is included in the approach followed, can a more complete view of syncretism be obtained. All this shows us that the study of religions is more likely to be influenced by the religions it studies than one would wish or expect.

We therefore suggest that the definition of syncretism ought to include the element of contesting. The seemingly irreconcilable objective and subjective options are not the only alternatives. Syncretism is in the first place *contested* religious interpenetration. Yet such a definition still remains closer to the subjective than to the objective definition. The latter is much broader and includes religious mixing which need not be the subject of controversy, and which may even go unnoticed. Such is the case when the result does not interfere with established clerical religion. Syncretism, then, can be defined as religious interpenetration, either taken for granted or subject to debate. This also implies that what is contested by some may be taken for granted by others, who may be opposed by the former, though not necessarily so.

Though not elegant as a definition, because of the inclusion of opposite characteristics, it has the advantage of bringing together —and going beyond— the objective and subjective types of definition, stressing the controversial nature of much syncretism. The phrase reflects the ambiguity caused by the trickiness of the term. In that sense, reviewing the problem of definition has helped us to define the problem.

The definition and approach we have suggested, have consequences for our research. In studying concrete cases of syncretism, we should ask ourselves to what extent the religious interpenetration under study is contested and by whom. The symbolic mechanisms must be analyzed. Changes in symbols, meanings, and patterns must be studied within the wider cultural and social context, including power structures. The position the authors of these changes and their critics occupy in society must be included in the research. Special attention should be paid to the relation between the symbolic and the social structures. How do they influence each other? What role does (the struggle against) syncretism play in the maintenance or undermining of social boundaries? Are there spontaneous, undiscussed forms of syncretism, acceptable to all?

In the study of the place of syncretism in dialogue the more general questions formulated in the preceding paragraph must return. The fear of syncretism must receive more attention since it may hamper interreligious contacts. The unnoticed nature of some forms of syncretism may, on the other hand, facilitate dialogue. Dialogue may be viewed as a process involving the meaning-makers of two or more symbolic systems. Another question which must be posed is: To what extent do relations of power within religious traditions influence the dialogue and possible accusations of syncretism? Who represents a religion in the dialogue? Is there participation by the laity? Is syncretism an issue in the discussion, and do so-called syncretists have any participation in the dialogue?

8. Epilogue

Finally, I must ask myself how objective or subjective I have been in discussing objective and subjective definitions of syncretism, and in pointing a way out of this dilemma. I have been able to uncover subjective elements in the objective approach. But have I myself escaped subjectivism?

It is better to be consciously subjective than seemingly objective. In my opinion, some phases in the course of an enquiry tend to be more open to subjectiveness than others. While the choice of a theme and opting to write for a certain public is a matter open to individual motives, the collection of data should be more objective, and open to verification by others. The choice of a theoretical model, however, is more subjective than objective.

One might therefore expect an option for one of the three types of social scientific models —functionalist, Marxist, symbolic— which we dealt with in preceding sections. We suggest, however, that the three be used as what they primarily are: heuristic instruments which may open our eyes to otherwise hidden aspects of syncretism (cf. Droogers 1985). The models may sometimes contradict one another, as is clearly the case with the functionalist and the Marxist model, each representing opposing ideologies. Yet social reality combines cohesion and conflict in a dialectical way. It is within this context, including the relations of power, that man acts as a meaning-maker, trying to make sense of both order and contradiction, at the social as well as at the symbolic level. The right to meaning-making may be at stake, as in the conflict between the clergy and the popular masses. The three models therefore belong together, even though their proponents would condemn this approach as eclecticism or even as scientific syncretism.

Yet even in defending this eclectic position, I have opted for a rehabilitation of lay people in religious matters. Their religion is as important a field for the study of religion as is erudite religion (Kamstra 1984). Lay people are active meaning-makers, despite the official clerical dominance, documented by students of religion.

The participation of the laity in a possible interreligious dialogue should be advocated, as they may represent the hidden face of a religion. The clergy of a religion should not monopolize the dialogue. This also means that the interclerical dialogue is only part of the possible encounter between religions. At the level of the common believers, a different dialogue should be stimulated. Since syncretism creates commonness, more than diversion, this dialogue may even be more promising than the 'official' one. If Christian organizations, like the World Council of Churches, defend the interests of the voiceless, then this should also be put into effect in questions of dialogue, transforming the voiceless into spokesmen.

I have taken some distance from a negative subjective definition. I have tried to rehabilitate popular religion and syncretism. I have also advocated dialogue. Yet as a Christian I must admit that the problem of the boundaries of syncretism is a real one. It was also for this reason that the controversial element has been maintained in the definition.

I would not, however, put unilateral emphasis on doctrinaire boundaries. In face of the current world problems, the practical questions seem more important in dialogue. Here again the so-called syncretists are often on more familiar ground than their clergy.

Bibliography

Asmussen, Jes Peter, Jørgen Lassøe, and Carsten Colpe, eds. *Handbuch der Religionsgeschichte.* Göttingen: Vandenhoeck & Ruprecht, 1975.

Baird, Robert D. *Category Formation and the History of Religion.* The Hague/Paris: Mouton, 1971.

Bax, Mart. "Religious Regimes and State Formation: Towards a Research Perspective." *Anthropological Quarterly* 60 (1987): 1-11.

Berner, U. "Heuristisches Modell der Synkretismus-Forschung (Stand August 1977)." In Wiessner, *Synkretismusforschung,* pp. 11-26.

——. "Das 'Synkretismus-Modell' als Instrument einer historischen Religionsphänomenologie." In Wiessner, *Synkretismusforschung,* pp. 27-37.

Binsbergen, Wim van, and Matthew Schoffeleers, eds. *Theoretical Explorations in African Religion.* London: KPI, 1985.

Bourdieu, Pierre. "Genèse et Structure du Champ Religieux." *Revue Française de Sociologie* 12 (1971): 295-334.

Colpe, Carsten. "Synkretismus, Renaissance: Säkularisation und Neubildung von Religionen in der Gegenwart." In Asmussen et al, *Handbuch,* pp. 441-523.

——. 1975. "Die Vereinbarkeit historischer und struktureller Bestimmungen des Synkretismus." In Dietrich, *Synkretismus,* pp. 17-30.

——. 1977. "Syncretism and Secularisation: Complementary and Antithetical Trends in New Religious Movements." *Numen* 17, 158-76.

——. 1979. "Synkretismus." *Der kleine Pauly,* V, pp. 1648-1652.

——. 1987. "Syncretism." *The Encyclopedia of Religion,* XIV. Ed. Mircea Eliade. New York/London: MacMillan, 1987, pp. 218-27.

Crick, Malcolm. *Explorations in Language and Meaning: Towards a Semantic Anthropology.* London: Malaby, 1976.

Dietrich, Albert, ed. *Synkretismus im Syrisch-Persischen Kulturgebiet: Bericht über ein Symposium in Reinhausen bei Göttingen in der Zeit von 4 bis 8 Oktober 1971.* Göttingen: Vandenhoeck & Ruprecht, 1975.

Droogers, André. "Symbols of Marginality in the Biographies of Religious and Secular Innovators: A Comparative Study of the Lives of Jesus, Waldes, Booth, Kimbangu, Buddha, Mohammed, and Marx." *Numen* (1980):105-21.

——. 1981. "Sincretismo." *Estudios Teológicos* 21, 139-50.

——. 1985. "From Waste-Making to Recycling: A Plea for an Eclectic Use of Models in the Study of Religious Change." In Binsbergen et al, *Theoretical Explorations,* pp. 101-37.

Hartman, Sven S., ed. *Syncretism, Based on Papers Read at the Symposium on Cultural Contact, Meeting of Religions, Syncretism, held at Abo on the 8th-10th of September, 1966.* Stockholm: Almqvist & Wiksell, 1969.

Hoens, D. J., J. H. Kamstra, and D. C. Mulder, eds. *Inleiding tot de Studie van de Godsdiensten*. Kampen: Kok, 1985.

Humanitas Religiosa: Festschrift für Haralds Biezais zu seinem 70 Geburtstag. Stockholm: Almqvist & Wiksell, 1979.

Kamstra, Jacques H. *Synkretisme: Op de Grens tussen Theologie en Godsdienstfenomenologie*. Leiden: Brill, 1970.

——. 1975. "Het Spinneweb." In Sperna Weiland, *Antwoord*, pp. 175-96.

——. 1984. "Een Moeilijke Keuze: De Godsdienst van de Gewone Man." *Nederlands Theologisch Tijdschrift* 38, 253-79.

——. 1985. "Religie en Syncretisme." In Hoens et al, *Inleiding*, pp. 210-23.

Kraemer, Hendrik. *De Wortelen van het Syncretisme*. 's-Gravenhage: Boekencentrum, 1937.

——. 1938. *The Christian Message in the Non-Christian World*. London: Edinburgh House Press.

——. 1956. *Religion and the Christian Faith*. London: Lutterworth Press.

——. 1962. "Synkretismus, II: Im Wirkungsbereich der Misssion." *Die Religion in Geschichte und Gegenwart: Handwörterbuch für Theologie und Religionswissenschaft*, VI. Tübingen: Mohr, pp. 567-68.

Leeuw, G. van der. *Phänomenologie der Religion*. Tübingen: Mohr, 1956.

Mulder, D. C. " 'None Other Gods' — 'No Other Names.' " *The Ecumenical Review* 38 (1986): 209-15.

Pannenberg, Wolfhart. *Basic Questions in Theology*, II. London: SCM, 1970.

Pye, Michael. "Syncretism and Ambiguity." *Numen* 18 (1971): 83-93.

Ortiz, Renato. "Du Syncrétisme a la Synthèse: Umbanda, une Religion Brésilienne." *Archives de Sciences Sociales des Religions* 40 (1975): 89-97.

Ringgren, Helmer. "The Problems of Syncretism." In Hartman, *Syncretism*, pp. 7-14.

Rudolph, Kurt. "Synkretismus vom Theologischen Scheltwort zum religionswissenschaftlichen Begriff." In *Humanitas Religiosa*, pp. 193-212.

Spencer, Robert F., ed. *Forms of Symbolic Action: Proceedings of the 1969 Annual Spring Meeting of the American Ethnological Society*. Seattle/London: University of Washington Press, 1969.

Sperna Weiland, J., ed. *Antwoord: Gestalten van Geloof in de Wereld van Nu*. Amsterdam: Meulenhoff, 1975.

Thils, Gustave. *Syncretisme où Catholicité*. Tournai: Casterman, 1967.

Thomas, M. M. "The Absoluteness of Jesus Christ and Christ-centered Syncretism." *The Ecumenical Review* 37 (1985): 387-97.

Turner, Victor W. "Forms of Symbolic Action: Introduction." In Spencer, *Forms of Symbolic Action*, pp. 3-25. 1969a.

——. *The Ritual Process: Structure and Anti-Structure*. London: Routledge and Kegan Paul, 1969b.

Visser 't Hooft, W. A. *No Other Name: The Choice Between Syncretism and Christian Universalism*. London: SCM, 1963.

Wiessner, Gernot, ed. *Synkretismusforschung: Theorie und Praxis*. Wiesbaden: Harrassowitz, 1978.

Willemier Westra, Allard Dirk. *Axe, Kracht om te leven: Het Gebruik van Symbolen bij de Hulpverlening in de Candomblé-Religie in Alagoinhas (Bahia, Brazilië)*. Amsterdam: CEDLA, 1987.

Chapter 2

Syncretism and Dialogue: A Philosophical Analysis

Hendrik M. Vroom

In this contribution, a conceptual analysis of syncretism and dialogue is presented. In contrast to encounter and mutual action —which can be seen as important preconditions for real dialogue— dialogue is conceived of as deliberate discussion concerning interpretations of humankind, the world, and the transcendent. In this analysis of the logic of religious belief, syncretism is conceived of as the incorporation by a religious tradition of beliefs and practices incompatible with its basic insights. Integration of foreign beliefs requires reinterpretation of old beliefs and a re-configuration (particularly) of basic insights. By such a hermeneutical process a religious tradition can accommodate profound change; it can, however, be changed to the point of losing its original identity. Such processes do indeed occur through religious inter-penetration as well as through contact with secular world-views.

1. Introduction

In this contribution, we will attempt to clarify a little the concept of dialogue, and especially the concept of syncretism, through an analysis of the logic of religious belief.

We will first make a few remarks by way of introduction. One could start by asking: What 'is' syncretism? Syncretism would then be portrayed as something present amidst many other religious phenomena. Recall, however, Van der Leeuw's consideration of the nature of phenomena —of *was sich zeigt*— and the difficulties facing such a view —reminiscent of Plato's ideas— of a phenomenon as a kind of reality in and behind concrete appearances (Van der Leeuw, 634). The term syncretism could better be used to indicate and analyze a certain aspect of the mutual influence between religious traditions. We therefore prefer a stipulative definition of syncretism. It is clear from Drooger's survey of the discussion of the term syncretism, that it involves a process in which beliefs and practices from one religious current or world and life view are adopted by certain people in another religious current, and subsequently assimilated or repudiated. It seems to me that the various authors cited by Droogers have focussed on important notions of the process of syncretism. Kamstra rightly interjects the element of *foreign-ness* (Kamstra, 9-10, cf. p. 27). Pye points out the *ambiguity* proper to elements newly to be incorporated in the meaning of beliefs and symbols. Droogers himself defines syncretism as *contested interreligious interpenetration.* As far as I am concerned, all these elements are illuminating for the analysis of the process one has in mind with the term syncretism. I believe that these perspectives can be bundled together within the context of an analysis of *religious belief* by speaking of *incompatible beliefs and practices.* I will define syncretism in the first instance as the incorporation of incompatible beliefs from one religion by another. Being incompatible is not the same as being contested, because non-compatibility is not a psychological or anthropological category, but a logical one. Nobody can believe that the earth is flat *and* round simultaneously, nor that people live only once *and* many times. That is a matter of logic. People may, however, differ on these issues; their approval or repudiation can entail all sorts of psychological and social issues, but that is not the concern of this paper. Some of the elements of the discussion on the meaning of syncretism can be assumed by the notion of incompatibility: foreignness, contradiction, and contesting. The point, however, is the alleged incompatibility of beliefs. We will return to the notion of ambiguity when dealing with religious traditions as historical and hermeneutical processes wherein the beliefs of a tradition are subject to reinterpretation and rearrangement.

We will focus primarily on beliefs. This is not in the least to suggest that practices cannot be incompatible. They certainly can. To give just one example: one can recommend practices which foster an attitude of 'unattachment,' compassion, and neighbourly love. Such practices are incompatible with actions which stimulate an intransigent and belligerent attitude. Beliefs and practices are in fact intertwined in the religious experience of reality. In our logical analysis, though, our concern is with the (in)compatibility of beliefs.

2. Encounter and dialogue

One could, concurring with Wilfred Smith, state that religious traditions are in a continual process of interpenetration. Adherents of one religion derive insights and practices from adherents of other religious traditions (Smith, 21ff.). That applies not only to religious traditions, but also to currents within a certain religion. What are the conditions for the possibility of such mutual interchange?

If person A says that he holds belief *p* to be true, then his assertion contains an invitation to his conversation partner B to acquaint himself with belief *p* and to experience the *subject* under discussion in accordance with *p*. If, for example, A says to B that 'Mohammed was a very special person,' then A is claiming to articulate a true insight about Mohammed. B can concur; he can contradict the statement; or he can interpret the assertion differently, in that 'very special' obtains a different meaning within his philosophy of life than within that of A. Among the conditions for the possibility of such an exchange of ideas belong the facts that people have certain properties in common, that they can acquire knowledge of matters with which they are initially unacquainted, and that they can converse about various aspects of their experience of life and their interpretation of reality. In our example, people have the property that they can be impressed by what certain people say and do; B can learn something about Mohammed; A and B can converse about their view of Mohammed. More generally, we will mention the following conditions for the possibility of such a dialogue:

1) the existential structure of man,
2) the possibility that people are concerned with the same matters,
3) the possibility of a discussion about a persuasion.

I add here that the existential structure of man is a point of debate between religions, that some 'matters' of which religious traditions speak (e.g. *moksha* and *nirvana*) are not wholly, and certainly not easily, accessible and open to discourse, and finally, that 'discursive thought and discourse' about such matters is not simple (Vroom, Chap. 8 & 9).

We wish to conceive of the dialogue between adherents of various religious traditions as deliberate discussion of interpretations given by various religious traditions (and persuasions in general) with regard to humankind, the world, and the transcendent. For the remaining human contact between adherents of divergent religions, one can reserve the term *encounter*. Such encounter, as well as mutual action to foster humanitarian goals, can be seen as a great help in coming to real mutual understanding. Not every encounter is a dialogue, however, and it is easy to see that a dialogue without encounter and sympathy is not very fruitful.[1]

[1] On dialogue as encounter and as life-style, see the *Guidelines on Dialogue with People of Living Faiths and Ideologies*, 2nd edn. (WCC: Geneva, 1982): 10. See also the "Rules for Dialogue," drawn up by R. MacAfee Brown, and originally published ca. 1960 in connection with Catholic-Protestant ecumenical discussion, but "recognized as embodying sound general principles for any form of bridge-building encounter," according to the editors of *Study Encounter*, *I*, 1965, p. 133f.

3 Syncretism

One of the questions entailed by the theme of this volume, *Dialogue and Syncretism*, is whether someone from one religion who *learns* something from a person of another religion is thereby being syncretistic, i.e. adopting beliefs which are *incompatible* with the insights in his own tradition. What applies for beliefs can also be said with reference to practices. After the previous assessment of *dialogue*, I will now pass on to a more elaborate exposition of syncretism. I will first present a few results from a study on the theme of *religion and truth*, which are of importance to our topic.

How one views syncretism, and the relationship between religious traditions depends to a large extent on one's view of the nature of a religious belief-system. If one regards the content of religions as a coherent entity, then religion A cannot adopt a belief from religion B, unless this belief is isolated from B and adapted (assimilated) to the entire belief-system of A. If adaptation is impossible, then A cannot adopt a belief from B. Hendrik Kraemer has spoken about religion in this manner (Kraemer 1938: 148f., 172; 1958: 38, 66; cf. 112). He regarded religions as closed cultural units in which the meaning of each element is determined by the whole. In terms of this view, the adoption by one religion of elements from another is religious syncretism: every foreign belief is incompatible.

If one does not view religions as coherent belief-systems, but as multi-faceted belief-systems, in which basic insights are related to one another in a looser fashion, then matters lie differently. We will proceed from the assumption that the religious content of a tradition is a more or less fluid configuration of beliefs. These beliefs are compatible in the sense that a certain coherence exists between them, or at least that they are reconciled in some interpretational scheme. By reinterpretation of foreign beliefs, incompatibility between beliefs in a belief-system is avoided. Every religion is immersed in a continual hermeneutic process in which the transmitted religious inheritance is reinterpreted. Every tradition is involved in a process of interchange with the culture in which the adherents live; this is commonly designated by the term contextuality. Certain beliefs are basic within a tradition; the accompanying religious experience is nurtured by rites. Beliefs which are not considered central to a tradition by its adherents are particularly subject to reinterpretation; a relatively broad measure of freedom to incorporate 'foreign' beliefs appears to exist at the 'boundaries' of the belief-system. This view, which I have elsewhere explicated and defended in detail, implies that interreligious encounter and exchange is a normal phenomenon (Vroom, Chap. 9, § 3). Suppose that religion C contains beliefs (1) through (8), and religion D beliefs (2), (3), (4), (5), (9), (10), and (11). Examples will follow below. The question arises as to whether C can assimilate belief (9) from D. This question springs from religion C's claim to truth: religion C aspires to as comprehensive a view as possible on all of reality as people experience it; religion D claims that belief (9) is true. In terms of religion C, (9) must be wholly or partially accepted or rejected. Since religion C does not form a strict coherent entity, whose unity is such that assimilation of (9) would disintegrate its unity, the adherents of religion C can consider adopting (9) in their belief-system. One would, of course, expect that a belief from another religious tradition will not be adopted without further ado, but that it will be interpreted in connection with other beliefs, thus producing (9´). If religion C assimilates belief (9) from D, a new configuration emerges, C´: (1) through (8), (9´). The new element, (9´), stands within configuration C´. The meaning of other elements can also be altered by the assimilation of (9´): (7´), (8´), etc. The order of importance of the various elements can also shift due to the adoption of new beliefs. Suppose that (6) and (7) are essential to C, and that (9) is in some tension with (6); then the equilibrium in religion C can shift, so that (6) is explained differently (6´) in (C´), and possibly receives a position of less importance in the whole, in order to integrate (9´).

We will now give an example in which the issues of incompatibility, coherence, and contradiction play a role. Suppose that religions C and D contain the following beliefs:

Religion C

- (1) Eternal salvation is received only through grace.
- (2) People must effectuate their blessedness in this life.
- (3) God has created the world, and has placed man above plants and animals; man is, if all is well, a reasonable, loving, and responsible being.
- (4) God is transcendent.
- (5) Evil is a reality in a world full of sin.
- (6) God has revealed Himself in the history of Israel and especially in Jesus Christ.
- (7) The Bible is the source and norm of Christian tradition.
- (8) In the ecclesiastical tradition, the Bible is explained and articulated with the guidance of the Holy Spirit.

Religion D

- (2) People must effectuate their blessedness in this life.
- (3) God has created the world, and has placed man above plants and animals; man is, if all is well, a reasonable, loving, and responsible being.
- (4) God is transcendent.

- (5) Evil is a reality in a world full of sin.
- (9) Mohammed is a prophet.
- (10) The Koran is the perfect revelation of God.
- (11) The Islamic community explicates the Koran.

The question is what will now transpire if religion C incorporates belief (9). One must not say too easily that this is entirely impossible, because in the course of the ages, religious traditions have incorporated many ideas of a foreign provenance. It is therefore sometimes said that every religion is a syncretic entity. But if religion C would adopt belief (9), then both (6) and (9) would have to be reinterpreted to retain a certain amount of coherence between the beliefs. Room would have to be created within (6) for a history of God with people outside one's own tradition; (9) would have to be reinterpreted so that (9´) is compatible with (6´). And the existence of a partial contradiction between (9) and (9´) cannot be excluded, as appears from a further elaboration:

- (9A) Mohammed is the greatest prophet, whose word is purer than that of all previous prophets (at least insofar as they have been passed on).
- (9A´) Mohammed has prophesied fundamental truths about God, and is a prophet through whom God has reached many people.

By incorporating 'foreign' beliefs and reinterpreting old ones, a religious tradition can thus accommodate profound change. We will present another example (for a more extensive consideration, we refer to the contribution by Kranenborg); it is also conceivable that religion C assimilates a belief from *religion E*:

- (12) One must acquire 'blessedness' in a long series of rebirths.

This belief would be incompatible with (1) and (2), which speak of salvation through grace alone and of a single existence. One cannot believe (1) together with (12). (12) would therefore come in (2)'s stead. (1) would also have to be reinterpreted, like this, for instance:

- (1´) Man needs grace in order to attain eternal salvation.

In this way (1´) becomes compatible with the beliefs of Jodo-shin-shu Buddhism, in which (13) is accepted next to (12):

- (13) By the grace of Amida —on which one concentrates by recitation of the words 'Namu Amida Butsu'— one can be reborn in the Western paradise regardless of one's *karma*, whence one can 'attain' *nirvana.*

The next question to arise, then, is the question as to the relationship between faith in Amida Buddha and Jesus Christ, (13) and (6) respectively.

In this analytical consideration, I will not delve into the question which could be asked in the theology of the various traditions, i.e., whether a certain synthesis with beliefs of other traditions is legitimate, and which criteria are valid within a religious tradition. We merely ascertain that such processes of assimilation do in fact take place. Foreign beliefs, which were previously held to be incompatible, are incorporated. The incompatibility is overcome by a (radical) reinterpretation of old and new beliefs. It is precisely the reinterpretation to which one is brought in incorporating foreign beliefs which gives evidence of the tension which people feel between the old and the new beliefs. Such tension is a matter of logic

In addition to the reinterpretation of old beliefs, yet another factor plays a role in the assimilation process, viz. the modification of the configuration of beliefs. By the configuration of beliefs, we understand the relations which exist between the various beliefs, and the central or less central position of beliefs within the multi-faceted belief-system. The example of religion C has been derived from Christianity. There has been discussion in the entire history of Christianity about the relationship between (1) and (2). The Protestant churches made (1) central within their belief-system (and in their religious experience). Alongside of that, (2) was given a place. In classical Roman Catholic theology, (2) stands central, although the necessity of grace is not denied. Accordingly, classical Protestant and Catholic theology each presented an interpretation of Christian faith. Neither denied the importance of grace *and* works, but they were ascribed a different relative weight, and divergent interpretations emerged, leading to vehement conflicts. The difference in belief-system (and religious experience) between one tradition and the other within Christianity was not slight. The cluster of beliefs (including a view on the relation between the different religions) is determinative for the possibility of the integration of beliefs from other traditions. In the example given, (12) is incompatible with (1). Only by reinterpretation of (1) can (12) be incorporated. As far as I can see, a current which regards (2) as more central than (1) will more easily admit of accepting (12) instead of (2).

The reinterpretation of (1) as (1´) allows more room for the acceptance of the teaching of reincarnation and the life of grace, as this is given form by the Jodo-shin-shu, but runs into other incompatibilities, particularly in respect of the relationship between *nirvana* and belief in God, and between faith in Amida Buddha and Jesus Christ.

Since religious traditions include many currents with divergent emphases, one may not place them over against one another as closed units. There is room for learning from other traditions. Since people aspire to an interpretation of the whole of the reality they experience, they will be inclined to integrate as many insights from elsewhere as possible. Which insights they consider important to integrate depends on various factors, including what is held to be true and what is considered to be of value (for better or for worse) in the culture in which one lives, and on what is impressive in other persuasions, impressive in the sense that justice is done to to essential aspects of being human. Interpenetration of religious traditions will be more common in a religiously pluralistic society than in a society with a single common world view.

Syncretism is, we can now say, the phenomenon of adopting or wanting to adopt beliefs which are incompatible with beliefs that are logically basic to a belief-system. Due to syncretism basic beliefs are reinterpreted in such a way that they (a) are radically modified in their meaning and (b) are no longer basic to the configuration of the belief-system. The original identity of a such a configuration is thereby changed.

I believe in this way to have done justice to the discussion of syncretism as Droogers has presented it. The notion of 'foreignness' is expressed in the assimilation of beliefs from another provenance, necessitating a thorough reinterpretation. The notion of reinterpretation is entailed by the ambiguity which Pye describes. Droogers himself speaks of "religious interpenetration, either taken for granted, or subject to debate." The analysis given here illumines the reasons for debate and contradiction; these lie in the incompatibility. This incompatibility is not only a matter of inconsistency of beliefs, but also of religious experience. The religious experience for example, of 'being sustained by grace' and 'not having to do it oneself,' is in conflict with the feeling that one must obtain salvation for oneself by observing the *Shari'ah,* for example, or by doing good works. Incompatibility can also surface in the rites and liturgies of a religion, since different practices evoke and nurture diverse religious experiences.

Finally, I must examine the incompatibilities which lie in religious traditions themselves. Since religious beliefs stand in close connection to fundamental human experiences, tension can exist between the various basic beliefs. An example which has already been mentioned of belief is (5): the existence of evil. The question of how one can relate the goodness of God or the Divinity to such awful misery surfaces in all kinds of religions. Religious belief-systems contain within themselves tensions between insights which are recognized to be true. These tensions, however, are interpreted in such a way as not to issue in direct contradiction. The well-known example of a contradiction is (a) God is good; (b) God is all-powerful and has made all things; (c) much misery exists. A classical manner of reconciling these three insights with each other is the assumption of (d), that the suffering governed by God has a purpose (unfathomable for human thought). Nowadays the tension between these perceptions is often mitigated by reinterpreting the 'omnipotence' of God, in the sense that God must countenance affliction for reasons too deep for human comprehension, or by denying that God actually desires suffering. In this way people reconcile the basic beliefs that God is the powerful Creator and that God is full of love with the reality of suffering in the world. Religious belief-systems thus incorporate their own incompatibilities; they have tempered these in their belief-system by placing certain relations between the beliefs which are experienced as incompatible, and by ascribing some beliefs priority (e.g., (a) God is good). These beliefs are closely related to those aspects of human experience which are fundamental to a certain religious tradition; the conscious experience of this is evoked and 'nurtured' by those traditions.

Syncretic processes display a different kind of incompatibility, since they disturb the balance which has grown between the basic beliefs of a belief-system and necessitate a new configuration of beliefs. What distinguishes syncretism, viewed in this manner, from the normal hermeneutic process which religious traditions undergo, is that the new insights are incompatible with basic beliefs of a tradition, as it has grown at a certain stage, or with basic beliefs that are essential to the identity of a religious tradition (e.g., Sinai, or the enlightenment of the Buddha). Syncretism denotes the adoption of beliefs which alter the essential experience and the central beliefs of a tradition. A legitimate reason can therefore exist for contesting syncretism, i.e., this incompatibility and the aspiration to keep certain beliefs pure, both in reflection as well as in experience. It is plain that abuse of power can play a role in repudiating the incorporation of other beliefs; abuse of power, however, has also often played a role in the syntheses which religions have entered into with each other and with secularized life.[2]

In summary, by dialogue, we understand discussion with followers of other persuasions. In this dialogue, one can learn from others. One then adopts elements from another persuasion or religious tradition and assimilates them into one's own belief-system. One can speak of syncretism if beliefs from one tradition are transferred to another, with whose basic beliefs they are felt to be in serious tension.

---

[2] It should be kept in mind that the original context of the critique of syncretism and 'religion' in dialectical theology was the era of German fascism, with its appeal to the laity, as well as to theologians and philosophers. I am afraid that there is no reason to idealize the religion of the laity and the masses, nor for that matter, the religion of popes, bishops, and synods. True religious life and insight seem rare.

Bibliography

Kamstra, J. H. *Synkretisme: Op de Grens tussen Theologie en Godsdienstfenomenologie.* Leiden, 1970.

Kraemer, H. *Godsdienst, Godsdiensten en het Christelijk Geloof.* Nijkerk, 1958.

——. *The Christian Message in a Non-Christian World.* London, 1938.

Leeuw, G. van der. *Phänomenologie der Religion.* Tübingen, 1963.

Smith, Wilfred C. *Towards a World Theology.* London, 1981.

Vroom, H. M. *Truth and Religions.* Currents in Encounter II. Amsterdam/Grand Rapids, 1988.

Chapter 3

Syncretism and Dialogue: Christian Historical and Earlier Ecumenical Perceptions

Jerald D. Gort

The purpose of this essay is to provide a birdseye view of the historical Christian attitudes to other religions. It is argued that with the exception of the first 250 years of its existence Christianity's attitude on this score has been predominantly negative, but that from around the turn of the present century a new, more congenial, and generous Christian stance has been in the making. With respect to this latter period, the examination is limited to developments on the Protestant side of Christianity. An attempt is made to identify some of the more important causal factors involved in the evolution of the newer attitude, whereby particular attention is given to developments in the thinking of the ecumenical movement during its earlier period from 1910–1963.

The basic issues involved in what for this symposium we have termed *syncretism and dialogue* are by no means exclusively or even largely modern but without doubt extremely old, probably nearly as ancient as human religious experience itself. Surely from the very inception of intergroup encounter and discourse *homo religiosus* has been faced with the necessity of forming an opinion regarding the beliefs and cultic practices of others. Historically all religions have had to decide time and again what stance to adopt vis-à-vis the differing belief systems with which they have come into contact.

1. Historical Attitudes

For Christianity, too, this question has always been a matter of central concern: What is the proper Christian attitude toward the world, toward other cultures, other religious traditions and their adherents?

Should the posture the church assumes relative to other faiths be one of respect, recognition, and conciliation or of repudiation, rejection, and confrontation? Should Christianity seek to transform other religions from within or attempt to displace them from without? Should it ally and link itself to or set itself off in isolation from them? Ought it to view its relationship with them in terms of continuity or discontinuity? At times both approaches have been in simultaneous evidence within the church. Indeed, some find this to be the case in the New Testament itself, where, it is argued, an "inclusivist" line, that of Luke-Acts, which leaves room for a "positive . . . appreciation for the operation of God's Spirit outside Christianity" exists alongside an "exclusivist" witnessing line that stresses the absolute finality and uniqueness of Christ and the Christian faith (Race, 10, 11, 38-41). Usually in Christian history, however, now the one then the other of these two main models of interreligious encounter has been in the ascendant.

During the second and third centuries, leading Christian thinkers exhibited no small degree of esteem for the faiths of other peoples. According to the great Apologists, Justin Martyr (ca. 100–ca. 165) and Clement of Alexandria (ca. 150–ca. 215), nothing good or true anywhere in the world exists independently of the operation of God's salvific grace and revelatory activity. Making use of various concepts and insights borrowed from Stoicism, they taught that the religious life of humankind belongs in reality to the Christian economy by virtue of the fact that all humans possess a *logos spermatikos* through which they participate in the eternal divine *Logos,* i.e., in Christ. The religious and philosophical traditions of humanity, they reasoned, function as a *praeparatio evangelica,* as schoolmasters (*paedagogoi*) that make people receptive to the repleteness of truth revealed in Jesus Christ. Unfortunately, this felicity of attitude, this initial generosity of mind and spirit which made it possible to hold the beliefs and convictions of others in such high regard was to be nipped in the bud before it could fairly flower and bear ripened fruit.

From about the middle of the third century, the affirmative openness which had informed early patristic theology gradually gave way to increasingly negative feelings on the part of the church toward the world around it. A second period in the theology of religion began to emerge, the watchword of which became: *extra ecclesiam nulla salus.* As originally formulated by Origen (ca. 185–ca. 254) this adage was clearly pastoral in intent and purpose. Ere long, however, it was given a dogmatic, stringently minimalist-exclusionist twist by Cyprian († 258), who contended that no salvation whatever is to be found outside the boundaries of the juridically, hierarchically ordered Christian church: "He cannot have God for his Father who does not have the Church for his mother" (cited in Kelly, 206). Subsequent to, and as a consequence of, the Constantinian establishment this Cyprianic rigorism hardened even further. The religions and cultures of 'non-Christian' peoples came to be perceived as expressions of heathen unbelief and iniquitous superstition, the 'outside world' as the kingdom of darkness requiring to be incorporated into the enlightened *corpus Christianum*. For the next 1500 years or better the climate of Christian thinking in respect of other religions would be almost wholly governed by that perception and, concomitantly, a massive fear of syncretism.

Of course, the desire to avoid syncretism need not in and of itself be adjudged unreasonable or invalid. To any religion syncretism *narrowly defined* poses a genuine threat and can never be a matter of mere indifference. Syncretism in this sense can be said to occur when two religions, belief systems, messages of salvation are merged in such a way that the essence of the one or the other or both is radically modified, changed into something different from what it was originally. Although from a strictly descriptive perspective even this kind of syncretism is rightly seen as a neutral phenomenon, from the prescriptive point of view of the religions undergoing or threatened by such modification it is understandably interpreted in *malam partem* as representing, in Luzbetak's term, "a theologically untenable amalgam" (cited in Schreiter, 146). Clearly, all religions, Christianity not excepted, have a legitimate right to try to ward off syncretism thus conceived. That "the importance of keeping the gospel message pure and unadulterated has been a constant concern of the Christian church" (Schreiter, 144) presents no difficulty.

The problem arose when 'syncretism' came to be so broadly defined that the possibility of any positive relationship between Christianity and other traditions was a priori precluded. And the root cause of this problem lay in Europe's historically overweening sense of comprehensive superiority. Its culture (in reality a melange of various cultures), its religion (in truth shot through with 'heathen' elements), its time-bound understanding and contextually conditioned expression of the Christian faith, were quite directly and speciously identified with the truth of the gospel and thus accorded universal normativity. This habitude of self-consecration made the Western church prone to view the displacement of other religions and cultures as the only admissible resultant of its encounter with them and correspondingly to classify *any other* outcome[1] of such encounter as *ipso facto* syncretistic. In other words, it was not the rejection of syncretism narrowly defined but rather exaggerated self-esteem that led, via an ever widening application of the concept of syncretism, to European Christianity's traditionally preponderating antipathy toward the views and ways of life of other peoples.

Certainly, there were those who now and again challenged the prevailing mood by advocating or employing a more accommodating model of encounter with other traditions: Pope Gregory the Great (ca. 540–604),

[1] For a helpful survey and analysis of the various possible outcomes of interreligious encounter see Schreiter, pp. 144-58.

Raymond Lull (ca. 1235–ca. 1315), Bartholomew de las Casas (1474–1566), Matteo Ricci (1552–1610), Robert de Nobili (1577–1656). Other names could be mentioned here as well. And even in the 19th century, when missions and North Atlantic colonial expansion were very nearly hand in glove, even in this era of "imperialized Christianity" (Pobee, 9), the heyday of the "*conquista*-oriented theological vision" of the North Atlantic church (Mundadan, 22), a few Western voices were raised in protest against the unyieldingly antagonistic attitude of European missions toward the religions of Asia and Africa. One example that may be cited here is that of the Swiss Reformed pastor, Ernst Langhans, who in 1864, according to Fritz Blanke, published an extensive, well-documented critique of the missionary enterprise of his day, in which he took strenuous exception to, among other things, the "dogmatic" and "tactless" manner in which most missionaries approached people of other faiths. Langhans complained, Blanke reports, that "es den Heidenen klargemacht [wird], daß sie allesamt vom Teufel tyrannisiert sind, und daß ihrer Götter Verkörperungen des Teufels darstellen" (Blanke, 119). Educated Indians and Chinese, he observed caustically, were supposed to be pleased to be greeted " 'von einer unwissenden schwäbischen oder schottischen Kapuziner' mit der Behauptung, 'du bist ein Lügendiener, ein Satansdiener' " (p. 121). Totally unconcerned about "die gegebenen Verhältnisse brechen [die Missionare] rücksichtslos in das heidnische Leben ein" (p. 121). Missionaries lacked the basic respect, he contended,

> die jeder sittlich gebildete Mensch der heiligen Gewissensüberzeugung seines Nächsten entgegenbringen soll. Jedes fremde Volks- und Gewissensrecht wird in Indien durch die Missionare mit Füssen getreten. Was würden wir in Europa sagen, wenn muselmanische Imans [sic] an Karfreitag oder aan Weihnachten in unseren Kirchen aufträten und das Christentum beschimpften? Wir würden solche Ruhestörer hinter Schloss und Riegel setzen. (p. 122-23)

Yet, all such important challenges were eventually suppressed or went largely unheeded; the lone voices were scarcely heard. The overall picture shows that the confrontation model, the *anathema sit* mentality continued virtually unabated; that when countering new religio-cultural traditions, Western Christianity very frequently allowed its behavior to be guided by an excessive fear of syncretism rooted in unbridled feelings of superiority.

2. Change of Mood and its Contributory Causes

In our day something new is afoot: the air is being cleared of the clouds of obscuring dust that accumulated throughout the years of Western delusion and domination. That the putative superiority of a supposedly Christian Western culture no longer obtains for most is reflected in a simple but powerful word from the Report of the 1975 Nairobi Assembly of the WCC: "No culture is closer to Jesus Christ than any other culture" (WCC 1976: 79). Christian theology, both Catholic and Protestant, has begun to concern itself ever more seriously with the study of other religions and interreligious dialogue. In the sequel an attempt will be made to trace in broad outline some important aspects of the *Entstehungsgeschichte* of this new climate, specifically within Protestant Christianity.[2] **First**, brief reference will be made to a number of external causal events. **Next**, the importance in this connection of ecumenicity as such will be argued. **Finally**, developments within the ecumenical movement during its earlier period from 1910 to 1963[3] will be adduced as an important factor in the evolvement of today's new disposition in respect of other faiths.

a. External Causal Factors

At the outset of the modern Protestant ecumenical movement, which began as a movement of international missionary cooperation, Western Christianity and its agencies of geographical outreach, its mission boards and mission societies, were still overwhelmingly informed by 19th century European presuppositions and certainties. However, in the years following upon the adjournment of the initial gathering of this movement, the World Missionary Conference held in Edinburgh in 1910, a series of events took place which were vastly to change the face of geo-political realities and world history, whereby the strong facade of European preeminence in human affairs would be cracked beyond repair. The process began in Europe itself with the Great War of 1914–1918. This sad spectacle of hatred and destruction among the Christian nations not only weakened Europe but also deeply eroded whatever faith Africans and Asians might still have had in the moral authority of the West.

Asian and African reactions to white racism had already been on the increase, and now the debacle in Europe led many in these regions to a positive reassessment of their own cultures. Existing and new movements for national autonomy and self-determination, linked with a renascence of traditional religions, began to gather force everywhere in Asia and Africa. These nationalist alliances became ever more vociferous in their opposition to Western influences, including that of Christianity, which for so long had been associated with European colonialism. In the past Christianity had often viewed the other religions as enemies; in this new situation *it* became the enemy. World War II, the second bankruptcy of European culture within 20 years, ushered in the period of decolonialization and

[2] Developments within Catholicism on this matter are of course equally important, but they are a subject for another essay.

[3] The reason for the choice of 1963 as *terminus ad quem* for this survey is based on my judgement that it constitutes a watershed of sorts between an older and newer period in the history of thinking with respect to the other religions.

nation-building. Europe as center, waxing for so long, was now clearly on the wane. All of this could not but help to force Western Christianity to a reappraisal of its basic assumptions, not only with respect to itself but also to other cultural and religious traditions.

b. Ecumenicity itself as causal factor

From the very beginning ecumenical contact formed an important stimulus to greater tolerance toward others on the part of Western Christians involved in it. The great significance of this should not be underestimated. A new store of receptive catholicity was gradually built up within the Western church and missionary organizations simply by virtue of the fact that Christians from differing confessional, cultural, and racial backgrounds were being brought into direct communication with one another. Encounters of this kind could not fail eventually to have a profoundly broadening effect upon the attitude of participating individual Christians, churches, and mission agencies regarding traditions outside their own limited spheres of life and experience. Exposure to the piety, convictions, and commitments of others led for many to release from the narrow confines of the confessionalism to which they had been held in previous thrall. The ecumenical coming together of Christians, even apart from the substantive deliberations in which they engaged, was itself a pedagogical exercise in the opening of new horizons, in the relativizing first of parochial and later also European theological and ecclesiastical points of view.

c. Ecumenical perceptions: 1910–1963

In this paragraph a broad survey will be given of the highlights of ecumenical discussions on the Christian relation to other religions as well as of a number of other closely related developments in thinking with regard to mission that, it will be argued, contributed significantly to the evolution of the new mood referred to above.

(i). From hesitant respect to open dialogue

Concern at the 1910 Edinburgh conference was for the most part centered on "the problems and possibilities of missionary practice: methods, strategy, and tactics" (Gort, 2). Yet some of its deliberations and findings clearly prefigured and even laid the foundation for later developments in ecumenical thinking having a direct or indirect bearing on the question of the proper valuation of other faiths. The report of its Commission IV, for example, advocated an understanding and sympathetic attitude to the "non-Christian religions"; though only Christianity can truly satisfy the "elemental needs of the human soul," all other religions "disclose that in their higher forms they plainly manifest the working of the Spirit of God" (cited in Bassham, 19). The real debate on the other religions, however, would emerge only in the 1920's and 1930's in connection with the bitter theological controversy that divided Western Christianity into two disputatious camps, referred to as the 'Continental' and the 'Anglo-Saxon' schools of thought.

At the following ecumenical gathering, the 1928 Jerusalem conference of the International Missionary Council (IMC), this controversy caused deep disagreement on many a point. Respecting other religions, the 'Anglo-Saxon' position was that these faiths contain much that is good and worthy, that also in these traditions God has not left Himself without witness, and that Christianity's relation to them is rightly conceived as one of continuity and fulfillment. The other religions were viewed as potential allies in the 'coming great struggle' against irreligious secularism and atheism, which since the Russian Revolution in 1917 had been running like a fire through especially the Western world. The 'Continentals,' strongly influenced by the views of Karl Barth, were deeply opposed to the 'syncretistic' and 'social-gospel' tendencies in the 'Anglo-Saxon' school and maintained that Asian and African religions exist in a state of total darkness. These traditions must be rejected in their entirety as hindrances to human conversion, which is directly effected by the gospel, the supernatural grace that strikes the human heart like an unmediated flash of lightning. In the end, Jerusalem tried to synthesize these two views.

In 1932 the issue of the other religions was addressed in a very controversial way in a report, *Re-thinking Missions: A Laymen's Inquiry After One Hundred Years,* edited by William Ernest Hocking. In this publication it was argued that the traditional goal of mission, conversion to Christianity, should be replaced by the reconception of all religions as equally valid manifestations of truth and parallel ways of salvation called to live in peaceful coexistence, whereby each would be involved in "stimulating the other in growth toward the ultimate goal, unity in the completest religious truth" (Hocking, 44). The relativist thesis of this publication raised a great deal of opposition in ecumenical circles, and in 1936 Hendrik Kraemer was asked to write a study on the proper Christian stance toward other religions in preparation for the next IMC gathering in Tambaram, India in 1938. The resulting book, *The Christian Message in a Non-Christian World,* stressed the uniqueness of God's revelation in Jesus Christ as disclosed in the Christian Scriptures. Kraemer allowed for the existence of a general revelation of God in the world, to which, however, it is not possible for people outside of Christ rightly to respond: without faith in Him they remain caught in their sinful rebellion against

God. The only true salvation in the world is to be found solely in Christ. To Kraemer the relationship between Christianity and other religions was one of dissimilarity, antithesis, discontinuity. Kraemer's book was the object of intense discussion at Tambaram, but his position was not accepted by this gathering, which took an official stance on this matter almost identical to that adopted by Jerusalem: Christians must recognize the good in other religions but at the same time never fail to witness to Christ as fulfillment of that good.

The matter of Christian relations with other faiths did not come up for serious discussion again until 1954 at the Evanston Assembly of the WCC. Under the influence of the Indian theologian, D. T. Niles, Evanston acknowledged that the renascence of Asian religions "necessitates a new approach in our evangelizing task" (WCC 1954: 106). A long-term study was called for on "The Word of God and the Living Faiths of Men," to be carried out in close cooperation with the Christian Centers for the Study of Religion and Society which had been founded in many parts of the world during the 1950s at the instigation of the 1952 Willingen Conference of the IMC. The interim findings of this study, which were presented at the 1961 New Delhi Assembly of the WCC, stressed, among other things, the character of all religions as *living faiths,* whose adherents share in a common humanity, and the need for deeper examination of the relation of the gospel to other religious traditions (Samartha, 172). New Delhi identified *dialogue* as prerequisite for true Christian witness.

At the World Missionary Conference held in Mexico City in 1963 'dialogue' emerged as an articulated issue of permanent ecumenical concern. In one of its section reports, "The Witness of Christians to Men of Other Faiths," it is stated that the proper Christian approach to people of other religious convictions is one of love, respect, and patience (WCC 1964: 144). This kind of dialogical encounter includes "a concern both for the Gospel and for the other man. Without the first, dialogue becomes a pleasant conversation. Without the second, it becomes irrelevant, unconvincing, and arrogant" (p. 146). Christians should realize that it is *God* who is in dialogue with people and therefore ought to have the intention in their own dialogue "to move our partner and oneself to listen to what God in Christ reveals to us, and to answer him" (p. 47). Discussion on dialogue since Mexico City has consisted basically of further reflection on and development of these fundamental ideas. This conference may be seen as a significant watershed between the older and the newer attitude of Christians to other faiths.

The movement toward dialogue within the ecumenical movement did not occur in a vacuum but in the presence of a number of significant interrelated developments in the understanding of the nature and basis of mission, which in their own right also contributed to the emergence of today's newer mood.

(ii). From Western evangelistic outreach to holistic mission

The old perception of mission as word-proclamation of the gospel, as a task belonging to the Western church and its missionary sodalities, and as a movement from the North to the South and the East, began to be modified from the very beginning of the ecumenical movement. Though Edinburgh continued to see mission as evangelism, it clearly stated that the missionary task belongs to the whole church in the whole world: "The whole world is the mission field, and there is no Church that is not a Church in the mission field" (cited in Bassham, 17). Edinburgh recognized that ultimately only Asians and Africans would be capable of finishing the work of mission in their own lands and therefore emphasized the great importance of fostering the growth of mature and independent churches in the traditional 'mission fields.' An Indian Christian leader, V. S. Azariah, stated: "There can never be any progress [for Christianity in India] unless the aspirations of [Indian Christians] to self-government and independence are accepted, encouraged, and acted upon" (p. 18). To that end Edinburgh's chairman, J. R. Mott, traveled throughout Asia from 1912 to 1913, where he "convened twenty-one conferences from Columbo to Tokyo" (Hogg, 156), which later grew into National Christian Councils.

At Jerusalem the idea that the task of communicating the gospel in a given context belongs primarily to local Christians was given further support, partly due to the presence and influence of a relatively large number of 'younger church' representatives, who, in Mott's words, were received on a basis of "parity as to . . . status, participation, and interests to be served" (cited in Bassham, 21). If the Asian and African churches were really to become the bearers of mission in their own areas, every effort would have to be bent to strengthen them. Jerusalem also laid great emphasis on the social implications of the gospel: mission is not limited to evangelism but must also address problems such as racism, rural development, and industrialization. It is not surprising that Tambaram, the first ecumenical gathering in a third-world country, repeated and further explicated the theme of mission as the task of the whole church in the whole world. The 'Younger Churches' needed to be built up so that they could take their rightful place in the universal Christian community, sharing fully in its reflection on "the faith by which it lives, the nature of its witness, the conditions of its life and extension, the relationship it must hold to its environment" (p. 23). Tambaram also reiterated the holistic interpretation of Christian mission as having to do not only with individual salvation but also with the "realization of such ends as justice, freedom, and peace" (p. 24). Whitby, too, carried this development along by calling for a genuine "partnership in obedience," whereby Asian, African, and European churches would stand on an absolutely equal footing. And the insights of Willingen regarding the eschatological nature of mission, in the sense of both expectation and fulfillment, established that it is indeed possible for, and incumbent on, Christians to work here and now for holistic human salvation.

Growth in the self-reliance of the churches in Asia and Africa, the "coming of the Third Church" (Bühlmann), was greatly abetted by the founding of the World Council of Churches in 1948, an international fellowship in which these churches would be on a complete par with other churches, a forum in which their voice would be fully recognized in all matters pertaining to the life and work of the universal church. The integration of the IMC into the WCC in 1961 contributed to this process: now mission became organizationally as well as theoretically the concern and task of the worldwide church. As New Delhi put it: the unity which God wills is manifested as all Christians in each place "are united with the whole Christian fellowship . . . in such wise that ministry and members are accepted by all, and that all can act and speak together as occasion requires for the tasks to which God calls his people" (WCC 1962: 116). Mission is thoroughly holistic: "It is a commission given to the whole church to take the whole gospel to the whole world" (p. 85); thus, "We are concerned not with three continents but with six" (p. 250). All of these developments reached a culmination in Mexico City, after which they became more or less common coin. This latter conference concluded that "mission is rightly understood only if it is perceived as mission in, to, and from all six continents" (Gort, 7). This meant that "the new missionary frontier, which runs around the world, became the line between belief and unbelief in every country" (Bassham, 65).[4]

These developments in the perception of the nature of mission were fraught with great significance for the evolution of today's newer attitude to other religions. Earlier, Asian and African churches had been more or less restricted to bilateral relations with overseas missionary agencies and thus prevented from having contact with each other. Moreover, the Western agencies insisted on retaining responsibility for mission in these regions. This situation of isolation and dependence effectively cut the 'Younger Churches' off from meaningful encounter with their own cultural and religious heritages. The development of the concept of the 'whole church' may be seen as a protest against this state of affairs. But it would also pay off handsomely in terms of the advancement of the newer openness toward the other faiths. For Asian and African Christians would, of course, be much more likely than Western missionaries to seek to mediate the gospel via a positive approach to indigenous traditions, and their experiences and insights in this regard would gradually feed back into the evolution of a new ecumenical theology of religion. The notion of 'whole gospel' is also very interesting in this connection: it clearly

[4] This idea had already been adumbrated in L. Newbigin, *One Body, One Gospel, One World: The Christian Mission Today* (London: IMC, 1958).

helped to create the room for later ideas of interreligious cooperation at the political, economic, and social levels. And finally, the concept of 'whole world' implies that Christians are to view the adherents of other religions as believers, as people with a faith commitment of equal value and worth to their own. All three of these notions in their development throughout the years served as propellants to the movement in the direction of greater appreciation on the part of Christians for other cultural and religious traditions.

(iii). From missio ecclesiae to missio Dei

The ever growing ecumenical emphasis on mission as mission of the church, coupled as it necessarily was with a Christological conception of the basis of that mission, also had a *shadow side,* which gradually burgeoned until at its culmination at Tambaram. Especially in the post-Tambaram period the shadow side had practically come to supersede the light side of this development. From Edinburgh to Tambaram the notions of Christ as the source and the church as the bearer of mission evolved in tandem —each acting as propelling pawl, as it were, to the other's ratchet— first into Christo- and church-*centrism* and then into something very much like Christo- and church-*monism.* The mission belongs to Christ, Tambaram averred, and it is accomplished solely in and through the church. Though some of the discussion at the Amsterdam Assembly of the WCC evinces a less rigorous Christology, it would be Willingen that initiated a major changed in direction in ecumenical thinking on these issues, a change which was to provide great impetus to the ever quickening process of advance toward a more appreciative Christian attitude to other faiths.

Within the framework of the study project on "The Missionary Obligation of the Church," which had been endorsed by Whitby, several studies had been prepared for Willingen by, among others, J. C. Hoekendijk and a North American working group. Hoekendijk led a strong attack against the preoccupation with the church in missionary theology and in particular against the church-centrism which had been in such evidence since Tambaram. Missionary thinking that revolves around the church "is bound to go astray," he wrote, because it obscures the fact that it is actually the *world* that is the locus of mission (Hoekendijk 1952: 332). He argued for a concept of missionary apostolate whereby not the church but rather *God* is seen as the bearer, the author, and finisher of mission. Mission is *missio Dei.* What is at issue in mission is God's will and purposes for, and His saving actions in, the human world. There is also a *missio ecclesiae,* but it has no right of existence apart from God's mission. The *missio ecclesiae* is no more than a derivative of the *missio Dei.* The church is called to mission, but then as agent of and participant in what God himself is doing in His world. The church is "an instrument of God's redemptive action in this world . . . a means in God's hands to establish *shalom* in this world" (Hoekendijk 1950: 170). It is only as the church takes its eyes off its mission and itself and, standing at the foot of the Cross, fixes them on the world and God's mission therein that mission will be able to divest itself of all triumphalisms and take on a new character: that of self-denying servant in solidarity with all who hunger and thirst after justice and salvation. The report of the North American group evidenced the same views, but added one important aspect to the discussion, namely, that it is the *trinitarian* God who is the subject of mission in human history, and that Christian mission rooted in the Trinity would be led to "sensitive and total response to what the triune God has done and is doing in the world" (*Why Missions?,* 6).

Some of these insights, particularly those having to do with God's relationship to the world and the church, were not accepted by Willingen itself; they would begin only later to exert real influence. This conference did, however, retain in its statements explicit reference to the triune God as the source of mission. Two years later Evanston reaffirmed the older Christological foundation of the missionary task, but the following WCC Assembly at New Delhi put mission back on a very firm trinitarian basis. The deliberations of the Mexico City conference can in many respects be seen as a continuation of the Willingen discussions on *missio Dei* and related concepts. This conference recognized that the world is the arena of mission. If the church is to ascertain the proper shape and "forms of missionary obedience to which Christ is now calling" it, it will have to identify and link up with "everything God is actively doing in the world apparently independently of the Christian community" (WCC 1964: 157-58). The agenda for Christian mission is written by the Kingdom activity of the King in His world. The *missio ecclesiae* requires to be shaped by the *missio Dei.* Although Mexico City left a number of problems unresolved, it was clear by the time it adjourned that a major shift of emphasis had taken place in ecumenical mission theology: *from* the Christian church *to* the world, "where God is at work and where the church must go to find him and cooperate with him" (Bassham, 50). A year after Mexico City, Raymond Panikkar articulated this shift very trenchantly: "The Christian attitude is not ultimately one of bringing God *in,* but of bringing him *forth,* of discovering Christ; not one of command but of service" (p. 45).

Clearly, these movements from *missio ecclesiae* to *missio Dei,* from ecclesio-centrism to world-orientation, from Christo-centrism to trinitarianism also played a prime role in the emergence of the newer Christian attitude to people of other faiths and their cultural traditions. Recognition that the triune God is and always has been profoundly present and active in His world among all His people must of necessity lead Christians eventually to acknowledgement of the significance, the value and worth of all positive human religious response to the salvific revelatory initiative of this Creator, Saviour, and Paraclete.

3. Concluding Remarks

It is fair to say that in the 20th century a groundswell change has taken place in the attitude of Christians toward other religions. The period from 1910 to 1963 has witnessed a sure, even if at times spotty, growth within Protestant ecumenical thinking in the direction of greater openness and dialogue. In contrast with an earlier period, in which Western churches behaved as though they had rights of ownership to the gospel as well as to its systematic interpretation and missionary communication, today's situation shows definite evidence of a growing awareness of a worldwide Christian community that, constrained by its own faith, as the Yugoslavian 'evangelical' theologian Peter Kuzmic has recently argued, must engage in appreciative and cooperative encounter with "non-Christians where in the areas of science, art, literature, philosophy, and social work they are producing what may well be found on the new earth. As Calvin said: 'All truth is from God; and consequently . . . we ought not to reject it [wherever it is found]; for it has come from God' " (p. 152). Today there is a feeling among many Christians that the real task of mission consists in the attempt to bridge the gap between belief and unbelief everywhere in the world. Lesslie Newbigin's recent publications[5] suggest that the greatest contemporary missionary challenge may well lie in the West and that those who wish to meet that challenge will have to listen attentively to the voices of Third World Christians who have been in creative encounter with traditional cultures and religions (Newbigin, 146), i.e., they will be required to give careful ear to the "Third Church" which "is on the point of becoming the First" (Bühlmann, 24).

To be sure, there are those who continue to oppose dialogical encounter between people of differing faiths because they suppose it to be a 'new form of syncretism' or because they view it as a threat to mission and evangelism. This became clear, e.g., at the 1975 Nairobi Assembly of the WCC. The old debate on syncretism has by no means died away; and where it is carried on, it continues to be laden with the remaining realities of North Atlantic imperialized mission. Some Western Christians and missions continue to evince the "lingering effects of benevolent paternalism," the assumption of an earlier missionary generation "that their respective brand of Christianity was better than anything that the Third World could produce on its own" (Gensichen, 20). And there are a number

[5] In addition to *Foolishness To the Greeks*, see his *The Other Side of 1984: Questions For the Churches* (Geneva: WCC, 1984), and "Can the West Be Converted?" *International Bulletin of Missionary Research*, 11 (1987): 2-8.

of substantive theological problems that remain to be ironed out. Some of the questions raised by Mexico City have not yet been answered: What is the relationship between God's action in the church and His action in the world outside the church? Can a distinction be drawn between God's providential and God's redeeming action (WCC 1964: 157-58)? D. C. Mulder refers to similar problems in a recent essay (p. 215).

Despite this remaining opposition and these problems, it may be fairly said that dialogue is now widely recognized among Christians as the best means of assuring open, constructive interaction between people of different backgrounds and cultures; of "promoting positive communication with people outside of the life of the church, especially with people of other faiths" (Bassham, 90); and of discovering answers to the questions just mentioned. Within the churches "there is increasing knowledge of and sensitivity to other religions;" to many Christians "other religions are no longer simply odd and strange ways of life but challenging achievements and not rarely sources of at least complementary light and inspiration" (De Smet, 10, 9). Christian theology is beginning to think ever more seriously in terms of the *contextualization and inculturation* of the gospel by local Christian communities in converse with the world church and people of other faiths in the totality of their human settings; to speak of the "construction of local theologies" (Schreiter); to argue that the proper model of cross-cultural mediation of God's Word is that of *kenosis and skenosis,* initial emptying and new tabernacling (Pobee, 9).

With respect to the attitude to other religions Christianity seems indeed to be standing on the threshold of something new, to be experiencing the quickening movements of a consensus struggling to be gestated. It is difficult to look into the future and predict what, at a given point a number of years hence, the *Wirkungsgeschichte* of present insights will have proven to be. Today there are ample signs of things new aborning, things having to do with the number *three*: the dawning of the third millennium of the Common Era; the coming of the Third Church; a new sense among Christians of their vocation to self-denying unity, kenotic witness, and joint fellowship to the "third encounter" (Mundadan, 28) with the world of other cultures and religions, in which the triune God is salvifically present as Lord of the whole of creation and all of human history.

Bibliography

Bassham, R. C. *Mission Theology: 1948–1975, Years of Worldwide Creative Tension, Ecumenical, Evangelical, and Roman Catholic.* Pasadena: Wm. Carey Press, 1979.

Blanke, F. *Missionsprobleme des Mittelalters und der Neuzeit.* Zürich/ Stuttgart: Zwingli Verlag, 1966.

Bühlmann, W. *The Coming of the Third Church.* Slough: St. Paul Publications, 1976.

De Smet, R. "Christ and the Transforming Growth of the Religions." Public Lecture, Free University of Amsterdam, May 19, 1988; – Mimeo. with bibliography, 10 pp.

Gensichen, H-W. "Mission For Hope — Hope For Mission: A Missiological Meditation." *Mission Studies: Journal of the International Association For Mission Studies* V–1:9 (1988): 15-21.

Gort, J. D. *Your Kingdom Come: Melbourne, Australia, 12–25 May, 1980.* Amsterdam: Free University.

Hocking, W. E., ed. *Re-Thinking Missions: A Laymen's Inquiry After One Hundred Years.* New York: Harper & Brothers, 1932.

Hoekendijk, J. C. "Call to Evangelism." *International Review of Missions* XXXIX:154 (1950): 162-75.

——. "The Church in Missionary Thinking." *International Review of Missions* XLI:163 (1952): 324-36.

Hogg, William Richey. *Ecumenical Foundations: A History of the International Missionary Council and Its Nineteenth-Century Background.* New York: Harper, 1952

Kelly, J. N. D. *Early Christian Doctrines.* London: Adam & Charles Black, 1965.

Kuzmic, P. "History and Eschatology: Evangelical Views." In *In Word and Deed: Evangelism and Social Responsibility.* Ed. B. J. Nicholls. Grand Rapids: Eerdmans, 1985, pp. 135-64.

Mulder, D. C. " 'None Other Gods' — 'No Other Names.' " *The Ecumenical Review* 38 (1986): 209-15.

Mundadan, A. M. "Gospel of Hope For the Third Millennium: A Reflection From India." *Mission Studies: Journal of the International Association For Mission Studies* V–1:9 (1988): 22-29.

Newbigin, L. *Foolishness to the Greeks: The Gospel and Western Culture.* Geneva: WCC, 1986.

Panikkar, R. *The Unknown Christ of Hinduism.* London: Darton, Longman & Todd, 1964.

Pobee, J. S. "Christian Mission Towards the Third Millennium: The Gospel of Hope." *Mission Studies: Journal of the International Association For Mission Studies* V–1:9 (1988): 6-14.

Race, A. *Christians and Religious Pluralism: Patterns in the Christian Theology of Religions.* London: SCM, 1983.

Samartha, S. J. *Living Faiths and the Ecumenical Movement.* Geneva: WCC, 1971.

Schreiter, R. J. *Constructing Local Theologies.* Maryknoll: Orbis Books, 1984.

Why Missions? Preparatory Studies for the Missionary Obligation of the Church. Committee on Research in Foreign Missions, NCCC/USA, Mimeo, 1952.

World Council of Churches. *The Evanston Report: The Second Report of the WCC.* Ed. W. A. Visser 't Hooft. London: SCM, 1954.

——. 1962. *The New Delhi Report: The Third Assembly of the WCC, 1961.* Ed. W. A. Visser 't Hooft. New York: Association Press.

——. 1964. *Witness in Six Continents: Records of the Meeting of the Commission on World Mission and Evangelism of the WCC held in Mexico City 8–19 December 1963.* Ed. R. K. Orchard. London: Edinburgh House Press.

——. 1976. *Breaking Barriers: The Official Report of the Fifth Assembly of the WCC, Nairobi 23 November–10 December 1975.* Ed. D. M. Paton. Grand Rapids: Eerdmans.

Chapter 4

Biblical Presuppositions For and Against Syncretism

Anton Wessels

This article wishes to make clear that Asian and African contributions to contextual theology are too lightly accused of syncretism on the basis of references to the Old Testament.
To demonstrate this, the Old Testament is examined to discern its attitude toward the relationship of God (Yahweh) to both El as well as Baal. It is apparent that a close relationship exists between faith in Yahweh and the surrounding Canaanitic culture and religion. The Old Testament nowhere speaks negatively of God when called El. This is not the case, however, when God is called Baal, as is manifest in the conduct of the prophets Elijah and Hosea. Adoption occurs in the both cases, however. 'Yahwism' adopts certain aspects of both El and Baal. The question which ought to be posed is: Who has 'overcome' whom? In my opinion it is necessary to speak not only of *cultural* or *literary* dependence but of *religious* dependance as well. Such an understanding can contribute to greater nuance in appraising forms of syncretism elsewhere.

"I am firmly convinced that there is in the Bible another attitude to people of other faiths that Christians in Asia and elsewhere need to recover and celebrate." (Ariarajah, xiv)

1. Introduction

It is not unusual that Asian and African contributions to Christian theologizing are quickly regarded as syncretistic by theologians from the West. What is then meant is that some theologians have allowed themselves to be influenced more (or sometimes completely) by their own cultural *context* than by the *text* (of the Bible or of *the* Christian message) in interpreting the Christian message within their own Asian or African context. They thereby betray the pure interpretation of the Biblical message, according to this line of reasoning.

I will leave undiscussed here the assumption which this view couches that the precise content of the pure message of the Bible can easily be ascertained. The concern of this article is another line of enquiry. Negative appraisals of Asian and African contributions to theology often proceed from certain Biblical presuppositions. What is particularly appealed to in this context is the opposition of the Old Testament prophets to the idolatry of the Baal cult such as the confrontation between the prophet Elijah and the priests of Baal on Mt. Carmel (I Kings 18). A remonstrant finger is raised, as it were, against forms of syncretism which are supposedly currently emerging in Asia and Africa.

In this article the issue is how exactly the relation between faith in Yahweh and the surrounding culture stands in the Old Testament. Is the issue there really, or even primarily, vehement opposition to syncretism as the above-mentioned presuppositions seem to suggest? Is it exclusively the protest of the prophets against syncretism which rings out here? (Lanckowski, 227-43). Or does the Old Testament era manifest the entry of the message of Yahweh into Canaanite culture, in the same way that the modern era speaks of African and Asian contextualization? How was the faith of the Israelites, coming into the land of Canaan from a Bedouin background, related to the culture and the religion of the indigenous population of Canaan? Were there also, in addition to the anti-Baalism (and thus anti-syncretism) expressed on Mount Carmel at Baal-Peor (Elijah), forms of adoption or assimilation of elements from the Canaanite cultural and religious context which did not fall under the verdict of the prophets? Was there only discontinuity between faith in Yahweh and the religion of the inhabitants of Canaan, or was there also continuity? Is the assumption true that there was a *cultural* syncretism for some time after the immigration of the Israelites into Canaan, but no corresponding *religious* syncretism, and that wherever the latter threatened to emerge, it was opposed by the prophets? (Colpe, 220). Is it possible to speak only of *literary* influence on the Old Testament by the mythology of fertility, without any concomitant influence in the area of 'dogmatics,' as someone else posits? (Cf. Worden, 273-97).

It is not possible to examine the entire Old Testament with regard to these questions within the scope of one article. For our aim it is sufficient to give a number of important examples of the interrelationship obtaining between faith in Yahweh and the Canaanite context. To this end, we will endeavour to say something about the relationship between faith in Yahweh and the Canaanite context in general (§ 2) in order subsequently to pause at Yahweh and El (§ 3), and at Yahweh and Baal (§ 4). Consideration must be given to the relation between El and Baal in order to obtain a picture of Canaanite contextualization. I will then focus on the two figures who epitomize the struggle against Baalism: Elijah and Hosea. In the conclusion I will pose the problem of what it means when one faith (in Yahweh) 'overcomes' another (Canaanism).* It is possible that the answer to this question could lead us to a more nuanced appraisal of Asian and African contributions to theology in terms of syncretism.

2. Faith in Yahweh and the Canaanite context

The faith of Israel did not come about all at once. It has a history, and crystallized slowly over the centuries through mutual interchange with its Canaanite environment. The Hebrew nomads who entered the land of Canaan in various phases, and settled there, came into contact with a population which possessed various religious conceptions and a culture of its own. The religion which thus emerged in Israel is the result of a process of give and take, of rejection and acceptance of what was encountered in the Canaanite context.

Thus faith in one God is the result of a development. It is sometimes said that we ought to speak of an initial henotheism (only one of the gods really deserves worship) rather than monotheism (faith in one God; F. M. Müller.) Faith in Yahweh, in the exclusivist sense, emerged slowly. Initially the existence of numerous gods was assumed, as Psalm 82 witnesses: God stands in the council of gods. He enacts judgment amidst the gods.

There seems to be no doubt that from the period of the conquest of Canaan by the Israelites until deep into the time of the Kings, Yahweh worship was mingled in one way or another with expressions of what is called popular piety. Ashera, the consort of the fertility god Baal was worshipped along with Baal. The Ashera symbol stood on the 'high places' of Canaan —in the form of a tree or a wooden pole— next to the altar of Baal. The worship of Baal and Ashera was never completely eliminated until the time of the exile. Just how long this mingling continued to exist can be seen from II Kings 21:7, among others, which mentions that a statue of Ashera was even found in the Jerusalem temple — something which is condemned, however.

An indication that one can speak of a process of Canaanizing is the fact that the Old Testament contains frequent usage of Canaanite metaphors, formulations, and ideologies, particularly in describing the character of Yahweh's actions. Michael David Coogan reaches the following conclusion in his consideration of Canaanite religion: "In the light of Canaanite religious and mythological literature, the declaration of the prophet Ezekiel to Jerusalem is strikingly apposite: 'Your origin and your birth are of the land of the Canaanites' (Ezekiel 16:3)."

---

* The term 'overcome' is the standard translation of the German *aufheben*, which is used in describing interaction and has the dual meaning of 'to raise to a higher level' and 'to abolish.' Wherever it thus appears in this article it will bear the same ambiguity.

A well-known example of *literary* dependence and affinity with the Canaanite context is the frequent use of the number *seven* in the Bible. God called Moses on the seventh day (Exodus 24:16); the creation took place in seven days; the fall of Jericho happened on the seventh day; after seven priests had blown seven trumpets and had marched around the city seven times. This predilection for the number *seven* has Canaanite precedents. As another example, the emphasis on of the initial *childlessness* of Abraham, Isaac, and Jacob is to be regarded as a Canaanite commonplace (Coogan, 52-53). Furthermore, when the Old Testament deals with what the duties of the king, namely, the care for the powerless in society —the poor, the widows, and the orphans (for example in Psalm 72 where the ideal king is described)— this corresponds to what is said concerning the duties of the king in the Canaanite context (Coogan, 56-57).

The building of the temple also points to a Canaanizing of the religion of Yahweh. Although it is true that various sanctuaries eventually had to make way for the one sanctuary in Jerusalem, Solomon nevertheless made use of an existing Jebusite cult location in the building of his temple in Jerusalem (II Samuel 24), and probably built according to a Phoenician model (I Kings 5; 7:13-51; Schoneveld, 8-88).

3. Yahweh and El

El is the name for the supreme god of the Canaanite pantheon. More has become known about El, primarily due to the discoveries of the texts from the ancient Canaanite port of Ugarit. The study of the Ugaritic texts enables us to form a better picture of Canaanite religion in the second millennium B.C. The god El apparently was a kind of 'High God' and stood at the head of the pantheon. He was the first in the council of the gods. He created heaven and earth, as well as the other gods and is called the father of years, father of the gods and of mankind, king and the eternal wise one. He was the Holy One and was appraised as the friendly and merciful God. His judgeship is also intimated (Blommendaal, 162-63). Several of these Ugaritic Canaanite traits of El can be found in the narratives of the patriarchs, which narrate how the patriarchs worshipped God at various locations under the name of El. Yahwism accepted these sanctuaries (Seebasz, 80). At these various sites, the patriarchs did not worship various *local* gods, but they encountered —this is how it should be viewed— El as so many manifestations of the one Creator God, known by various corollary names. Thus, Abraham first encountered God in Salem (Jerusalem) as *El 'Elyôn,* God the very Highest. Upon returning from his clash with the five kings, Abraham is greeted by Melchizedek, the king of Salem and priest of *El 'Elyôn,* Creator of heaven and earth (Genesis

14:18-22). On his ninety-ninth birthday, Abram receives a theophany from God *El Shaddai*, God the All-Mighty (Genesis 17:1).

Another name, by which El is designated in Beersheba, is *El 'Ôlam*, the Everlasting (Genesis 21:33):

> Abraham planted a tamarisk tree in Beersheba, and called there on the name of the Lord [Yahweh], the Everlasting God [*El 'Ôlam*].

The name *El-Roi*, 'God of Seeing,' occurs in the story about Hagar:

> For she [Hagar] said: Have I even here seen after him who sees me? (Genesis 16:13)

The Jacob cycle provides yet another appellation:

> And Jacob came to Luz (that is, Bethel), which is in the land of Canaan, he and all the people who were with him, and there he built an altar, and called the place *El-Bethel*, because there God had revealed himself to him when he fled from his brother. (Genesis 35:6, 7; compare Gen. 28:16, 17 —*El Shaddai*— the Almighty in Hebron, or El of the cosmic mountain, Exodus 6:2; Cross, 122.)

We can also infer how El was appraised in Israel from the several of personal names in which El occurs. The names Elkanah, 'God has created' (I Samuel 1:1; 2:11, 20), and Asahel, 'God has made' (II Samuel 2:18ff.; 3:27, 30), underscore El's role as Creator. The name Abiel, 'God is my father' (I Samuel 9:1; 14:51) points to His fatherhood, and the name Elhanan expresses the merciful character of God (II Samuel 21:19; Blommendaal, 163).

It is amply clear from these stories of the patriarchs and these personal names that this God (El) was known to the inhabitants of the land. We must undoubtedly speak of a certain continuity between the religion of the patriarchs and that of their environment. In the God who revealed himself to them, they recognized the newly lighted face of that God whom they had already worshipped as king of all gods and creatures, as Creator of heaven and earth; the one who was called 'El' in Canaan (Cross, 120).

It is striking that, unlike Baal, El is nowhere criticized in the Old Testament and his name remained in use in personal names. El was never seen as a rival to Yahweh as Baal was. When the Israelites introduced Yahweh to Canaan upon entering the land El's high status continued to be acknowledged and was only slowly replaced by Yahweh as the highest and only God. In a text such as Deut. 32:8, 9 ('The Song of Moses'), the author sees El as the highest God:

> When the Most High [*El 'Elyôn*] gave to the nations their inheritance, when he separated the sons of men, he fixed the bounds of the people according to the number of the sons of God [Heb: 'Israel']. For the Lord's [Yahweh] portion is his people, Jacob his allotted heritage. (Deuteronomy 32:8, 9)

One could say that El has been fused with Yahweh in one way or another.

> . . . the Yahweh cult, although taking the lead, did not fight the El cult, but endeavoured to assimilate both cults. Thus the El cult was conceived of as an older form of belief, and although it was lifted to a higher level by the Yahweh epiphany, it continued to be a recognized form of belief in the true God, and the God of Abraham, Isaac, and Jacob, in spite of the difference of the names, was identified in His essence with Yahweh. (Eissfeldt, 35)

El has therefore ceded much to Yahweh, such as the aspects of creator-god, king, and father and Yahweh has adopted and incorporated various traits of El; recall, for example, the sacrificial customs, cult songs, and such. "El is the special contribution of Canaan to the world. He is fused with the stern God Yahweh, and thus has become the expression of all fatherliness, being mild and stern at the same time" (Eissfeldt, 37). What the nature of this contribution entails can well be presented in brief by referring to the conclusion of Blommendaal's study:

> The world-wide vision, which witnessed to the ultimate encounter between Yahweh and the nations, and their being drawn into His salvation (cf. Isaiah 2:2-4; 25:6; 45:22), must be considered the most important fruit of the development of universalism in the Old Testament, for which the El-tradition was of such extraordinary importance. Boundaries were broken down and a perspective towards unimagined vistas was opened up, above all, towards the Kingdom of God, where people of all races and languages could meet one another as people about the throne of their Creator, King, Judge, and Father, where righteousness and justice ruled and that *kabod* (glory) was brought to God which was due Him. [pp. 171-72]

Blommendaal considers El as foundation and exponent of Old Testament universalism. That is to say, that certain universalist representations of El from Canaanite religion were of fundamental significance for the universalism in the Old Testament. These universal traits have been transferred to Yahweh. Yahweh thus becomes the Creator of the world and king of the gods and of all people, to whom is due the praise of the entire creation (pp. 14-15). Blommendaal also mentions the social-ethical element as one of the most striking aspects of the 'Elistic' terminology: in connection with this, Yahweh is portrayed as the God of righteousness and justice, who stands on the side of the just and upright, who takes on the cause of the miserable, the oppressed, and the socially dispossessed, and who turns against the oppressors and the godless (p. 170).

4. Yahweh and Baal

Baal (literally: 'Lord,' or owner; plural: Baalim) is a West-Semitic name for god. The god, Baal, is connected with the weather. He is a god of vegetation, the god of fertility. Ashera or Astarte is often mentioned with him in one breath. Baal often adopted a local character, such as Baal Berit(h), the city god of Shechem (Judges 8:33; 9:4), or Baal Zebub of Ekron (II Kings 1:2, 3, 6). He is also worshipped as Baal *shamem*, 'god of the heavens.' The sanctuary at Baal Peor was apparently used by Moabites and Israelites over a long period of time (Numbers 23-25).

Initially, as with El, Baal would probably have been seen as the equivalent of Yahweh. An indication of this is the fact that Baal occurs in the names of the sons of Saul and David. The name of one of Saul's sons, Ish Baal, is later changed to Ish Boseth ('man of shame'), possibly because the name of Baal was no longer a name for God (I Chronicles 8:33; 9:39; II Samuel 2:8).

The Israelites started to worship the Canaanite fertility god Baal once they had exchanged nomadism for a sedentary agricultural life in Canaan. It was, as it were, necessary to turn to the god of the land, Baal, in the new farming situation, since this god could give rain and fertility. It is very probable that many of the customs/rites which were connected to working the land, had a religious character and were in that sense tied to Baal. It cannot be denied that Yahweh took over many of Baal's features. A number of examples can clarify this:

- When it is said that Yahweh "rides on the clouds" (Psalm 68:34; 104:3), this is a metaphor borrowed from Baal.
- When there is mention of the conflict between *Yahweh and the sea,* a manner of expression is employed which has been derived from the myth of Baal's conflict with the sea (cf. Job 26:12, 13; Psalm 89:10; Isaiah 27:1), even though the Biblical narrative typically describes the event as *historical,* namely, the journey through the Red Sea or through the Jordan (Psalm 77:15-20; Isaiah 51:9, 10; Psalm 114:1-3).
- When it is said in Jeremiah 9:21 that, "Death has come up into our windows," such an expression can only be properly understood against the backdrop of the myth about Baal's building of his house, whereby he hesitated in putting in a window. Popular belief held that the god 'Death' entered through the window.
- When a narration describes how Yahweh blesses with fertility, expressions are employed which were previously also used of Baal.

It is also clear that the Canaanite fertility myth influenced the literature of the Israelites. No one described this environment in which the fertility myths were popular better than Hosea, even though he simultaneously opposed it fiercely. His manner of description testifies to literary dependence:

> And in that day, says the Lord, I will answer the heavens and they shall answer the earth; and the earth shall answer the grain, the wine, and the oil, and they shall answer Jezreel. (Hosea 2:20-21)

Thus a whole series of gods take part in the growing process. Yet this activity must be credited to Yahweh alone according to Hosea. "It is significant that Hosea . . . should be the one who depends so much upon Canaanite literature for the expression of the true doctrine," in view of the fact that he condemns "the Canaanite practices of unfaithful Israelites" (Worden, 289-97).

It must be clearly pointed out that this also issued in a confrontation between Yahweh and Baal. The anti-Baal attitude comes into the foreground most clearly in the case of the prophets. Baal was viewed increasingly as an idol by Israel's prophets. The Canaanite fertility cult was regarded as a seduction to which the Israelites only too often succumbed. This was seen as an evil and as adultery against Yahweh. (Compare Jeremiah 13:26-7; Isaiah 57:3; Ezekiel 16:36-40; Hosea 2:2; 7:4.)

5. Elijah

The prophet Elijah is known above all as the prophet who turned against King Ahab and his serving of Baal. He also opposed King Ahaziah's consultation of Baal Zebub of Ekron (I Kings 1:16). Elijah accuses Ahab of forsaking Yahweh and his covenant:

> And he answered, "I have not troubled Israel; but you have, and your father's house, because you have forsaken the commandments of the Lord [Yahweh] and followed the Baals." (I Kings 18:18)

Elijah seizes the opportunity of the great drought to demonstrate that not Baal, the rain god who was thought to provide rain and fertility every season, but Yahweh has the power to provide rain. Elijah was convinced that rain and fertility, as well as healing and sickness, were exclusively dependent on Yahweh (Jacob, 250-51).

On Mt. Carmel, which was located in the border area between Israel and Phoenicia which had been annexed to Israel by Ahab in the ninth century, the famous confrontation took place between Elijah —whose name, Yahweh (and thus not Baal) is God, sounds like a program— and the Baal priests (I Kings 18). A Baal sanctuary must have been situated there very early on.

The divine verdict on Mt. Carmel concerns the reconquest of a local sanctuary, where the Baal of Carmel was worshipped, for the service of Yahweh (I Kings 18:30). Elijah confronted the people with a fundamental decision between Yahweh and Baal (the Phoenician Baal of the heavens, or Melkart, the city god of Tyre, whence came Ahab's wife Jezebel; Mulder 1979).

Elijah is seen, on the one hand, as the one who saved faith in Yahweh from a demise into syncretism. On the other hand, it can also be said that this Elijah, who so ardently opposed the Baal priests and who was the real instigator of the violent action of king Jehu against the service of Baal, received a revelation from God on Mt. Horeb not in the thunder storm, but in the sighing of a mild wind. This Elijah, who obtained refuge from a Phoenician widow in Zarephath (I Kings 17:9), had to learn that God's revelation is not exhausted by the storm (I Kings 19).

6. Hosea

The prophet Hosea lived in the Kingdom of Israel (ca. 750–722) and experienced both its flourishing and its decay. The theme of his book can be indicated by the word 'adultery': the love of Yahweh for his people, as opposed to the unfaithfulness of the people towards God. The bond of marriage between God and his people is broken because Israel combines the fertility rites with the worship of Yahweh. The marriage between Yahweh and his people is rent, indeed, has deteriorated into prostitution, if accompanied by fertility rites and symbols.

Hosea permits Israel's first 'husband' to complain about the 'whore' Israel, since she does not acknowledge that Yahweh, not Baal, provides grain and oil (Hosea 2:7).

> . . . a spirit of harlotry has led them astray, and they have left their God to play the harlot. (Hosea 4:12)

The religion which is practised is self-made (cf. Hosea 8:5). The people have even made golden and silver idols of which nevertheless divinity cannot be predicated (Hosea 8:4):

> And now they sin more and more, and make for themselves molten images, idols skillfully made of their silver, all of them the work of craftsmen. (Hosea 13:2)

> And we will say no more, "Our God," to the work of our own hands. (Hosea 14:3)

The consequences of Baal worship are impurity and death (Hosea 6:10; 13:1). Yahweh is especially incomparable in that he cannot be molded into an image. The reality of the gods stands or falls with the product of human hands while the reality of Yahweh occurs in freedom: "I shall love them freely" (Hosea 14:5; Wolff, 402-3).

Hosea has become the prophet who epitomizes the opposition to syncretism in the religion of Israel. He wanted to be an upright adherent of Yahweh in the midst of the agricultural civilization of Northern Israel, where he chiefly appears. Yet at the same time he is again an example of someone who has derived much from that Canaanite environment and who articulates his message in its language. He who was so opposed to illegitimate syncretism himself participated in Canaanizing in a certain sense. Hosea does not employ the 'violent' methods of an Elijah, nor does he choose the way of the Rechabites, who 'opted out' (Jeremiah 35:1-19). This last group, under the aegis of Jonadab, endeavoured to spiritually continue the nomadic existence in Canaan. They rallied to the side of

King Jehu (I Kings 10:15), who had made anti-Baalism a matter of state (I Kings 10:15, II Kings 10), a policy which suffered shipwreck.

In his struggle against Baal, Hosea employed a 'homeopathic' method, as Jacob has so accurately expressed it. He employs evil in order to subsequently heal it. He himself descended into the arena of Baal worship and is thus personally very involved in bearing out his message of resistance. And it was this personal experience which would decisively influence his message (Jacob, 251). Hosea must enter into a marriage with an immoral woman. The intention of such a 'sacred marriage' (*hieros gamos*) was to foster the fertility of the land. The highest class of temple prostitutes, as representative of the mother goddess, probably entered into 'sacred marriage' with a youthful deity in order to guarantee the fertility of the land.

Although this custom occurred in Israel (Genesis 38:21f.; Numbers 25:1; I Kings 14:24; Jeremiah 3:2; Hosea 4:12ff.) and there was also a relation between sacrificial meals and sexual rites (Isaiah 57:5, 7; Ezekiel 22:9; Hosea 4:12ff.) such practices evoked the opposition both of certain kings, e.g. King Asa (I Kings 15:12), King Jehoshaphat (I Kings 22:46), and King Josiah (II Kings 23:7), as well as of prophets, especially Hosea. The law also condemns this prostitution (Leviticus 19:29; Deuteronomy 23:17; Kittel, VI, 579-95).

Hosea transformed the meaning of this 'sacred marriage' by his own marriage. On the one hand, he delivered criticism of the cult, but on the other, he conserved and reappraised ('overcame') positive elements in an authentically Yahwist climate. The ritual of the 'sacred marriage' became the expression of the *history* of God's marriage to his people. Hosea borrowed a large number of images from Canaanite religion, in order to subsequently utilize them to express the love of God: in the first place the love of a spouse, but also that of a father (cf. Hosea 11:1, 3, 4, 8).

> In order that Yahweh might be able to claim sole and total adoration of his faithful, it was indispensable that the figure of the jealous God and of the warrior, which was the characteristic trait of the God of Moses, be complemented by the figure of the loving God, tender, and compassionate, just as it was inevitable that the religion of the desert be complemented by that of the farmland, and that agriculture be placed under the independence of Yahweh. [Jacob, 258]

7. Conclusion

When speaking of the relationship between faith in Yahweh and the Canaanite context, one could speak of the 'overcoming' religion, a term which has been employed when referring to situation in which the Christian faith addresses a particular foreign religious and cultural context. As has already been noted, the word 'overcome' can have two meanings when so employed. It can mean to 'abolish,' and it can mean to 'raise to a higher level.' The important question then is: What exactly is 'overcome' by what? It is commonly thought, in terms of the Canaanite context, that Yahwism —faith in Yahweh— 'overcame' faith in El of Baal, and was not itself 'overcome.'

J. H. Bavinck spoke of *possessio* in connection with the relation of Christian faith to other religions: "Christian life does not accommodate itself to pagan forms of life, but takes possession of them and, in so-doing, renews them" [Bavinck, 181]. Elements from other religions are 'taken into possession' by Christian faith. In this sense one could speak of Yahweh taking possession of El. But the question which surfaces here is, Who really possesses whom? Can one also say that El 'took possession' of Yahweh, or 'overcame' Yahweh, in the case of the relationship of El to Yahwism?

This survey warrants the conclusion that the Old Testament shows that faith in Yahweh is related to the Canaanite context (culture and religion) in such a way that it would be incorrect to advance exclusively the antithetical (anti-Baal) line.

– In the first place, such an antithesis does not exist between Yahweh and El. The kind of resistance directed against Baal does not occur with respect to El. One can state that Yahweh has adopted various traits of El. One can surely posit that in certain regards, El was the giver and Yahweh the receiver (Blommendaal).

– We have spoken of literary and cultural dependence, and illustrated this with examples. Worden speaks of the many Old Testament echoes of the Ugaritic literature. He often calls the *literary* dependence striking, and speaks of much borrowing (Worden, 276). But it seems to me untenable to maintain that a *religious* dependence could be denied completely. *Form* —temple building, and hymns, for example— and *content* cannot so easily be disengaged from one another. In addition to speaking of the 'overcoming' of El by Yahweh, one must therefore also speak of the converse, namely, the 'overcoming' of Yahweh by El. Many important qualities of El, particularly such universalist qualities as Fatherhood and Kingship, were incorporated by Yahweh.

This survey has also taught us that one cannot speak only of antithesis in the relationship to Baal, one cannot speak only of antithesis. Yahweh's relationship to Baal is not just negative, as is usually thought. There is undoubtedly literary influence but it seems to me untenable to speak only of a literary influence (for example, the fertility myths) on the Old Testament, and to deny a concomitant influence in the area of 'dogmatics' (Worden, 273-97). Likewise, it is inappropriate to speak only of Israel's *cultural* syncretism after the immigration into Canaan, but not of its *religious* syncretism (Colpe, 220). (Literary) form and (religious) content are not so easily separated.

Nomadic, Sinaitic Yahwism fused together with Canaanism. It might be true that Canaanism was engulfed (*bewältigt*) in this process, but this has still led to a modification of both (Maag, 134-53). In Canaan the Israelites assimilated themselves, in a certain regard, to the religious forms which flourish in a sedentary society, even though they did not thereby disavow their nomadic or semi-nomadic derivation. Nomadic religion is little concerned with cultic regulations; piety consists primarily in obedience and trust in the power of God. Nomadic religion is one of promise. God is a shepherd to them, and not a king (!), as for the Canaanites.

When the prophet Hosea speaks of the love of Yahweh, his description is coloured strongly by the Baalite context. Hosea was able to convey his message about the love of Yahweh for his people by employing the language of that context and by indeed actually (recall his marriage) immersing himself in it completely, while simultaneously transforming and 'overcoming' it.

There is a place for 'overcoming' in the sense of rejecting and abolishing, but there is equally an opportunity for a manner of 'overcoming' in the positive sense of the word, "one of the most successful attempts at purification and deepening in the religion of the fathers" (Jacob, 251).

Labuschagne views the Yahwist as a theologian who has explicated the traditions of the fathers within the context of faith in Yahweh. The Yahwist viewed the divine images consorting under various names not as idols, but as pre-Yahwist manifestations of God: Yahweh was present incognito before the time of the patriarchs. He appeared to King Abimelech (Genesis 20:3); He spoke on several occasion to Balaam (Numbers 22-24); He not only led Israel out of Egypt, but also the Philistines out of Caphtor (Amos 9:7), and used the Assyrians as a (disciplinary) rod (Is. 10:5), as well as Cyrus (Isaiah 44:28; 45:1). Without realizing it, those who did not know Yahweh were involved in His actions and history. In pre- and extra-Israelite history, Yahweh is the unknown God. Labuschagne considers it characteristic of faith in Yahweh that it is very much a reformation of that knowledge of God which is already present (Labuschagne, 11-12, 14). Israel's prerogative, in his view, consists in infinitely deepening the knowledge of God by a most intimate relationship with God in history and by means of the activity of the prophets (Labuschagne, 16).

This implies that there is and indeed remains an antithesis. Elijah's confrontation on Mt. Carmel is the most outspoken example of this. Over and against the 'philo-Canaanite tendency' which is encountered in the patriarchal narratives of Genesis, there is the statement in Exodus, that "You shall make no covenant with them or with their gods" (Exodus 23:32). The opposition is focussed in two areas. In the first place it focusses on the area of (temple) prostitution, which at times cannot be distinguished from ordinary prostitution, and which is related to the fertility rites (as those at Baal-Peor). In the second place, the Old Testament condemns human sacrifice. In concrete terms, the issue is primarily the sacrifice of children to Moloch, sometimes mentioned in the same breath with building high places for Baal; the sanction against those sacrifices according to the law of Moses is the death penalty (Leviticus 18:21; 20:2-5; II Kings 23:10; Jeremiah 32:35; compare Acts 7:42). This custom apparently occurred within Israel as well. (Deuteronomy 12:31; Psalm 106:37, 38 —"they also spilled innocent blood, the blood of their sons and daughters, which they sacrificed to the idols of Canaan.") A concrete example which is mentioned is that of King Ahaz who sacrificed his son (II Kings 16:3; II Chr. 28:3). The same is mentioned of King Manasseh (II Kings 21:6; II Chr. 33:6).

To return to our point of departure, we ought to operate more cautiously than is sometimes the case, in my opinion, when evaluating the contributions of Asians and Africans to theology. One ought not to reject syncretism with a simple appeal to Elijah's example. In Old Testament Yahwism, there was apparently a place for a 'yea-saying' attitude toward Canaanite culture, as well as for condemnation, thus providing a place for authentic contextualization. Such an analysis can be a road marker for theologians in appraising contextualization, admonishing a watchful eye for both sides of 'overcoming,' and for the reciprocity of the process.

A repudiatory line is present in the Old Testament —opposing Baal— which can be used as an enduring example of warning in the struggle against syncretism. But the question of contextualization is not being dealt with legitimately if the other side, as was ascertained in the case of 'Canaanite contextualization,' is not taken into account as well.

Bibliography

Ariarajah, Wesley. *The Bible and the People of Other Faiths.* Geneva, 1985.

Bavinck, J. H. *Inleiding in the Zendingswetenschap.* Kampen, 1954.

Blommendaal, J. *El als Fundament en als Exponent van het Oud-testamentisch Universalisme.* Utrecht, 1972.

Colpe, Carsten. "Syncretism." *Encyclopedia of Religion,* XIV. Ed. Mircea Eliade. London/New York, 1987.

Cross, Frank Moore. "Yahweh and the God of the Patriarchs." *Harvard Theological Review* 55 (1962): 250-259.

Eissfeldt, Otto. "El and Yahweh." *Journal of Semitic Studies* 1 (1956): 25-37.

Jacob, Edmond. "L'Héritage Cananéen dans le Livre du Prophète Osée." *Revue d'histoire et de Philosophie Religieuses* 43 (1963): 250-250

Kittel, G. *Theologishes Wörterbuch zum Neuen Testament.* Stuttgart, 1959.

Labuschagne, C. J. "De Godsdienst van Israël en de Andere Godsdiensten." *Wereld en Zending* 4 (1975): 7-16.

——. 1978. *Schriftprofetie en Volksideologie.* Nijkerk.

Lanczkowski, G. "Zur Entstehung des antiken Synkretismus." *Saeculum* 6 (1955): 227-43.

Maag, Victor. "Malkut JHWH." *Supplements to Vetus Testamentum* 7 (1959): 129-53.

Mulder, M. J. *De Naam van de Afwezige God op de Karmel: Onderzoek naar de Naam van de Baäl van de Karmel in 1 Koningen 18.* Leiden, 1979.

Schoneveld, J. *Solomo: De Vorst van Israëls Gouden Eeuw.* Baarn, 1959.

Seebass, Horst. "Die Gottesbeziehung zur Götterwelt der Völker im Alten Testament." In *Christliche Grundlagen des Dialogs mit Weltreligione.* Eds. W. Strolz and H. Waldenfels. Freiburg, 1983.

Strolz, Fritz. "Jahwes Unvergleichlichkeit und Unergründlichkeit: Aspekte der Entwicklung zum alttestamentlichen Monotheismus." *Wort und Dienst.* Jahrbuch der Theologischen Schule Bethel. 1977, p. 10.

Vorlaender, Hermann. "Aspekten van Volksvroomheid in het Oude Testament." *Concilium* 4 (1986): 57-63.

Wolff, H. M. "Jahwe und die Götter in der alttestamentlichen Profetie." *Evangelische Theologie* 29 (1969): 397-416.

Worden, T. "The Literary Influence of the Ugarit Fertility Myth on the Old Testament." *Vetus Testamentum* 3 (1953): 273-97.

Chapter 5

Syncretism and Intra-religious Normativity Illustrated by the Phenomenon of Sacred Scriptures

Rein Fernhout

This article investigates three cases of 'syncretism' with respect to the phenomenon of Sacred Scripture. It appears that the so-called 'receiving' religions view the characteristics of syncretism concerned in a totally different way than does scholarly research, and perhaps than does the 'donor' religion. The conclusion reached is that the 'receiving' religions do not view themselves as 'recipient' at all, but to the contrary, view themselves as 'original' in one way or another. As a consequence, there was no margin for dialogue in the cases described. It appears, moreover, that much scholarly research itself actually behaves in precisely the same way as a 'receiving' religion.

1. Introduction

There are three religions which ascribe authority to the Scriptures of another religion: Mahāyāna-Buddhism recognizes the Tripiṭaka of Hīnayāna, Christianity shares the Tenach (=Old Testament, Jewish Bible), with the Jews, and Islam appeals respectively to the Scriptures of both Jews and Christians. Perhaps it is not wholly correct to distinguish between Mahāyāna and Hīnayāna as two separate religions, but for the subject of our enquiry, it makes no difference. From a scholarly point of view, the syncretic pattern is clearly recognizable in all three cases. There is a 'donor religion,' which originally acknowledged the authority of the Scriptures concerned; there is a 'receiving religion,' which claims adherence to the same Scriptures; and this claim is justified by 'resymbolization' or 'reinterpretation.' Moreover, controversy arises not so much within the receiving religion as between the 'donor' and the 'receiving religion.'

It is the aim of this paper to investigate whether this scholarly approach is congruent with the views of the religions themselves. I have therefore opted to take as my point of departure the so-called receiving religions with the following query: 'Do they see themselves as receiving religions, and do they consider their conception of the Scriptures to be reinterpretation?' The term 'normativity' is used to characterize the existential frame of this 'seeing': it is a matter of truth or untruth, and ultimately of salvation or non-salvation. Intra-religious normativity entails acceptance of the conceptions of one's own religion as binding.

In describing religious views, I will adhere to current beliefs expressed by the Sacred Scriptures themselves, or opinions in line with them. Christianity is dealt with last, because the phenomenon is the most complicated and integrated in this religion.

2. The Tripiṭaka: Buddha's 'tactics'?

Many hitherto unknown Scriptures have made their appearance among Mahāyāna-Buddhists, e.g. the Aṣṭasāhasrikā Prajñāpāramitā, or 'The Perfection of Wisdom in Eight Thousand Lines,' and the Saddharma Puṇḍarīka, or 'The Lotus of the True Law.' How does Mahāyāna view the relationship between these Scriptures, which have appeared more recently, and the Tripiṭaka of Hīnayāna?

In answer to this query, it is above all necessary to define the nature of the Tripiṭaka, as it is conceived of by Buddhists. According to the Tripiṭaka itself, it was fixed orally during a council which followed immediately upon the death of Buddha (*Cullavagga* 11; 1880: 284-93). The Tripiṭaka of the Theravāda, the only extant school of Hīnayāna, speaks of only two of the three parts of the Tripiṭaka, namely the *vinaya* (rules for monks and nuns) and the *sūtra* (expositions of Dharma). However, Buddhaghosa (4th century A.D.), the famous commentator of this school expressly states on more than one occasion that the *abhidharma* (scholastic analysis of Dharma) was also included (Norman, 8). The Tripiṭaka is valued as the canonical Word of Buddha (*buddhavacana*). In these Scriptures, however, there are passages which originate from someone other than Buddha himself. In such a case, we may assume that the speaker was somehow personally authorized by Buddha (MacQueen 1981: 304-10; Bond, 22-31). Even a text which emerged several centuries after Buddha's death is based solely on materials which Buddha himself left behind with a view to a future author, according to Buddhaghosa, at least in terms of its method and contents. It should therefore be considered Buddha's Word (*Atthasālinī*, ed. Müller, 4-6). The text at issue, however, is found in the *abhidharma*, and already formed part of the canon.

Mahāyāna does not deny the authenticity of the Tripiṭaka as Buddha's Word, but ascribes these Scriptures to Buddha's 'tactics' (*upāyakauśalya*), e.g. in the second chapter of the Lotus of the True Law. It was an exposition of the Law for people with little comprehension. At present, however, in the view of Mahāyāna, instruction of a higher nature has emerged, and all who can grasp it need not bother with the former explications any longer. The practical consequence of this is that the Tripiṭaka has become a *scriptura otiosa* for Mahāyāna.

In formal respects, however, Mahāyāna is dependent on the Tripiṭaka. It claims that its own Scriptures are no less Word of Buddha than the canon of Hīnayāna. The Scriptures themselves refer to Buddha or some eminent disciple of his as their point of origin. The doctors of Mahāyāna point out the places where, and sometimes even the dates when, Buddha preached the doctrines of these Scriptures (Lamotte: 382-83). According to the Tibetan author Bu-ston ('Butön'; † 1364), the Mahāyāna Scriptures were fixed in a fashion similar to the Tripiṭaka, during a second council held at precisely the same moment, but with more participants, i.e. a million bodhisattvas (Bu-ston, 101). While waiting for the time that mankind would be ripe for them, the Scriptures were entrusted to mysterious god-like beings and 'nāgas,' or snakes. Some of these Scriptures, Bu-ston says, were found by the great Buddhist sage Nāgārjuna (2nd century A.D.), whose very name indicates his connection to the snakes (p. 124). MacQueen suggests that the Mahāyāna Scriptures themselves actually made use of an extended conception of the 'Word of Buddha,' which was already virtually present in the Tripiṭaka, and was indeed articulated by Buddhaghosa: A Word of Buddha need not always have been literally spoken by Buddha himself. Unlike Hīnayāna, however, Mahāyāna applied this concept not to a closed canon, but to one which was in principle open, according to MacQueen (1982: 60).

Hīnayāna rejects the claims of Mahāyāna. The first Mahāyāna Scriptures which reached Sri Lanka, were officially burned (Walpola Rahula: 92). According to the Tibetan Buddhist historian Tāranātha (b. 1575), Hīnayāna invented the pretense that Nāgārjuna was their author, instead of accepting that he had received the Scriptures in question from the *nāgas* (1869: 1; 1980: 109). This rejection on the part of Hīnayāna already occurs in the Mahāyāna Scriptures themselves. The Lotus of the True Law describes how a multitude of five thousand monks, nuns, and others refused to listen to Buddha's exposition of the True Law, because they regarded themselves as being adequately instructed by the Tripiṭaka (cf. the prose between *Saddharmapūṇḍarīka* 2:37 and 2:38; 1912: 38-39; 1960: 163). The Perfection of Wisdom in Eight Thousand Lines warns the adepts of Mahāyāna that —like Buddha himself!— they will undergo the temptations of the evil Māra, who, disguised as a monk, will say to them: "What at present you have heard is not Word of Buddha but poetical fiction; what I will say to you, however, that is said by Buddha himself, that is Word of Buddha" (*Aṣṭasāhasrikā Prajñāpāramitā*; 1888: 328; 1960: 163). The paradoxical result of incorporating this repudiation on the part of Hīnayāna in the Scriptures, is that it integrates it in the very Word of Buddha, as understood by Mahāyāna!

From the point of view of normativity there is a striking asymmetry in the ways in which Mahāyāna and Hīnayāna appraise each other. Hīnayāna sees in Mahāyāna a 'receiving religion' which has unjustly appropriated the concept 'Word of Buddha,' and has degraded the status of the Tripiṭaka by reinterpreting it as Buddha's 'tactics.' Mahāyāna not only denies both, but its denial implies that Mahāyāna has a better understanding of the Scriptures of Hīnayāna than the adherents of this religion themselves have. According to Mahāyāna the adherents of Hīnayāna believe themselves "to have reached what they did not reach and to understand what they do not understand" (*Saddharmapūṇḍarīka*, ibid).

3. Tenach and New Testament: Adulterated Scriptures?

The Koran calls Jews and Christians "people of the Scripture" (*ahl al-kitāb*), owing to their possession of the Sacred Scriptures, viz. the Tôrāh and the Psalms of the Jews, and the Gospel of the Christians. Each of these Scriptures, like the Koran itself, is related to the name of a prophet, respectively: Moses, David, and Jesus. The message of the Koran is the same as that of the other Scriptures, but in the Arabic language (Koran, Sura 41:43-44). The Koran and the other Scriptures therefore confirm one other. When in doubt about the revelation which he received, Mohammed could take counsel from those who had 'read the Scriptures' before him (Sura 10:94). Conversely, the 'people of the Scripture' must accept the mission of Mohammed (Sura 2:41). The relation between the Koran and the Scriptures of the Jews and Christians is placed within the framework of a dispensation of prophets. Each period has its own prophet and Scripture, and the prophet of a succeeding period confirms the Scripture(s) of the preceding prophet(s). Jesus confirms the Tôrāh, and Mohammed confirms the Tôrāh and the Gospel (Wessels, 146). Since this confirmation is reciprocal in Mohammed's case, his coming is presaged both in the Tôrāh and in the Gospel. The latter even contains a synonym of his name, Ahmad (Sura 3:81; 7:157; 61:6). However Mohammed is 'the seal of the prophets' (Sura 33:40). That is to say, his message is the final revelation (Bowman, 6-7).

This final revelation brings about the re-emergence of the religion of Abraham, who was neither Jew nor Christian, but a Muslim (Sura 3:67). The Koran harks back to the original religion of mankind (Roest Crollius, 125-26). This horizontal extension is combined with a vertical one. The 'Original Scripture' to which the Koran refers (*umm al-kitāb*; Sura 13:39) is seen by Muslims as a heavenly prototype of all Scriptures, of which the Koran is the Arabic version. With the dawning of the theme of the eternity of the Koran in Muslim theology, many theologians identified the Original Scripture with the eternal Koran (Gardet, 470).

Although the Jewish and Christian contemporaries of Mohammed rejected Mohammed's message, this naturally did not imply that he was mistaken, according to the Koran. On the contrary, the rejection fits completely into the prophetic model. The 'children of Israel' were always disobedient to their prophets; some they called liars and others they killed (Sura 5:70). The depravity of Jews and Christians even goes so far that they do not shrink from adulterating their own Scriptures. The technical term for this adulteration is *tahrīf*, 'distortion' (GRIC, 126-27). In the case of the Jews this distortion is described as the consequence of punishment from Allah, who hardens their hearts because they do not believe in his messengers (Sura 5:12-13). They degrade themselves from 'people of the Scripture' to violators of Scripture.

This raises the question regarding what value Muslims can attach to the Scriptures of the Jews and the Christians in their present form. Some Muslims suppose that the 'distortion' has to do with the exegesis and not with the text of the Scriptures, but this opinion met strong opposition (Jomier, 122-30). However the alternative of a fully corrupted text undermines the cogency of the predictions of Mohammed's coming which are present, according to the Koran, in the Scriptures of the Jews and the Christians. It is therefore generally assumed that these Scriptures are not wholly adulterated, but only to a certain extent. The resulting unreliability is not a serious problem for the Muslim, for he does not need these Scriptures anymore in practice. The exegesis of the Koran includes the principle of 'abrogation' (*nasḳ*): a prescription which is revealed later abrogates an earlier one. This principle is applied to the relation between the Koran and the preceding Scriptures as well. The Koran "abrogates all that is antiquated in previous revelations and renders the remainder superfluous by superseding it" (Vadja, 265). The result of 'distortion' on the one hand, and 'abrogation' on the other, is a complete 'otiosizing' of the Tôrāh, the Psalms, and the Gospel.

The same asymmetry which we found in the controversy between adepts of Mahāyāna and of Hīnayāna can also be discerned in the conflict between 'the people of the Scripture' and Islam. Jews and Christians do not want their Scriptures to be involved in a 'syncretic process.' Islam, however, not only denies being a 'receiving religion' and the fact that its interpretation of these Scriptures can be considered as a reinterpretation, it also accuses Jews and Christians of not understanding, and even not wanting to understand, their own Scriptures. By virtue of its use of the concept of 'distortion,' Islam went much further in such reinterpretation than did Mahāyāna with regard to the Tripiṭaka. Yet the practical effect is the same in both cases: the Tenach and the New Testament became equally *scripturae otiosae* as the Tripiṭaka

4. The Tenach: Old Testament?

In the last chapter of the Gospel according to Luke, the risen Christ explicates 'Moses,' 'the Prophets,' and 'the Psalms' as presaging his suffering, his resurrection, his glory, and the preaching of 'repentance for forgiveness of sins' (Luke 24:25-27, 44-47). At one of the verses concerned, a modern commentator remarks: "The sense of Christ's words . . . is that from one end of the Hebrew Scriptures to the other, they bear testimony about him and his fate" (Fitzmyer, 1567). This conviction is not a special characteristic of Luke, but is shared by all the authors of the New Testament.

Within this framework the same themes return which we found with Islam and even with Buddhism. Just as the Prophetic office of Mohammed is said to be predicted in the Scriptures of Jews and Christians, so Jesus' Messiahship is presaged by the Tenach, according to New Testament authors. Furthermore, the Tenach appears to be a *praeparatio evangelica*, looking forward to the 'fullness of time' (Gal. 4:4), which recalls the role which Mahāyāna and the Koran assigned respectively to the Tripiṭaka and the earlier Scriptures. Interesting examples of this theme are to be found in Paul,in the Epistle to the Hebrews, and in my opinion, in Revelation as well, where apocalyptic images from the Tenach take on tremendous and fascinating new dimensions. Here too there seems to be 'abrogation': the Jews thought that the prescriptions of the Tôrāh had been suspended by Christ or by his followers. According to New Testament authors, however, it is only now that the real significance of the Tôrāh is manifest. The Sermon on the Mount is testimony to the fact that Jesus did not come "to abolish, but to fulfill" the Tôrāh (Matt. 5:17). The prologue to the Gospel according to John seems to contrast the Tôrāh given by Moses to grace and truth, which came by Jesus Christ (John 1:17). On closer examination, however, Jesus Christ appears to be the ultimate realization of what the Tôrāh intended (Gese, 188-90). Paul calls the Tôrāh 'a schoolmaster unto Christ'; it cannot save its pupils, but it leads them to a crucified Saviour (Gal. 3:19-25). The Epistle to the Hebrews explains the cultic portions of the Tôrāh as 'foreshadowing' the great cult, with Jesus Christ as high priest and sacrifice.

The Epistle to the Hebrews is important in still another respect. Some words from the Psalms and Isaiah which are regarded as predictions are ascribed to the pre-existent Christ (Heb. 2:11-13; 10:5-7): Jesus is not only the fulfillment of the predictions, but their origin as well! This line is continued in the first Epistle of Peter. The Spirit of Christ had caused former prophets to testify to his suffering and glory, and even wanted to them to know that this testimony was not intended as a service to themselves but to the people to whom the Gospel of Jesus Christ would be preached (I Peter 1:11-12). One step further yet, scarcely a step, and the whole Tenach would be inspired by Christ himself. "Damit ist eine Vorstellungshorizont erreicht, wie er dann in der Alten Kirche 'Gemeingut' geworden ist" (Plümacher, 20).

The real significance of the Tenach is not always seen, according to the New Testament authors. The men of Emmaus even heard the reproach: "O fools and slow of heart to believe in all that the prophets have spoken!" (Luke 24:25). All the more serious is the lack of understanding from the side of unbelieving Jews. Referring to a well-known passage from the Tôrāh (Ex. 34:33-35), Paul writes: "... whenever Moses is read, a veil lies over their heart; but whenever a man turns to the Lord, the veil is taken away" (II Cor. 3:15-16). Thus according to Paul the Tôrāh itself contains a paradigm of how it is misunderstood. The end of Acts (28:23) describes how Paul is "trying to persuade them [the Jews] concerning Jesus, from both the Law of Moses and from the Prophets, from morning until evening." When they, or at least a part of them, reject the message, Paul declares that their hardening was already adumbrated by Isaiah (Acts 28:25-27). The resemblance to what the Koran says about the rejection of Mohammed by the Jews is striking. The unbelieving Jews are condemned by their own Scriptures (Gnilka, 153-154).

It is evident that the New Testament authors do not see he Christian faith as a 'receiving religion' which borrowed and reinterpreted the Tenach of the Jews. On the contrary, according to these authors the Jews place themselves outside their own religion by refusing to understand that their Scriptures give testimony concerning Jesus Christ. The asymmetry and other characteristics we noticed in both the other cases are present here too. There is, however, one big difference in relation to Mahāyāna and Islam: the Tenach does not become an otiose Scripture. A comprehensive and integral understanding of the Tenach as testimony of Jesus Christ emerges. In entire agreement with this is the term 'Old Testament' which came into circulation in the Church towards the end of the second century for the Tenach.

5. Syn-, re-, dia-?

The normativity of Mahāyāna, Islam, and Christianity precluded their receiving Scriptures from another religion. On the contrary, the origin of their own religion is identical with that of the earlier Scriptures. The prefix *syn-* of syncretism is not applicable from the point of view of normativity: There is no combining of elements from diverse religions. According to their own understanding, therefore, there is no reinterpretation of the status or contents of those Scriptures either. The earlier Scriptures always had the meaning which appears in the new situation, although this meaning was perhaps not always perceived as such. Hence the prefix *re-* of reinterpretation is not applicable either. Furthermore the asymmetrical character of the controversies has the consequence that there can be no dialogue. Mahāyāna, Islam, and Christianity, inasmuch as they are treated in this paper, are unable to see their opponents as other than people who not only do not understand Mahāyāna etc., but as people who do not understand, or who even refuse to understand, their own Scriptures, and consequently, themselves as well. In such a situation, there is no room for the *dia-* of dialogue.

As a matter of fact, much scholarly research seems to confirm the arguments of those who reject the claims of Mahāyāna, Islam, and Christianity. Concerning the late appearance of the Mahāyāna Scriptures, Lamotte writes: "Pour nous, la raison de ce retard est obvie: ces textes ne furent point connus au début pour le seul motif qu'ils n' existaient pas encore" (p. 383). According to Paret, the critical passages in the Koran concerning Jews and Christians are the product of a disappointed Mohammed, "er mußte nunmehr versuchen, die tatsächliche Gegebenheiten mit seinem Heilsgeschichtlichen Weltbild in Einklang zu bringen" (p. 127). Dunn holds the view that many passages in the New Testament disclose the coalescence of a tradition regarding Jesus and an Old Testament text to form a new text of mixed nature, "or to give the original text a meaning which its original wording could hardly bear" (p. 96). Such remarks, which could be multiplied, would be grist for the mill of Hīnayāna, etc., in their struggle with what they view as the annexing, rather than merely the 'receiving' religions.

Aid from these quarters, though, is not without its consequences for the 'donor religions' themselves. Their ideas concerning their own Scripture(s) are subject to the same relativity of scholarly thought. Properly speaking, scholarship often behaves as a 'receiving religion' in this connection. It reinterprets the observed facts and places them within a framework of probability and rationality which is believed to be generally acceptable. This framework functions as a kind of basic normativity, which encompasses all human phenomena. Though not a part of my investigation, I presume that this basic normativity enables an open-minded interreligious dialogue concerning 'syncretism,' 'reinterpretation,' 'donor,' and 'receiving religion.' But then all the religions concerned would have to accept the same kind of position with regard to this basic normativity as Mahāyāna, Islam, and Christianity assigned to their 'predecessors.' That is to say they would have to be just like scholars say they are.

Bibliography

Aṣṭasāhasrikā Prajñāpāramitā.
Mitra, R., ed. Calcutta, 1888;
Vaidya, P. L., ed. Darbhanga, 1960;
Conze, E., tr. *The Perfection of Wisdom in Eight Thousand Lines and Its Verse Summary.* Bolinas, Calif., 1973.

Bond, G. D. *'The Word of the Buddha': The Tripiṭaka and Its Interpretation in Theravāda Buddhism.* Colombo, 1982.

Bowman, J. "Muḥammad the *Nabī Kāmil.*" *Hamdard Islamicus* 8, no. 2 (1985): 3-9.

Buddhaghosa, *Atthasālinī.*
Müller, E., ed. London, 1897;
Tin, Maung and C. A. F. Rhys Davids, trs. 2 Vols. London, 1920–1921.

Bu-ston, *History of Buddhism,* II: *The History of Buddhism in India and Tibet.* Tr. E. Obermiller, Heidelberg, 1932.

Cullavagga.
Oldenberg, H., ed. *The Vinaya Piṭakam,* III. London, 1880;
Horner, I. B., tr. *The Book of the Discipline,* V. London, 1952.

Dunn, J. D. G. *Unity and Diversity in the New Testament.* London, 1977.

Fitzmyer, J. A. *The Gospel according to Luke,* 2 Vols. The Anchor Bible 28^{a}. New York, 1981–85.

Gardet, L. "Kalām." *Encyclopaedia of Islam^{2},* IV. Leiden/London, 1978, pp. 468-71.

Gese, H. *Zur biblischen Theologie: alttestamentliche Vorträge.* Munich, 1977.

GRIC (groupe de recherches islamo-chrétien). *Ces Écritures qui nous questionnent: La Bible et le Coran.* Paris, 1987.

Gnilka, J. *Die Verstockung Israels: Isaias 6:9-10 in der Theologie der Synoptiker.* Munich, 1961.

Jomier, J. *Le Commentaire Coranique du Manâr: Tendances Modernes de l'exégèse Coranique en Égypte.* Paris, 1954.

Lamotte, É. "Sur la formation du Mahāyāna." In *Asiatica.* Festschrift F. Weller. Leipzig, 1954, pp. 377-397.

MacQueen, G. "Inspired Sypeech in Early Mahāyāna Buddhism."
I. *Religion* 11 (1981): 303-19;
II. *Religion* 12 (1982): 49-65.

Norman, K. R. *Pāli Literature.* Wiesbaden., 1982.

Paret, R. *Mohammed und der Koran: Geschichte und Verkündigung des arabischen Propheten.* Stuttgart, 41976.

Plümacher, E. "Die Heiligen Schriften des Judentums im Urchristentum." *Theologische Realenzyklopädie,* VI, pp. 8-22.

Rahula, W. *History of Buddhism in Ceylon: The Anurādhapura Period.* 2nd edn., Colombo, 21966.

Roest Crollius, A. *The Word in the Experience of Revelation in Qur'ān and Hindu Scriptures.* Rome, 1974.

Saddharmapūṇḍarīka.

Kern, H. and B. Nanjio, eds. St. Petersburg, 1912;

Vaidya, P. L., ed. Darbhanga, 1960;

Kern, H., tr. *The Saddharma-Puṇḍarīka or The Lotus of the True Law.* SBE 21. Oxford, 1884.

Tāranātha.

Schiefner, A., tr. *Geschichte des Buddhismus in Indien.* Petersburg, 1869;

Lama Chimpa Alaka Chattopadhyaya, tr., Debiprasad Chattopadhyaya, ed. *History of Buddhism in India,* I. Calcutta, 1980.

Vadja, G. "Ahl al-Kitāb." *Encyclopaedia of Islam*2, I. Leiden/London, 1978, pp. 264-66.

Wessels, A. *De Koran Verstaan: Een Kennismaking met het Boek van de Islam.* Kampen, 1986.

Chapter 6

The Dialogue Of Touchstones as An Approach to Interreligious Dialogue

Maurice Friedman

Dialogue means openhearted address and response between persons of different religions. It does not assume agreement, and it is able to tolerate not only opposition but contradiction. It honours the witness of others while making one's own, giving rise to a 'community of otherness' that does not demand or need a common myth. This way of being faithful and diverse at the same time leads to the mutual confirmation of the dialogue of touchstones of reality, offering a third option to absolutism and relativism. The fellowship of the committed can dialogue across denominational lines, leading to a faithful pluralism that does not assert that all religions are the same or have the same goal. Buber and Heschel witness to this approach.

Martin Buber said that when he first went to school in the Austro-Hungarian Empire, all the teachers desired to appear tolerant of the small group of Jewish students and no attempt at conversion was ever made. Yet the recital of the Trinity creed morning after morning for eight long years, during which ritual the Jewish students stood looking at the ground, stamped itself upon his soul as no intolerance could have done. "To have to participate as a thing in a sacral rite in which no dram of my being could take part," he said, resulted in a life-long antipathy to all missionary effort among people with religious roots of their own. Asked once to speak to an annual luncheon of clergymen about Buber's view of Christianity, I concluded with this story, only to be followed by a benediction in the name of Christ!

What was so difficult for Buber and me in these situations? It was not that our religious position as Jews was attacked but that it was ignored. This 'unanimity' of the majority which overlooks the presence of another vital attitude, remains a central problem for all Jews in trying to come to terms with Christianity. One result of it has been an unconscious disparagement of Judaism that is so much a part of our culture that the average secular Jew shares it — a tendency to look on the religion of the 'Old Testament' as a lower, inferior religion of a jealous, wrathful God in opposition to the New Testament's religion of love. Another is that even liberal Jews are often quite unable to have an honest dialogue with Jesus and Paul and the Gospels.

Yet if Judaism is to come of age intellectually in our day, it must be able to enter into this dialogue without fear of losing itself. This fear leads many Jews, including rabbis, to suppose that Martin Buber's influence on contemporary Christian thought must somehow mean that he is not really Jewish. But real dialogue, as Buber himself taught, means going out to meet the other and holding your ground while you meet him. Speaking of Hasidism Buber wrote: "It has often been suggested to me that I should liberate this teaching from its 'confessional limitations,' as people like to put it, and proclaim it as an unfettered teaching of mankind."

> Taking such a 'universal' path would have been for me pure arbitrariness. In order to speak to the world what I have heard, I am not bound to step into the street I may remain standing in the door of my ancestral house: here too the word that is uttered does not go astray.[1]

When Rabbi Joseph Soleveichik, the leading thinker of Orthodox Jewry, warns against Jewish-Christian dialogue about faith, I cannot take him seriously. But neither can I get excited about *official* Jewish-Christian dialogues. I am convinced that wherever committed people come together they can talk with one another if they share some real concern. There is a new spirit of openness abroad among a great many Catholic, Protestant, and Jewish thinkers. Real listening is already a form of responding, and real response is not only dialogue but sharing from a different side in a common reality. In a "Third Hour" discussion at Emmaus House in New York City between an eminent Catholic theologian and myself, I asserted that Judaism could not be expected to enter fully into dialogue with Catholicism when even after Vatican II the Church still claims to have superseded the people of the covenant as the 'true Israel.' His complete agreement with what I said was an honest recognition of difference that was already a step toward overcoming it. I recall in contrast a day that I led for an adult-education group at the Graduate Theological Union more than a quarter of a century ago. After I had given my opening lecture, a woman missionary from the Netherlands said that it was dangerous for the group to allow Martin Buber or me to put forward our views since we were Jewish, and the orientation of the group was Protestant Christian. I wanted to reply to what she said, but the famous Transactional Analysis ("I'm OK, You're OK") woman who led the meeting immediately declared a recess and even afterward made it impossible for me to respond!

[1] Martin Buber, *Hasidism and Modern Man*, ed. & trans. with an Introduction by Maurice Friedman (New York: Horizon Books, 1958), p. 42.

I do not assume that the goal of dialogue is agreement or that dialogue is only of value if it leads to agreement. I believe in dialogue — not as debate or mere intellectual interchange, but as openhearted address and response. But I have no assumptions concerning its outcome. I do not even assume —how could I?— that there will always be genuine dialogue, even though both partners may genuinely desire it. We need to be face to face to talk. But that oppositeness all too often crystallizes into fixed opposition, and we run aground on what Martin Buber calls "the cruel antitheticalness of existence itself." The only perspective from which we can find comfort in the face of such tragic conflict is the Talmudic approach that holds that "every controversy that takes place for the sake of heaven endures." This is completely contrary to Aristotelian logic with its assumption that a statement and its opposite cannot both be true. To say that *both* sides will endure does not mean that eventually one will be proved right and the other wrong. The knowledge that the other also witnesses for his 'touchstones of reality' from where he stands can enable us to confirm the other in his truth even while opposing him. We do not have to liberate the world from those who have different witnesses from us. The converse of this also holds, namely, that each must hold his ground and witness for his truth even while at the same time affirming the ground and the truth of the other. If the witness of the other is genuine, it seems to me that it is always possible to respond and to move toward greater openness: I can open myself to what the other says; I can recognize the witness of the other even in opposing it; and I can reaffirm my own witness in dialogue with that of the other. Although I have no right to judge the touchstones of others either by evaluating them objectively or morally condemning them, the other needs to know that he is really coming up against us as persons with touchstones and witnesses of our own. Sometimes the strongest opposition is more confirming by far than someone who defends your right to your opinion but does not take it seriously.

During the four years of its existence I was the only non-Quaker member of the Working Party for the Future of the Quaker Movement. Despite its grandiose title, our Working Party really consisted of a small group of eight or nine intellectuals who met three weekends a year for intensive sharing of where we had come from, where we were, and where we felt we were going. Sometimes we thought of our sessions as autobiographical excursions, sometimes as confirming each other in our *daimons,* or callings, sometimes as a dialogue of metaphors, or the interchange of the myths that 'spoke to our condition.' We met across all differences in an intense mutual sharing and caring that went beyond the search for common formulae. My very presence in the group, as a Jew and not a Quaker, already implied that loyalty to the Society of Friends did not preclude fellowship with committed seekers outside of it. At times we had to make a distinction between the Society of Friends and the 'Quaker movement.' If the Society of Friends creates an environment in which its members feel at home, that raised for us the question of whether a feeling of belonging and being a vanguard movement, or thrust into the future, go together. There is a persistent danger of confusing affinity and community. Affinity is based on likeness, true community begins with the acceptance of otherness.

Our Working Party could never reach the place where it could agree on Christ-centeredness as a central term for everyone, not even excepting me. Nor could it reach the place where everyone would agree to dispense with that term. The greatness of what the Friends call the 'gathered meeting' lies in the fact that it does not start with an *a priori* unity but with a genuine trust. The genius of Quaker worship, at its finest, lies in the fact that it does not seek any sort of abstract or conceptual unity or criterion of faith. Nor can one speak of an experienced unity attained during the meeting — only community and communion, which enables us to be really different and yet together. To some members of the Working Party, Christ remained an ultimate beyond which they could not go to any sort of higher abstractions that would be more satisfactory to them. Yet in contrast to those who turn their Christology into an exclusive way to God, they were not imprisoned in it and had no trouble talking to non-Christians as well as to Christians for whom Christ was not central.

In the course of our Working Party's discussions of myth I glimpsed one further 'myth' —one might call it a 'metamyth'— which included both the individual daimons of the members of the group and that spirit which joined us together as a group. It was this myth that I called 'the Quaker movement.' Taking it out of the context in which it arose, I call it 'The Community of Otherness.' In contrast to the myths of process, evolution, and the unconscious which *we* had, *it* possessed *us*. We could not objectify or articulate it. It removed the very desire for a common myth; for it held us together, borne by a common stream. This inarticulable myth is perhaps greater than any myth that can only be lived out in the lives of individuals. Wherever persons of no matter what religion or none at all meet in a spirit of common concern, ready to encounter each other beyond their terminologies, this 'myth' can come into being and with it the lived reality of community.

What emerged for me from our four years of the Working Party as the uniqueness of the Quaker movement is also what I should like to point to as a model for meaningful dialogue in general — a way of being faithful and diverse at the same time. The appeal to unanimity and universality is a thing of the past. Relativism, its seeming opposite, is no more meaningful for the present situation, for it does not accept things as they happen in their *uniqueness*. It knows only *difference* — comparison and contrast in terms of categories.

In contrast to the either/or of absolutism and relativism, I offer as a genuine and more fruitful third option the mutual confirmation of the dialogue of touchstones of reality. This third option is difficult at first to grasp, for many people feel that we have to choose between an exclusivist truth and a hopeless relativism. I feel, in contrast to *both* positions, that the reality of pluralism must be the starting point of any serious modern faith. We should give up looking for the one true religion and consider our religious commitments as unique relationships to a truth that we cannot possess. We live our lives in a movement between immediacy and objectification. What matters is not the one or the other taken by itself but the spirit that leads us from the one to the other and back again. After we had given up trying to come to an articulated myth, movement, or future, we glimpsed the possibility that the distinctiveness of what we called 'the Quaker Movement' might be precisely a quality of gathered presence which would give us the trust that would enable us to affirm religious pluralism.

Is this not a hopelessly ideal approach in the face of a situation that can only be described as a congeries of babbling voices, each asserting itself against the other, each claiming sole truth or denying all truth? Not if we recognize that relativism is only the other side of the same coin as absolutism, that the relativist is the disappointed absolutist who says that if I cannot have one absolute truth, then I shall deny that there is any truth at all. We still long for what Dostoevsky's Grand Inquisitor called the 'unanimous ant heap,' a universal religion that will give us the security and comfort of never having to stand our own ground and to think for ourselves.

If we are honest with ourselves, we will recognize that such a universal religion is neither possible nor desirable. The longing for it is a throwback to the desire for a universal, objective Truth that we can possess rather than a touchstone of reality arrived at through obedient listening and faithful responding. If we look dispassionately at the contemporary scene, what is more, we shall recognize that not only are there a great many competing religions that show no slightest trace of merging into one, but also that there are many things that compete with religions for our attention and devotion in such a way that they, too, must be accounted religions in the sense of idols that claim our ultimate allegiance and swallow up our total existence. It little matters whether that idol be money, Moloch, magic, materialism, the family, the party, the nation, or even the new world-order.

If we return to the adherents of the religions themselves, we find that the seeming agreement among the members of particular churches and synagogues and religious fellowships is often only illusory. People confess the same faith but mean totally different things by it, or mean nothing at all. How many of us "affirm before the world and deny between the rocks," as T. S. Eliot puts it in "Ash Wednesday"? The fact is that what Abraham Joshua Heschel called *religious behaviorism,* the fad of joining for the sake of joining, is so predominant among those who are religious today that it is very difficult in practice to say which particular religious group is what I call a *community of affinity,* or *like-mindedness,* and which is what I call a *community of otherness.* The former is a pseudo-community based on the false security of commonly-ascribed-to catch phrases or the equally false security of belonging just for the sake of belonging and promoting the religious institution as an end in itself. The latter is the fellowship of really other persons brought together in the struggle for a common cause, one to which they relate from unique perspectives and life-stances yet which they share and find real fellowship in that sharing.

The true fellowship of the committed is made up of those who can meet and talk with one another because they really care about one another and the common goal they are serving, however differently that goal may be stated. This fellowship is often found not within but *across* organizational, institutional, and denominational lines. It is my experience that I can talk to a committed person of any religion or even no religion at all better than I can talk to an uncommitted person of my own religion so long as that commitment does not fall into the idolatry of objectifying one's touchstones into universal truths that one wishes to impose upon others and force everyone to ascribe to. If this is so, then the answer to the dilemma of cultural relativism is not a new universalism or a new absolutism, or even some 'perennial philosophy' that claims to have found the true essence of all religions. It is a faithful pluralism — a mutually confirming dialogue of touchstones.

We do not need to use the same words as others or even to affirm that beneath our different words and images we really mean the same thing in order to share a meaningful religious fellowship. In contrast to those like Aldous Huxley, Henri Bergson, and Erich Fromm, who have claimed a perennial philosophy that obliterates essential differences, we can accept the fact that we not only have different paths, but also that these different paths may lead to different places. What matters is that in listening to the other we hear something genuine to which we can respond. Real religious fellowship does not begin with creed or catechism but with genuine trust. We receive from each other without ever being identical with each other; we are able to affirm and respond to what we receive, and grow through it. Some religions, to be sure, seek to articulate abstract criteria of faith and creed. But unless those abstractions are rooted in lived tradition and lived community of trust, they are worthless. The dialogue of touchstones is not between religions but between persons and groups. For all that we speak of Jewish-Christian dialogue, for example, it is always, in fact, only particular Jews and particular Christians who are in dialogue and never the religions as such. That becomes self-evident as soon as we recall that dialogue only takes place between persons. Religions and religious institutions, whatever else they may be, are not persons! There has thrived in our day, unfortunately, a form of pseudo-dialogue in which official representatives of religions carry on official dialogues that are neither genuine meetings of religions, for religions cannot meet, nor genuine meetings of persons because these persons speak only for their social role and do not stand behind what they say with their own persons.

Many share the illusion that if people could just arrive at the same terms, they would be in real communication and agreement. Actually, no real communication takes place except by one person speaking from one vantage point and the other listening and responding from a really other vantage point — the ground of his or her uniqueness. Useful as precision and definition are for the exact sciences, the true humanity and the very meaning of the dialogue of touchstones depends upon its being brought back to the fruitful disagreement of lived speech between persons whose meanings necessarily differ because of the difference of their attitudes, their situations, their points of view.

My word is a part of my witness. I cannot give it up. But I wish to witness to *you.* Therefore, I cannot impose my word on you. I want you to hear and respond to it *from your side* rather than passively accept it. All I can legitimately ask of you is to listen to me and to be actively what you are in response to me. If this is so, then we cannot have the notion of 'one truth' of which our individual truths are so many symbolic expressions. Every one of us has to witness from where he or she is. We shall never find a common philosophy, theology, or myth that unites us But we can share our myths with one another and grow in the strength to live without a single, all-encompassing myth. Despite our differences and contradictions, it is indeed necessary to continue talking and sharing; for this is the only direction in which we can hope to reach that 'community of otherness' to which I point.

We should give up the notion that some persons possess the spirit and others do not. The spirit that speaks through us is a response to the spirit that we meet in others, the spirit that meets us in the 'between.' The spirit may express itself in silence or in words or in both. The words that are spoken out of the silence of a fellowship bear witness to a gathered presence that transcends the particular set of words that each member of the fellowship may use. This gathered presence gropes toward and responds to the diversity of individuals without aiming at any final answers or conclusions. The spirit does not stand in contrast to words. It finds its true life in the encounter of words when that encounter means caring and concern, in the contending of words when that contending means witnessing and confirming. Our ultimate concerns touch one another through and beyond all words. This going *through* the word to a meeting *beyond* the word can be a more powerful witness to the imageless God than any dogma, creed, theology, or metaphysics.

The only perennial philosophy that I can and do espouse is that of openness — the witness to the ever-growing dialogue with committed persons of every religion and none. Each of the religions and each of the touchstones of reality that I have entered into dialogue with have pointed me toward greater openness, and each has opened for comrades on the way the possibility of a fuller and freer fellowship — a mutually confirming dialogue of touchstones.

Both Martin Buber and Abraham Joshua Heschel have given powerful witness to the dialogue of touchstones as an approach to interreligious dialogue. In the "Disputations in Religion" section of his essay "Dialogue" Buber writes:

> We expect a theophany of which we know nothing but the place, and the place is called community. In the public catacombs of this expectation there is no single God's Word which can be clearly known and advocated, but the words delivered are clarified for us in our human situation of being turned to one another. There is no obedience to the coming one without loyalty to his creature. To have experienced this is our way.
>
> A time of genuine religious conversations is beginning — not those so-called but fictitious conversations where none regarded and addressed his partner in reality, but genuine dialogues, speech from certainty to certainty, but also from one open-hearted person to another open-hearted person. Only then will genuine common life appear, not that of an identical content of faith which is alleged to be found in all religions, but that of the situation, of anguish and of expectation.[2]

In his essay "No Religion Is An Island" Abraham Joshua Heschel writes:

> Parochialism has become untenable.... Horizons are wider, dangers are greater... *No religion is an island....* Spiritual betrayal on the part of one of us affects the faith of all of us. Views adopted in one community have an impact on other communities. Today religious isolationism is a myth....
>
> The purpose of religious communication among human beings of different commitments is mutual enrichment and enhancement of respect and appreciation rather than the hope that the person spoken to will prove to be wrong in what he regards as sacred. Dialogue must not degenerate into a dispute, into an effort on the part of each to get the upper hand.... Does not the all-inclusiveness of God contradict the exclusiveness of any particular religion?... Is it not blasphemous to say: I alone have all the truth and the grace, and all those who differ live in darkness, and are abandoned by the grace of God?... Does not the task of preparing the kingdom of God require a diversity of talents, a variety of rituals, soul-searching as well as opposition? Perhaps it is the will of God that in this aeon there should be diversity in our forms of devotion and commitment to Him. In this aeon diversity of religions is the will of God...."The Torah speaks in the language of man." Revelation is always an accommodation to the capacity of man. No two minds are alike, just as no two faces are alike. The voice of God reaches the spirit of man in a variety of ways, in a multiplicity of languages.... Holiness is not the monopoly of

---

[2] Martin Buber, *Between Man and Man*, trans. by Ronald Gregor Smith with an Introduction by Maurice Friedman (New York: Macmillan Books, 1965), pp. 7f.

> any particular religion or tradition.... What then is the purpose of interreligious cooperation?... to cooperate in trying to bring about a resurrection of sensitivity, a revival of conscience; to keep alive the divine sparks in our souls, to nurture openness to the spirit of the Psalms, reverence for the words of the prophets, and faithfulness to the Living God.[3]

---

[3] Abraham Joshua Heschel, "No Religion Is An Island," in *Disputation and Dialogue*, ed. F. E. Talmage (New York: KTAV, 1975), pp. 345, 347f., 352-354, 357, 359.

PART II

CASE STUDIES

of

Interreligious Encounter and Syncretism

Chapter 7

Abū Ḥātim ar-Rāzī (10th century A.D.) on the Unity and Diversity of Religions

Hans Daiber

The present article describes the way in which the 10th century Muslim philosopher Abū Ḥātim ar-Rāzī attempted to account for and deal with the phenomenon of religious diversity. He defends the necessity and authority of Mohammed's prophecy against attack by contemporaries who denied divine inspiration or did not consider it essential. Remaining well within orthodox tradition, Abū Ḥātim claims that Mohammed's prophecy is necessary to authoritatively separate truth from accretions and errors, since these tend to be mixed in purely human knowledge. In distinction from narrower interpretations, however, he also wants to show that the content of prophecy is no denial of human reasoning, and therefore is no refutation of all other human knowledge. To the contrary, prophecy appeals to and even demands that people apply their minds. The attainment of the universal belief in one single God and in the justness of His laws is thus not only the historical result of prophetic revelations to mankind, but is also a permanently renewed intellectual process, the seeking for the universal meaning of the diverse forms of tradition and religion respectively. The present article approaches these issues in the light of present-day historical scholarship and in the context of intellectual discussion and cosmopolitan ferment during Abū Ḥātim's time.

As we know, the prophet Mohammed has adopted many biblical stories. For he considered himself the last link in a universal salvation-history with prophetic forerunners in Judaism and Christianity: divine revelation had already been revealed to the 'people of the book' before him (Paret, 92ff.). In later times, however, shortly after the Hidjra from Mecca to Medina (622 A.D.), Mohammed had modified his attitude (Paret, 117ff.). The obstinacy of the Medinan Jews induced this change of mind, which entailed that the divine message revealed to him had to replace the religious conceptions of Jews and Christians. He considered himself the restorer of the religion of Abraham, the religion which preceded Moses (Judaism) and Jesus (Christianity). In this sense, Mohammed regarded himself as the successor to earlier prophets in Judaism and Christianity; the universal, pre-Islamic divine knowledge would be transmitted via his person to people in an unadulterated manner. This also served to legitimate his religious-political authority.[1]

In view of this combination of political power with divine knowledge revealed to the prophet, unending debates arose after Mohammed's death on the legitimacy of the Caliphs (Sharon, ch. 2). Against the background of these debates, the philosopher Fārābī († 950 A.D.), in his book on "The Perfect State," argued the thesis that the leader of the perfect state, who was endowed with knowledge, the philosopher, had to be a prophet too. For his knowledge is inspired in him in the form of prophetical inspiration by the divine active intellect.[2] This combination of, respectively, authority and prophecy, knowledge and divine inspiration, can also be found in the case of the Ismaili scholar Abū Ḥātim ar-Rāzī, who died 17 years before Fārābī.[3] In his book on "The Proofs of Prophecy,"[4] he endeavours to prove, in accordance with the Mu'tazilite-Zaidite[5] and Ismaili tradition (Madelung 1961; 1977; Makarem, 35), that the imperfection of human knowledge requires prophetic inspiration. Divine knowledge was already revealed to Jews and Christians by earlier prophets. Abū Ḥātim takes up the Koranic view of universal divine knowledge, which had already been revealed to Jews and Christians, in an original manner. He offers an interesting explanation for the unity and diversity of religions. The occasion for his argument was a dispute with the famous physician and philosopher Abū Bakr ar-Rāzī in Rayy (today: Teheran) between 318/930 and 320/932–33, in the presence of the governor Mardāwīdjī, or perhaps already before 313/925 (Stern, 199, 202f.). Abū Bakr ar-Rāzī had denied the necessity of prophecy,[6] and had defended —following Aristotle's

---

[1] Cf. Suras 2:251(252); 4:54; 12:101(102).

[2] Daiber 1986b: 15f.

[3] His complete name is Abū Ḥātim Ibn Ḥamdān Ibn Aḥmad al-Warsinānī al-Laythī ar-Rāzī. Cf. Sezgin, 573; Poonawala, 36-39; Halm, 173f.

[4] Edited by Salah al-Sawy with introduction and notes. English introduction by Seyyed Hossein Nasr. Portions (3·3-13, 15; 69·3-76, 12; 104·3-116, 3) have been translated into French (Brion). Page (and line) numbers in the remainder of the article refer to this edition when no other author is specified.

Abū Ḥātim's argumentation was adopted a generation later by the Ismaili Ḥamīd ad-Dīn al-Kirmānī († 411/1020–21), who recapitulates the discussion between Abū Ḥātim and Abū Bakr in the introduction (pp. 9-19) to his *Akwāl adh-Dhahabiyya* (Sawy 1977b), a refutation of Abū Bakr ar-Rāzī's *aṭ-Ṭibb Ar-Rūḥānī.*

[5] Cf. al-Djāḥiẓ, *al-Djawābāt wa-stiḥkāk* (Hārūn, 320·3ff.); Germ. trans. Pellat, 104ff.; comments by Nagel, 147-49. On the Zaidites, especially al-Ḳāsim (785–860 A.D.), cf. Abrahamov.

[6] Strangely enough, Abū Ḥātim does not refer to Ibn ar-Rāwandī (830–910 A.D.), and does not criticize him, as was done more than a century later by the Ismaili al-Mu'ayyad fī d-dīn ash-Shīrāzī. The circumstance that Abū Ḥātim was better informed on Ibn ar-Rāwandī, who was incorrectly reckoned among those who deny prophecy by his posterity, perhaps forms a possible explanation. According to Ibn ar-Rāwandī, divine revelation does not contradict reason; he only denies the possibility of proving the infallibility (*'iṣma*) of the prophet. For this, and a

teaching of the eternity of matter, the impossibility of *creatio ex nihil,* and the createdness of form— the following thesis: the world came into being, when God showed mercy to the eternal soul and 'assisted her,' to lead the unsettled movement of the eternal soul to an orderly one[7] (Sawy, 20ff.). Abū Bakr defended his thesis of the eternity of the five principles, 'creator,' 'soul,' 'matter,' 'space,' and 'time,' in this connection (Sawy, 13; Mohaghegh, 16-23; Fakhry). He maintains the classical doctrine of atoms, by adding a Neo-Platonic component (Pines, 34ff.); his theories on space and time were apparently influenced by Proclus' *Institutio Theologica,*[8] to a greater degree than has been assumed up until now.[9]

Contrary to the Platonic/Neo-Platonic tendencies of Abū Bakr ar-Rāzī, his Ismaili opponent, Abū Ḥātim follows Aristotle's theories on time[10] and space;[11] there is no absolute, eternal time, and no absolute, eternal space. We cannot enter into details here, and shall focus our attention on Abū Ḥātim's emphasis on intellectuality, which enables man to speculate on space and time as something which can be imagined, but not as something absolute. For Fārābī (cf. p. 88, man can only consider what is conceivable to his imagination. Otherwise it does not exist, just as absolute space and time do not exist. God is of course an exception to the rule; God exists, but he transcends human experience, and his existence can be proven only from His creation.

In accordance with the Ḥanbalite and Mu'tazilite theology, no one can inquire into the nature (*kaifiyyā*) of the creator (Sawy, 38·6ff.); in conformity to the Koran's prescriptions,[12] man is asked to 'reflect' (*tafakkara, i'tabara*) on God's creation (39·13ff.). Here we find a kind of cosmological proof for God, the establishing of God's existence from his creation. This has a parallel in the *Kitāb al-'Aẓama* of his younger contemporary from Iṣfahan, Abū-Shaykh (274/887–369/997; Heinen, 37ff.) as well as in the *Kitāb ad-Dalā'il wa-l-i'tibār 'alā l-khalḳ wa-t-tadbīr* ascribed to al-Djāḥiẓ (9th century A.D.), which is actually identical with the *Kitāb al-Fikar wa-l-i'ti-bār* ascribed to Djāḥiẓ' contemporary Djibrīl Ibn Nūḥ Ibn Abī Nūḥ al-Anbārī (Daiber 1975: 159f.; Davidson, 219f.). These books follow patristic-Hellenistic tradition, which has been the point of

reverberation of it in Fārābī, cf. Van Ess 1978; 1980.

7 Davidson, 14f., has a short note on Abū Bakr ar-Rāzī, but unfortunately does not take into account this important report.

8 In connection with Abū Bakr ar-Rāzī's conception of space (Pines, 48), cf. 'magnitude' and 'extension,' Greek *mégethos* and *pléthos* of the *óntōs on,* in Proclus' *Institutio theologica* (Dodds 1963), proposition 86. Arabic translation (perhaps by Yaḥyā Ibn al-Biktrīḳ in the 9th century A.D.; Endress, 33); German translation p. 286f., s.v. *'iẓam/ 'uẓm – kathra.*

9 Pines only mentions a parallel with Proclus in his discussion of Rāzī's conception of time. Max Jammer unfortunately does not discuss our authors.

10 Aristotle, *Physics VIII* 8.256a, 11-12, and *IV* 14.223b, 21-23; cf. Daiber 1980: 365f. – Bilinski does not discuss our author.

11 Aristotle, *Physics IV* 4.212a, 20f., cf. Daiber 1980: 362.

12 38·6ff.; Abū Ḥātim refers to Suras 2:164(159); 3:189f.(186f); 13:3; 16:8-10.

departure for Islamic cosmology ever since the 9th/10th century A.D. (Radtke).

The commendation to think about God's creation received an interesting accentuation in Abū Ḥātim's case: By referring to the Koran (Sawy, 35f., citing Sura 3:93/87), he corroborates God's command to people of differing opinions (*al-mukhtalifūn*), to 'examine' (*an-naẓar*), and to "follow what is most excellent, suitable, true, and necessary" (36·5f.). According to Abū Ḥātim, the 'adherents of the laws' (*ahl ash-sharā'i'*) are also enabled to 'examination' and 'enquiry' (*baḥth*; 36·11ff.); this is totally different from 'controversy' (*djadal*), 'quarrel' (*khuṣūma*), or 'strife' (*tanāzu'*) which is indeed 'unbelief' (*kufr*; 36·11ff.). Abū Ḥātim is here criticizing the disputes of the *mutakallimūn*, the theologians; it is not legitimate to get the upper hand in a dispute in an unlawful manner, but it is legitimate to 'enquire' in a legal way (*bi-l-inṣāf wa-l-'adl*; 36·15ff.). Furthermore, radicalism in belief (*ta'ammuḳ fī di-dīn*) is not acceptable; this would be exaggeration (*ghulūw*) and has nothing to do with attaining an independent judgment (*idjtihād*; 43·6ff.).[13] Abū Ḥātim here explicitly criticizes the Kharidjite sect (43·9ff.), which had gained a reputation for radicalism in the early history of Islam, denying the claim of 'Alī and 'Uthmān to the caliphate (Levi Della Vida, 1ff.; Watt, 1ff.). The critical attitude toward *mutakallimūn* and Kharidjites was in agreement with the view of the Ḥanbalites.[14] Moreover, Abū Ḥātim ar-Rāzī's book shows a clearly anti-Kharidjite import in its thesis on the differences between people. The Kharidjites defended the equality of men, a similarity with the Old Arabic egalitarianism; the leader of the community does not —contrary to Shī'ite ideas— have any charisma. Just as in the Old Arabic tribal ideal, he is primus inter pares. The Kharidjite-Ibadite sect of Yazīdiyya, founded by Yazīd Ibn Abī Anīsa (or: Unaysa), of whom nothing more is known, even went so far, assuming the equality of Persians and Arabs, as to maintain that in the future there would be a Persian prophet who would replace Mohammed's revelation with a new one.[15] This revelation would be equally divine as those in Judaism and Christianity (Levi Della Vida, 1076b).

Against the background of such tendencies and trends, Abū Ḥātim apparently tried to develop his own opinions. He presupposes the diversity of men, giving way to pro-Shī'ite and anti-Kharidjite tendencies; he writes:

[13] In this usage of *idjtihād*, which must be accompanied by orientation to the prophetic revelation (*taḳlīd*; 72·13ff.; cf. below p. 97) according to Abū Ḥātim, he anticipates al-Ghazzālī. On Ghazzālī's conception of *idjtihād* as opposed to *taḳlīd*, cf. Lazarus-Yafeh, 488ff. Here too, Ghazzālī, while a critic of the Bāṭiniyya (= Ismailites; cf. below p. 98, n. 42) has at the same time been influenced by the Bāṭiniyya — as Jabre has already shown with other examples.

[14] Cf. Laoust, 55f. on the Ḥanbalite attitude towards the *kalām* of the *mutakallimūn*. He mentions the Ḥadīth scholar Abū Ḥātim ar-Rāzī († 277/890) on p. 56, 2, who should not be confused with the Ismaili, Abū Ḥātim.

[15] Cf. Goldziher 1971: 138f.; Watt, 27ff. (read Yazīd Ibn Abī Anīsa/Unaysa); add to the sources mentioned Sa'īd Ibn Nashwān al-Ḥimyarī († 573/1177), *al-Ḥūr al-'īn* (Muṣṭafā 175·5ff.).

> ... There are different classes of men as concerns their intelligence, insight, and power of distinction and perception. For men are not created equal to each other in their natures, as are animals, for instance, which do not differ[16] in their perception, as is needful in men. Since every class of animals is equal by nature, as regards their consciousness of the obligation to look for food and to reproduce, they do not differ in a comparable fashion as is the case with the diversity of intelligence and insight mentioned of human classes. (185·6-10; cf. 6·13ff.)

By way of explanation, Abū Ḥātim offers the notion that God "is too just, wise, and merciful to equate men with animals" (185·12f.).

Men are different from animals, but also differ among themselves: there are people who know (*'ālim*) and people who learn (*muta'allim*), leaders (*imām*) and people guided by them (*ma'mūm*).[17] God therefore forgives the weak, who are not obliged to the same extent as the strong (64f.); and for this reason, "it is possible that God bestows his wisdom and mercy on men, chooses them from his creation, makes them prophets, helps them, and gives them prophecy" (8·8-10; cf. 183·15ff.; 185·2ff.). People require guidance on account of these intellectual differences. The prophet is their guide par excellence, elected by God and equipped with divine knowledge. We find here the first beginnings of ideas which were later developed into a unique system of political philosophy by Fārābī.

The diversity of men and their need of guidance proves the necessity of prophecy in the eyes of Abū Ḥātim. He thus distantiates himself from his opponent, Abū Bakr ar-Rāzī, who had denied the existence of prophecy: man could obtain knowledge on his own, and has no need of any authority, such as a prophet. Man can even learn something from the imperfect knowledge of previous scholars and philosophers, because he can 'discover' (*istadraka*) 'other things' (*ashyā' ukhar*) through intelligence (*fiṭna*) and through intensive investigation (*naẓar*) and study (*baḥth*).[18] Abū Ḥātim was not blind to the inconsistency in ancestors serving as models on the one hand, and needing correction on the other (10·9ff.). Man has need of authority, according to him. God provides for the unity of men, despite

---

[16] *tafāḍalū*: the term can be found with this meaning in the later Fārābī too, *al-Madīna al-fāḍila* (Walzer, 226, 5; 230, 14). The diversity of ranks among people in different states is a central theme of Fārābī; cf. the commentary by Walzer, 423ff.

[17] Cf. 6·21ff.; 8·7f.; 55; 72·5ff.; 184·12ff. It is striking that Abū Ḥātim does not use the Ismailite term *dā'ī* instead of *'ālim*, perhaps because his book was written for a wider circle of readers; cf. Ivanow, 13f. and the end of this paper. This may also be an explanation for the fact that typical details of Ismailite doctrines are missing in Abū Ḥātim's book; cf. Madelung's overview (1977), or Makarem (1972). Finally, we should point out the parallelism between Abū Ḥātim and the later Fārābī with respect to this terminology (on the latter, cf. Daiber 1986b: 7f.).

[18] 11·2ff.; cf. 273·7ff., below p. 93, and on the contrast of this doctrine of intellect to the theory of intuition by illumination (*ishrāk*), see Nasr (cf. Sawy, 273ff., esp. 274·1ff.). This idea of 'progress' was certainly not new; compare the philosopher al-Kindī († after 866 A.D.), *Rasā'il al-Kindī al-falsafiyya* (Abū Rīda, 102), trans. Ivry, 57, commentary p. 126 (on the Aristotelian source of inspiration; Cortabarria, 210-12). Or compare Kindī's contemporary, al-Djaḥiẓ († 868 A.D.), Khalidi 1977; Enderwitz, 136ff.; furthermore, cf. Khalidi 1981; Daiber 1988b.

their different intellectual capacities and opinions, through the agency of prophetic authority.

The prophet is a teacher of men; among their ranks, they count the 'knowing (*'ālim*) and the ignorant (*djāhil*),' the 'virtuous (*ṣāliḥ*) and the vicious (*ṭāliḥ*),' the 'godfearing (*wari'*) and the desecrating (*muntahik*),' the 'wise (*'āḳil*) and the unwise (*ghabiy*)' (111·7ff.). For this reason, men must be 'forced'—writes Abū Ḥātim, referring to the Koran (Sura 8:39, 40)—"to accept the external form of their [i.e. the prophets'] prescriptions."[19]

> For the well-being (*ṣalāḥ*) of this world can only be completed by force (*ijdbār*), coercion (*ḳahr*), and suppression (*ghalaba*). For men's natures are different, just as are their intentions in their religious (*adyān*) and worldly affairs. (110, ult. ss.)

The authority of the prophet thus becomes a test of the obedience and disobedience of all men, who are to be guided by the revealed divine law (110·14ff.). Some of them must be forced, on account of their dissenting opinions; there is something akin to freedom of conscience though, and Abū Ḥātim ascribes to men the capacity to choose, referring to Sura 2:256(257); Sawy, 111·13ff.:

> God has ordered men to seek (*ṭalab*) the deeper meanings (*ma'ānī*) which exist beneath the external form of their laws, and which bring salvation. He has invited them to this in a most beautiful manner by forgiving them (*bi-l-i'dhār*), by warning them (*al-indhār*), and by [speaking to them in] beautiful exhortation, as, for example: 'Seek knowledge, even if it were in China!,' or,[20] 'The search for knowledge is a duty for every Muslim.' (112·2-5)

Ignorance is thus disobedience to the prophet

> who presents knowledge without any restriction of the law's content to those who deserve it, who are obedient, and who defend it against the unjust and the enemy who does not deserve it. (113·5-7)

Ignorance, which means acting without knowledge, "causes enmity and injustice (*baghy*)" (113·2ff., esp. 113·5), according to Abū Ḥātim. People without knowledge "mix heresies with the prophetic norms" (173·2f.; cf. 9ff.) which are passed on, and only do this, strictly speaking, "for the love of power and in the struggle for the irrelevant things (*a'rāḍ*: 'accidents') of the world" (173·4f.; cf. 186·6ff.). Wars between adherents of religions (*ahl al-milal*), consequently, arise 'mostly' because,

> they combat their opponents (*mukhālifūhum*); they struggle and fight for the world. Just as we see conflicts on behalf of kingdoms and towns in the country of Islam, the same happens with all adherents of religions in their countries. (186·11-13)

Abū Ḥātim adds that Muslims and non-Muslims by no means doubt their religion in so doing; however, "they have preferred world to religion, even

---

19 *qabūl ẓāhir rusūmihim*, 111·9.

20 Also recorded by Ibn Mādja († 273/886), *Sunan Muḳaddima 17.*

though they are convinced of the reward and punishment of those to whom these are promised and threatened."[21] He adds:

> Their natural desire drives them to this, and so dominates their intellect that they prefer the bad to the excellent (187·10f).

In addition, Abū Ḥātim notes the insatiability of men, who want to have more and more of the 'irrelevant things' ('accidents') of the world. (188·6ff.) In order to control this,

> God has elected leaders for men, who guide them and give them regulations, so that the world is kept in order, so that men act properly with respect to (their) religious and worldly affairs, and so that they can live and not die, as God —exalted is He— has said: 'Had God not driven the people, some by means of others' (Sura 2:251(252))[22] by what the prophets have prescribed for the people, by what they have laid down, and by what (people) have been induced to by them? (188·13-16)

Abū Ḥātim further remarks that, "certainly not everyone who wins can get the upper hand" (188, ult. s.); ultimately men must keep to religion and "are kept in check" (*yuqhar*) by religion (189·1f.; cf. also 189·14f.). He then presents the following –remarkable– statement:

> Were a Jew, a Christian, or any adherent of a non-Moslem religion to be desirous of gaining the upper hand in the country of Islam, he would not be in a position to do so, and would be unable to do it. Although they prefer irrelevant things ('accidents') of the world, they do not doubt religion (*milla*). (189·2-4)

This means that wars between adherents of different religions do not arise primarily for the sake of belief, but because of the insatiability and avarice of men for 'worldly things'; religious authority regulates the world, "keeping it in check." Man must keep to his religious duties, and is unable, contrary to what Abū Ḥātim's opponent Abū Bakr ar-Rāzī maintained, to attain knowledge and judgment by his own 'inventiveness' (*istinbāṭ*) and inspiration (273ff., esp. 274·1ff., note 18 above). He is dependent upon the divine revelation of the prophet, the leader of the religious community.

Abū Ḥātim adds a further remarkable proposition at this juncture: The learned books of the Greeks, such as Galen, Hippocrates, Euclid, and Ptolemæus, "are based upon true wisdom and well-arranged principles (*al-uṣūl al-muntaẓima*)" (275·15). This wisdom is not a privilege of the revelation of Islam; those who deliver divine wisdom have different names and belong to different religions; they are prophets, who —as was later explained by the philosopher Fārābī as well, expanding the thesis to include the peripatetic-Aristotelian doctrine (Alexander of Aphrodisias)[23]— received divine revelation in a dream (287f., 288·13ff.). Irrespective of

[21] 187·1ff. Abū Ḥātim here refers to the Mu'tazilite principle of *wa'd* – *wa'īd*. On this, cf. Daiber 1988a: 13, 15.
[22] The translation follows Arberry.
[23] Daiber 1986a: 737ff.; 1986b: 15.

their affiliation to a religious community, "they know the religious secret" (*'ālim al-ghayb*;[24] 318·16ff.; cf. 301·11ff.). The prophet is therefore "the first of the wise" (*al-ḥakīm al-auwal*; 314ff., esp. 318·4ff.), the mediator of divine revelation. Their intellect (*fiṭra*) and nature does not enable prophets and scholars "to ascend to heaven and to understand these secret things (*al-ghuyūb*); rather, God has informed them about these and has revealed (the secrets) to them" (301·11ff.).

As we have seen, Abū Ḥātim did not confine the presence of prophetic revelation to Islamic religion. And as was already emphasized by the Koran, the 'people of the Book,' Jews and Christians, are in possession of prophetic truth too; they have falsified it however (cf. above, p. 87. In Islam, the universal truth which was already present among earlier prophets has been restored, for they had mingled it together with error. In like manner, there are differences of degree between languages; best are —next to Arabic[25]— Syriac, Hebrew, and Persian. They have their origin in 'instruction' (*tauḳīf*) by God (290·2ff.), according to Abū Ḥātim's presentation of divine revelation as source of all knowledge, following through the early Islamic exegesis of Sura 2:31(29)[26] which has continued right through to widespread contemporary tradition.[27]

This 'revelationist'[28] theory appears to be combined with the thesis of the 'natural relation' between word and meaning, or language and content, in Abū Ḥātim — a thesis which had first been defended before Abū Ḥātim's time by the Mu'tazilite 'Abbād Ibn Sulaymān († 864 A.D.; Daiber 1975: 211), and which had been generally assumed by the Ismailiyya.[29] Discrepancies arise only when human interpretation of prophetic records mix truth and error. Abū Ḥātim writes:

> The exterior (pl. *ẓawāhir*) of the prophetic records in people's hands is true (*ḥaḳḳ*); the heresies which heretics combine with it are wrong, however. Whoever adheres to these records which are mixed with heresies, combines truth and falsehood. This has been done by Christianity in

---

[24] On the originally Koranic term *ghayb*, cf. Daiber 1975: 117ff.

[25] Cf. Abū Ḥātim, *Kitāb az-Zīna* (al-Hamadānī, 60ff.), on the superiority of Arabic to Hebrew, Syriac, and Persian.

[26] "And he taught Adam the names, all of them" (Arberry).

[27] As representatives of this doctrine, we find the Mu'tazilites Abū 'Alī al-Djubbā'ī († 915–16 A.D.) and his pupil Ka'bī, al-Ash'arī († 935–36 A.D.), and some grammarians from the 10th century; cf. Weiss, 33ff.; Haarmann, 149-69, esp. 153f.

[28] I have adopted this term from Weiss.

[29] Ibn Ḥawshab = Manṣūr al-Yaman († around 303/915), *Kitāb ar-Rushd wa-l-hidāya* (trans. Ivanow, 32ff.); or his *Kitāb al-'Ālim wa-l-ghulām* (cf. Poonawala, 64), English summary, Ivanow, 73; or Abū l-Fawāris al-Ḥasan Ibn Muhammad al-Mīmadhī (or al-Mihadhī/al-Mayhadhī, end of the 10th century A.D.), *Risāla ilā djamā'at ahl ar-Rayy*, summary Ivanow, 129ff.

> Rome, by Judaism in Khazar,[30] and by the Magians[31] living in some mountain regions. (173·14ff.)

Abū Ḥātim bases his explanation on the Koran (Sura 3:78(72); Sawy, 173·10ff.); people who had too little understanding, "the weak who did not recognize the truth of the books' contents" (173·7), have been misled by 'leaders' (*ru'asā'*) who have combined the records of the prophets with heretical doctrines[32] as a result of a variety of 'intentions' (*ahwā'*; 172·9f.). This was all the easier since the revealed Scriptures contain 'clear' (*wāḍiḥa*) as well as 'complicated' (*mustaghlika*) thoughts (*ma'ānī*; Sawy 71·14ff.; cf. 116·2ff.); "the majority of the prophetic utterances are rendered in a symbolical manner (*marmūz*)" (173·7f.; cf. 71·5). The symbol (*ramz*), or the parable (*mathal*), plays an important part in Abū Ḥātim's philosophy. He traces it in Islam (Koran) as well as in the Jewish and Christian religion by presenting many quotations and fragments from the Old and the New Testaments.[33] The conclusion which this yields is that, "the prophets' expressions and symbols vary in meaning" (156·2f.; cf. 94·3ff.), giving the impression that revelations contain contradictions (*tanāḳuḍ, ikhtilāf*; 72·7f.; 104·6ff.). Abū Ḥātim solves this by saying that prophets "do not differ in the principle of religion and in the confession of the unity (*tawḥīd*) of God" (156·3f.). Abū Ḥātim thereupon adds a complete creed which emphasizes the oneness and eternity of God, who has Himself created his creatures, not from something else which is eternal;[34] who has sent the elected prophets to men as messengers and warning; who will raise men from the dead in the future; who will reward or punish them; and who has imposed commands and prohibitions on them. Analysis of this creed demonstrates its affinity with the credo of the Ismailiyya;[35] it includes the *shahāda*, which has been modified in accordance with Abū

30 This is the district around Darband (Caspian Sea); cf. Wüstenfeld, 436, 14ff. on this and its religious minorities.

31 The Magians are sometimes called 'dualists' (cf. 131·7f.), i.e. adherents of the sects of Mani or Mazdak; cf. Monnot 1974: 77ff., on these adherents during Islamic times.

32 173·9ff.; cf. 171-77; disparate traditions arose about the prophet on account of this combining of truth with error (168·6ff.). Jesus is crucified according to the gospels, but not according to the Koran (Sura 4:157(156)); cf. Schumann, 37f.

33 94ff.; cf. the index, p. 345ff., which requires some correction. A precise comparison should include the Biblical quotations in Abū Ḥātim's unpublished *Kitāb al-Islāḥ* (cf. Ivanow, 118ff.; Poonawala, 38), and would be helpful for the identification of the *Vorlage* of the quotations. Ismailite circles were acquainted with Hebrew and Syriac, as is demonstrated by Kraus, 243-63. (Cf. A. Baumstark in *Der Islam 20* (1932): 308-13.)

34 This includes critique of Abū Bakr ar-Rāzī; cf. above p. 89 and below, note 37.

35 Cf. the creed of Abū Ya'ḳūb as-Sidjistānī († between 386/996 and 393/1002-3), *Kitāb Sullām an-nadjāt* (ed. Alibhai); belief in God, His unity, His books, His angels, His prophets, the Last Judgment, resurrection, heaven and hell, guarantee the salvation (*nadjāt*) of believers (cf. 150ff.).

Ḥātim's intentions,[36] and which incorporates elements of the orthodox creed;[37] Abū Ḥātim writes:

> The (prophets) unanimously confess: God is one single god; there is no (other) God besides Him; He is eternal, without any (second) eternal (god) besides Him; He did not cease to be and shall not cease to be; He is the creator of all creatures, which have not been created from something (else eternal); there is no creator besides Him; they have described Him —great is His reputation— with the most beautiful attributes, as He deserves. They concurred in the following opinion: He has sent the prophets as messengers of good news and as warning; He has chosen and elected them from His creation with the purpose of delivering His good news to them; He has created two places, one for troubles (*sa'iy*) and labour, the other for reward and punishment; He has imposed on them commands and prohibitions; He will raise them from the dead upon death, and will call them to account for their deeds, sentencing them accordingly; God 'may recompense those who do evil for what they have done, and recompense those who have done good with the reward most fair' (Sura 53:31/32). At the end stand paradise and hell. Here (the prophets) follow one way, not at all disagreeing, and demanding of all men that they praise God in their deeds, being unanimous in their principles. For example: practise prayer, giving alms, fasting, sacrificial ceremonies (*manāsik*), immolation (*ḳarābīn*), and all religious duties and norms. They do not disagree in any of these, and they all demand that these (be observed); they ascribed truth and prophecy to one another, and order (men) to follow the one way, by being subject (to God). They disagree, however, in the establishment of laws, as, for example, about the prayer-times, the number of bendings of the torso (along with two prostrations), the instructions on almsgiving, the times of fasting, and other practical rules by which God —mighty and exalted is He— has examined and put to the test His creation — just as Moses has ordered prayer, which forms the principle of religion in every law. He has, however, ordered (people) to orient themselves to Jerusalem in prayer; likewise, Jesus commanded prayer, with an eastward orientation. At the same time, (Jesus) ascribes truth as well as prophecy to Moses. (156·4-157·5)

Abū Ḥātim explains the fact that religions do not differ in their essence, but are different in the details of law, in their practices, as follows (157·6-10; cf. 158·3ff.; 172·13): The prophets have to be blamed for this because they intended,

> to make visible the obedient, in contrast to the disobedient... as God has said: 'And we did not appoint the direction thou wast facing, except that we might know who followed the Messenger from him who turned on his heels.' (Sura 2:143/138, tr. Arberry)

Such an explanation enables Abū Ḥātim to explain to his opponent Abū Bakr ar-Rāzī why religion seems to be true in a certain country at a certain

---

36 Instead of Mohammed, only 'the prophets' are mentioned.

37 There are some similarities to the Ḥanafite *Fikh akbar* (published in Ḥaidarābād 1321/1903, with commentary by Abū l-Muntahā); cf. the English translation, Wensinck, 188ff.; compare, for example, art. 5 (Wensinck, 190; commentary pp. 210-12) to Sawy, 156·5f. (The creation of the world not from something else eternal presupposes the denial of the Aristotelian proposition of the eternity of matter; cf. above p. 89 on this.)

time, but wrong in other countries at other times (171-172·3; 172·5ff.). God

> ... has sent the prophets in different epochs and times to warn (people), to inform them about the way of truth, away from falsehood, about the way of right guidance, away from error, and to free the traditional norms from heresies. (172·11f.)

At the same time, Abū Ḥātim seizes the occasion to point out the didactic value of the circumstance he describes (the seeming difference between religions): men must exert themselves, inspecting and examining these differences with their intellect. Man is put to the test (72·6f.), so that he can come to distinguish between truth and error (155·15ff.).

Abū Ḥātim never tires of stressing that man should not trust in subjective opinion (*ra'y*; 72·14; see above note 13), but is in need of the prophet, the 'teacher' who informs his pupil, offering the 'learning' about utterances which are difficult to comprehend (72·13ff.; see above note 17, and 71·14ff.), and who shows him how to distinguish between truth and error, and how to find the true meaning (*ma'ānī*) of the symbols, of the 'external' forms by way of 'interpretation' (*ta'wīl*).[38] The Koran orders people to turn to their messengers and 'scholars' (*'ulamā'*), according to Abū Ḥātim.[39] These 'scholars' are identified with 'the philosophers who speak the truth' (*al-falāsifa al-muḥiḳḳūn*; 131·6f.). They too speak in a 'corporeal' (*djismānī*) or in a 'spiritual' manner, as Abū Ḥātim explains with reference to the Neo-Platonic philosopher, Proclus.[40] The 'corporeal' manner of speaking is the parable, while the symbol and the spiritual manner is the 'meaning' (*ma'nā*).[41] Abū Ḥātim sometimes also employs the

---

[38] Cf. Sawy, 14·12ff.; 115·3ff. and Goldziher 1952: 181ff. on the Ismailite —originally Shi'te— term *ta'wīl*; also Halm, 22; 123, and the Index.

[39] Cf. Sawy, 115·7ff., which contains a reference to Suras 4:83/85 (Sawy, 115·10-12) and 4:59 (Sawy, 115·15-17). The last mentioned Sura also has been used by the Ismailite, al-Kirmānī († 411/1020–21) in his *Kitāb al-Maṣābīḥ fī ithbāt al-imāma* (Makarem, 38); the Zaydite al-Ḳāsim ibn Ibrahim, † 860 A.D., had already referred to the Sura as an argument for the necessity of the Imamate (cf. Abrahamov, 87).

[40] Abū Ḥātim has based his statement on a doxographical text which is ascribed to Ammonius, and which has been preserved in the unique Arabic manuscript, *Aya Sofya* (Istanbul) 2450, fol. 132 v·5, counting from below, and ff. (the ms. has BRMNS; this may be an incorrect rendering of BRḲL = Proclus). This distinction is indeed the Hellenistic antithesis between *sōmatikón* and *pneumatikón*, as Goldziher 1952: 182, has already shown. The passage in Abū Ḥātim —our oldest dated reference to the Ammonius text (cf. Daiber 1984: 259f.) — certainly proves that Ammonius' doxography (an edition is being prepared by Ulrich Rudolph, Göttingen) was the source of this distinction in Islam, and it may have first entered Ismailite circles here. It plays a central role in Ismailite philosophy (cf. Alibhai, 18ff.). Alibhai (74f.) was at a loss to explain the origin of this distinction, and assumed a Christian Neo-Platonic source.

[41] 107·7-9; cf. 126·11f. and 105. Abū Ḥātim subsequently validates this distinction by appealing to Democritus (following the Ammonius text —see previous note— fol. 134r·12ff.) and Pseudo Apollonius (= Bālīnās), *Sirr al-khalīka* (Weisser 2·5f. = Sawy, 107·12ff.). The *Sirr al-khalīka* is cited by Abū Ḥātim several times, not only in his *A'lām an-nubūwa*, but also in his *Kitāb az-Zīna* (cf. Daiber in *Der Islam 59*

terminology of 'external' (*ẓahr, ḳahir*) and 'internal' (*baṭn, bāṭin*; 105·1ff.). He refers to a tradition ascribed to the prophet Mohammed and to ʿAlī, and follows old Ismaili terminology.[42] There are people among the philosophers too, however, who mix up truth and error. They are called *mutafālsifa*, 'those who affect to be philosophers' (131f.), and have developed diverging opinions. Abū Ḥātim has demonstrated this in a long doxographical chapter on the disagreement of these philosophers in their doctrines about elements (Sawy, 133-38, summary pp. 149-51); he uses translations or partially lost Greek works in this chapter.[43] Aristotle is apparently reckoned among the true philosophers, for his symbolical utterances are misunderstood by some people, as Abū Ḥātim declares, and they therefore fail to classify him as a 'monotheist' (*muwaḥḥid*).[44]

Despite this high estimation of the true philosophers, they do not attain the rank of the prophet Mohammed, just as the prophets before Mohammed did not. Thus, Moses, Jesus, Mohammed, and the other prophets "have all been recognized by their perfection, intellect (*ʿaḳl*), judgment (*tamyīz*), guidance, and by their commendable qualities" (73·15f.). But Moses and Jesus are inferior to Mohammed (89·10ff.), and

> the peoples which have seen Mohammed for themselves agree in their estimation of Mohammed as perfect in his intellect (*ʿaḳl*), mercy (*ḥilm*), patience (*anāt*), leadership, and guidance of all men. (73·17-19)

Abū Ḥātim has therefore devoted a long chapter to describing the good qualities (*shamāʾil, ḥilya*) of the prophet Mohammed (77-93). Here as well as in the *tafḍīl*, the priority of Mohammed over other prophets, Abū Ḥātim adheres to the orthodox picture of the prophet as the ideal of the perfect moral life (Andrae, 190ff., 245ff.); as bearer of prophetic knowledge, the prophet is equipped at the same time with ethical qualities which clearly betray influences of the Platonic doctrine (Plato, *Rep. IV* 435B ff.) on the cardinal virtues of 'wisdom' (cf. Gr. *sofía*), 'abstinence' (cf. Gr. *sōfrosýnē* with *tawāḍuʿ*; Sawy, 84f.), 'courage' (compare Gr. *andreía* with *shadjāʿa;* Sawy, 80-82), and 'justice' (cf. Gr. *dikaiosýnē*);[45] they are

(1982): 328f.).

42 Cf. the Ismailite Ibn Ḥaushab (see note 29 above on him), *Kitāb al-ʿĀlim wa-l-ghulām*; summary by Ivanow, 69ff.; Halm, 23; Makarem, 49; Esmail and Nanji, 239ff. —They are called *'Bāṭiniyya'* by their critics because of their allegorical interpretation, distinguishing between the allegorical, 'interior' (*bāṭin*) meaning of a word, and its 'external' (*ẓāhir*) meaning; cf. Hodgson; Goldziher 1956/ English translation McCarthy, 175ff.; cf. the analysis by Goldziher and Jabre, 415ff. —Ghazzālī's book was refuted by the Ismailite, Ibn al-Walīd († 612/1215), *Dāmigh al-bāṭil wa-ḥatf al-munāḍil* (Ghālib).

43 On the not yet completely identified sources, cf. Daiber 1980: 178 (add the quotation from Ps. Apollonius, *Sirr al-khalīḳa* (see note 41 above), p. 28·1f.; 7-9 = Abū Ḥātim ar-Rāzī, Sawy, 140·4-6.

44 72·15ff. Perhaps Abū Ḥātim has the so-called 'Theology' of Aristotle in mind here, an Arabic redaction of Plotinus' *Enneads*; cf. Kraye, Ryan, Schmitt, eds., and the review by Daiber in *Der Islam* *65* (1988): in press.

45 Cf. 94·5f. on justice (and veracity = *ṣidḳ*) as a feature of the prophets.

combined with the Aristotelian doctrine of the happy mean (Gr. *mesótēs*).[46] Abū Ḥātim here presents a combining of the traditions of the Islamic prophetic ideal with Greek ethics. This combination reappears and is developed further by later philosophers such as Fārābī (Daiber 1986a: 751f.), Miskawayh († 421/1030),[47] and Rāghib al-Iṣfahānī († circa 502/1108).[48]

Abū Ḥātim ar-Rāzī's orthodox idea of the priority of Mohammed over earlier prophets appears to be combined in an original manner with his thesis about the universality of divine knowledge, which had already been revealed to earlier prophets. Mohammed is not only the last prophet who confirms the authenticity of earlier prophets; according to Koranic-orthodox doctrine[49] he is indeed the best prophet as well.[50]

Non-Islamic traditions of prophetic revelations contain clear signs of Mohammed's prophecy (195ff.); the book of Daniel in the Old Testament, to be precise, Daniel's interpretation of Nebuchadnezzar's dream, is the clearest reference to Mohammed's future prophecy: the fourth kingdom prophesied by Daniel may be the Islam which follows upon the Jews, the Christians, and the Magians (53·1ff., note 31 above).

Islam, then, is the completion of what had already been announced to earlier prophets and wise men, namely, the belief in one, single God, which had already been announced by earlier prophets. Their symbols and parables, however, have not been understood by people. Only the Koran, God's message to men as delivered by the prophet Mohammed, is the perfect formulation of belief in one single God; the miracle of the inimitable Koran thus proves the superiority of Islam to other religions all the more (191-94, and on the Koran, p. 227-70.).

Former prophetic revelations remain important nevertheless, as a passing on of the universal belief in one single God, and as presaging the coming of the prophet, Mohammed. Their mistakes, as well as those of philosophers in the past, are caused by the mixing of truth and error. Mankind can attain salvation (*nadjāt*) by seeking (*talab*) 'the well ordered sense' (pl.*al-ma'ānī al-mu'talifa*) of 'the exterior shape of laws' (*ẓāhir ash-sharā'i'*), namely, of God's word. This is the only way to avoid error (*ḍalāl*) and controversy (*ikhtilāf*), and to have guidance (*hidāya*; 110·9ff.).

Moreover, the pre-Islamic revelations form an informative example for the present. They not only prove the necessity of a prophet, and of the superiority of the prophecy of Mohammed; they also show how ignorance

46 Cf. Aristotle, *Nichomachean Ethics II* 1107a ff.; the Arabic term is *i'tidāl*, see Sawy, 85f., where we find an interesting description of its effect on the physiognomy (*firāsa*) of the prophets.

47 *Tahdhīb al-akhlāk*. Cf. Daiber in *Orientalistische Literaturzeitung 67* (1972), col. 370ff., on Miskawayh, whose recourse to the terminology of the current prophetic picture deserves to be investigated.

48 In his book, neglected up until the present, *adh-Dharī'a ilā makārim ash-sharī'a* (new edition by al-'Adjamī).

49 Sura 33:40 on Mohammed as seal (*khātam*) of the prophets. Cf. Speyer, 422f.

50 On this interpretation of *khātam*, cf. Freedman.

and the mixing up of truth and error result in apparent contradictions between divine revelations. People, with their different capacities, are confronted by them, as with a temptation, and are asked to look at them with their mind, to examine them, and to reach the true, universal meaning of all religions. The attainment of the universal belief in one single God and in the justness of His laws is thus not only the historical result of prophetic revelations to mankind, but is also a permanently renewed intellectual process, the seeking for the universal meaning of the diverse forms of tradition and religion respectively.

With these fascinating ideas, which reappeared shortly afterwards in the *Rasā'il Ikhwān aṣ-ṣafā'* (Goldziher 1952: 189ff.), an encyclopedia compiled by sympathizers of the Ismailites before 959/960 A.D. (Diwald, Introduction, esp. pp. 15ff.), Abū Ḥātim sketched a design for a universal religion which enables the peaceful co-existence of different forms of religions. Although the idea of the identity of prophetic messages from different times is not quite new[51] and may be inspired by the Koranic tradition about the renewal of the religion of Abraham by Mohammed — the Ismaili, Abū Ḥātim ar-Rāzī lent it a new currency; his reaction to Abū Bakr ar-Rāzī's denial of prophecy has issued into a very impressive proposal on the universality of religious knowledge.

Abū Ḥātim wrote his validation of Mohammed's prophecy at a time of peaceful co-existence between different religions and sects in the Islamic empire. He cites books of Jews, Christians, and Greeks. He has perhaps written his book for the benefit of non-Islamic readers as well, in accordance with a principle of Ismaili apologetics, viz. the conversion of people by referring to their own doctrines.[52]

[51] Lewis, p. 31, note 94, refers to the Jewish sect of the 'Īsawiyya in Iṣfahan. During the reign of the Omayyad Caliph 'Abdalmalik, its members defended the assertion that Jesus and Mohammed were true prophets.

[52] Lewis, p. 31, note 94, refers to the Jewish sect of the 'Īsawiyya in Iṣfahan. During the reign of the Omayyad Caliph 'Abdalmalik, its members defended the assertion that Jesus and Mohammed were true prophets.

Bibliography

Abū Rīda, 'Abdalhādī Muḥammad, ed. *Rasā'il al-Kindī al-falsafiyya*, I. Cairo, 1950.

Abrahamov, Binyamin. "Al-Ḳāṣim Ibn Ibrāhīm's Theory of the Imamate." *Arabica* 34 (1987): 80-105.

al-'Adjamī, Abū l-Yazīd, ed. *Rāghib al-Iṣfahānī: adh-Dharī'a ilā makārim ash-sharī'a*. Cairo, 1985.

Alibhai, Mohamed Abualy. *Abū Ya'qūb al-Sijistānī and Kitāb Sullām al-Najāt: A Study in Islamic Neoplatonism.* Thesis, Harvard, 1983.

Andrae, Tor. *Die Person Muhammeds in Lehre und Glauben seiner Gemeinde.* Archives d'Études Orientales 16. Stockholm, 1918.

Arberry, Arthur J. *The Koran Interpreted.* 1964; rpt. Oxford, 1986.

Bilinski, Janusz. "The Concept of Time in the Ismailitic Gnosis." *Folia Orientalia* 23 (1985–86): 69-110.

Brion, Fabienne. "Philosophie et Révélation: Traduction Annotée de Six Extraits du Kitāb A'lām an-nubūwa d'Abū Ḥātim al-Rāzī." *Bulletin d'Philosophie Médiévale* 28 (1986): 137-62.

Cortabarria, A. "El Metodo de Al-Kindī visto a travers de sus Risālas." *Orientalia Hispanica,* I, part 1. Ed. J. M. Barral. Leiden, 1974, pp. 209-225.

Daiber, Hans. Review of *The Refinement of Character,* as trans. by Constantine K. Zurayk. *Orientalische Literaturzeitung* 67 (1972): 370-373.

——. 1975. *Das theologisch-philosophische System des Mu'ammar Ibn 'Abbād as-Sulamī († 830 n. Chr.).* Beiruter Texte und Studien 19. Beirut/Wiesbaden.

——. 1980. *Aetius Arabus.* Akademie der Wissenschaften und der Literatur, Veröffentlichungen der Orientalistichen Kommission 33. Wiesbaden.

——. 1983. "Democritus in Arabic and Syriac Tradition." *Proceedings of the 1st International Congress on Democritus,* B. Xanthi, October, 1983, pp. 251-65.

——. 1986a. "Prophetie und Ethik bei Fārābī († 339/950)." In *L'homme et son Univers au Moyen Âge* 2. Philosophes Médiévaux 27. Louvain-la-Neuve, pp. 729-53.

——. 1986b. *The Ruler as Philosopher.* Mededelingen der Koninklijke Nederlandse Akademie van Wetenschappen, afd. Letterkunde, nieuwe reeks, vol. 49, no. 4. Amsterdam/Oxford/New York.

——. 1988a. *Wāṣil Ibn 'Aṭā' als Prediger und Theologe.* Islamic Philosophy and Theology: Texts and Studies, II. Leiden.

——. 1988b (forthcoming). "Die Autonomie der Philosophie im Islam." *Proceedings of the 8th International Congress of Medieval Philosophy.* Helsinki, August 24-29, 1987.

Davidson, Herbert A. *Proofs for Eternity, Creation, and the Existence of God in Medieval Islamic and Jewish Philosophy.* New York/Oxford, 1987.

Diwald, Susanne. *Arabische Philosophie und Wissenschaft in der Enzyklopädie: Kitāb Iḫwān aṣ-ṣafā' (III): Die Lehre von Seele und Intellekt.* Wiesbaden, 1975.

Dodds, E. R., ed. Proclus, *Institutio Theologica.* Oxford, ^{2}1963.

Enderwitz, Susanne. *Gesellschaftlicher Rang und ethnische Legitimation.* Islamkundliche Untersuchungen 53. Freiburg, 1979.

Endress, Gerhard, ed. *Proclus Arabus.* Beiruter Texte und Studien 10. Beirut/Wiesbaden, 1973.

Esmail, Aziz and Azim Nanji. "Ismāʿīlīs in History." In Nasr, *Ismāʿīlī Contributions,* pp. 227-58.
Ess, Josef van. "Al-Fārābī and Ibn Al-Rēwandī." *Hamdard Islamicus* 2, no. 4 (1980): 3-15.
——. "Ibn Al-Rēwandī, or the Making of an Image." *Al-Abḥāth* 27 (1978–79): 5-26.
Fakhry, Majid. "A Tenth Century Arabic Interpretation of Plato's Cosmology." *Journal of the History of Philosophy* 6 (1968): 15-20.
Freedman, Yohanan. "The Finality of Prophethood in Sunni Islam." *Jerusalem Studies in Arabic and Islam* 7 (1986): 176-215.
Ghālib, Muṣṭafā, ed. Ibn al-Walīd, *Dāmigh al-bāṭil wa-ḥatf al-munāḍil.* Beirut, 1982.
Goldziher, Ignaz. *Die Richtungen der Islamischen Koranauslegung.* Leiden, 1952.
——. ²1956, ed. Ghazzālī, "Faḍā'iḥ al-Bāṭiniyya." In *Streitschrift des Ġazālī gegen die Bāṭinijja-Sekte.* Leiden.
——. 1971. *Muhammedanische Studien,* I. Halle, 1888; rpt. New York: Hildesheim.
Haarmann, Ulrich. "Religiöses Recht und Grammatik im klassischen Islam." *Zeitschrift der Deutschen Morgenländischen Gesellschaft,* Suppl. II (1974): 149-69.
Halm, Heinz. *Kosmologie und Heilslehre der frühen Ismāʿīlīya.* Abhandlungen für die Kunde des Morgenlandes 44, 1. Wiesbaden, 1978.
al-Hamadānī, Ḥusain Ibn Fayḍallāh, ed. Abū Ḥātim: *Kitāb az-Zīna,* I. Cairo, ²1957.
Hārūn, ʿAbdassalām Muḥammad, ed. *Rasā'il al-Djāḥiẓ* 1-4. Cairo, 1979.
Heinen, Anton. *Islamic Cosmology.* Beiruter Texte und Studien 27. Beirut/Wiesbaden, 1982.
Hodgson, M. G. S. "Bāṭiniyya." *Encyclopedia of Islam²,* I. Leiden/London, 1960, pp. 1098-1100.
Ivanow, W. *Studies in Early Persian Ismailism.* 2nd rev. edn. Bombay, 1955.
Ivry, Alfred L. *Al-Kindī's Metaphysics.* Albany, 1974.
Jabre, Farid. *La Notion de Certitude selon Ghazali.* Beirut, ²1986.
Jammer, Max. *Das Problem des Raumes.* 2nd edn., Darmstadt, 1980.
Khalidi, Tarif. "The Idea of Progress in Classical Islam." *Journal of Near Eastern Studies* 40 (1981): 144-46.
——. 1977. "A Mosquito's Wing: Al-Jāḥiẓ on the Progress of Knowledge." *Arabic and Islamic Garland: Historical, Educational, and Literary Papers presented to Abdul-Latif Tibawi.* London, pp. 277-89.
Kraus, Paul. "Hebräische und syrische Zitaten in ismāʿīlitischen Schriften." *Der Islam* 19 (1931): 243-63.
Kraye, Jill, W. F. Ryan, and C. B. Schmitt. *Pseudo-Aristotle in the Middle Ages: The Theology and Other Texts.* Warburg Institute: Surveys and Texts, XI. London, 1986.

Laoust, Henri. *La Profession de Foi d'Ibn Baṭṭa*. Damas, 1958.
Lazarus-Yafeh, Hava. *Studies in Al-Ghazzali*. Jerusalem, 1975.
Levi Della Vida, G. "Kharidjites." *Encyclopedia of Islam*², IV. Leiden/London, 1978, pp. 1074-77.
Lewis, Bernard. *The Origins of Ismā'īlism*. Cambridge, 1940; rpt. New York, 1975.
Madelung, Wilfred. "Das Imamat in der frühen ismailitischen Lehre." *Der Islam* 37 (1961): 43-135.
——. 1977. "Aspects of Ismā'īlī Theology: The Prophetic Chain and the God Beyond Being." In Nasr, *Ismā'īlī Contributions*, pp. 51-65. (Also in Madelung, *Religious Schools and Sects*. London, 1985. Variorum Reprints.)
——. 1978. "Ismā'īliyya." *Encyclopedia of Islam*², IV. Leiden/London, 1978, pp. 198-206.
Makarem, Sami Nasib. *The Doctrine of the Ismailis*. Beirut, 1972.
McCarthy, J. *Freedom and Fulfillment: An Annotated Translation of Al-Ghazālī's al-Munqidh min al-Dalāl and Other Relevant Works of Al-Ghazālī*. Boston, 1980.
Mohaghegh, Mehdi. "Rāzī's Kitāb Al-Ilm Al-ilāhī and the Five Eternals." *Abr Nahrain* 13 (1972–73): 16-23. (Also in *Filsuf-i-Rayy Muhammad Ibn-i-Zakariya-i-Razi*. 2nd enlarged edn. Teheran, 1974. Eng. section pp. 28-35.)
Monnot, Guy. *Penseurs Musulmans et Religions Iranniennes*. Études Musulmanes 14. Paris, 1974.
Muṣṭafā, Kamāl, ed. Sa'īd Ibn Nashwān al-Ḥimyarī, *al-Ḥūr al-'īn*. Teheran, 1972.
Nagel, Tilman. *Studien zum Minderheitenproblem im Islam*, II: *Rechtleitung und Kalifat*. Bonner Orientalistische Studien (NS) 27. Bonn, 1975.
Nasr, Seyyed Hossein, ed. *Ismā'īlī Contributions to Islamic Culture*. Teheran, 1977.
——. 1982. "Intellect and Intuition." In *Islam and Contemporary Society*. Ed. Salem Azzam. London/New York, pp. 36-46. (Also in *Studies in Comparative Religion* 13, no. 1-2 [Lancaster, 1979]: 65-74.)
Paret, Rudi. *Mohammed und der Koran*. Stuttgart, ⁵1980.
Pellat, Charles. *Arabische Geisteswelt: Ausgewählte und übersetzte Texte von Al-Ǧāḥiẓ*. Zürich, 1967.
Pines, Solomon. *Beitrage zur islamischen Atomenlehre*. Berlin, 1936.
Poonawala, Ismail K. *Bibliography of Ismā'īlī Literature*. Malibu, 1977.
Radtke, Bernd. "Die älteste islamische Kosmographie: Muḥammad-i Ṭūsīs 'Aǧā'ib al-maḫlūqāt." *Der Islam* 64 (1987): 279-88.
al-Sawy, Salah, ed. Abū Ḥātim ar-Rāzī, *A'lām an-nubūwa*. Teheran, 1977.
——. 1977b, ed. Ḥamīd ad-Dīn al-Kirmānī, *al-Akwāl adh-dhahabiyya*. Teheran.
Schumann, Olaf H. *Der Christus der Muslime*. Missionswissenschaftliche Forschungen 10. Gütersloh, 1975.

Sezgin, Fuat. *Geschichte des Arabischen Schrifttums,* I. Leiden, 1967.

Sharon, Moshe. *Black Banners from the East.* The Max Schloessinger Memorial Series Monographs, II. Jerusalem/Leiden, 1983.

Speyer, Heinrich. *Die biblischen Erzählungen im Koran.* Hildesheim, New York, 1971.

Stern, S. M. *Studies in Early Ismā'īlism.* The Max Schloessinger Memorial Series Monographs, I. Jerusalem/Leiden, 1983.

Walzer, R. *Al-Fārābī on the Perfect State.* Oxford, 1985.

Watt, W. M. and M. Marmura. *Der Islam,* II. Stuttgart, 1985. Die Religionen der Menschheit 25, 2.

Weiss, Berhard G. "Medieval Muslim Discussions of the Origin of Language." *Zeitschrift der Deutschen Morgenländischen Gesellschaft* 124 (1974): 33-41.

Weisser, Ursula, ed. Ps. Apollonius, *Sirr al-khalīḳa.* Aleppo, 1979.

Wensinck, A. J. *The Muslim Creed.* London, 1965.

Wüstenfeld, F., ed. Yāḳūt, *Mu'djam al-buldān,* II. Leipzig, 1867; rpt. Teheran, 1965.

Chapter 8

New Religious Movements and Syncretism in Tribal Cultures

Harold W. Turner

The spectrum of forms provided by new religious movements arising in the interaction between Christianity and the primal religions offers special insights into syncretic processes. The series of changes represent stages —each indispensable to conversion but each insufficient in itself and an obstacle if it becomes terminal. In the dimension of world-views there is affinity with primal religions at the ontological level but major cosmological differences. Here there are syncretic stages in the changes towards a contingent view of the universe, the new ways to control power and to view time, in the development of an open society, and in the internalization of evil as individual sin.

The Free University, Amsterdam, may be said to have been founded as a Christian answer to a syncretistic new religious movement. In late 19th century Europe the great Abraham Kuyper saw around him a certain return to religion in reaction to the rationalism and irreligion of the Enlightenment and the French Revolution, and the positivism and materialism of his own century. He saw this return taking the form of a "warm stream of mysticism" related to "some intangible infinite." This new syncretistic religion selected from the Christian past, placed it in an evolutionary context, and led to a naturalistic and individualistic private faith. Being "banished to the retreats of sentiment," it could not encourage intellectual activity nor provide a common and public truth and world view that embraced the spiritual and the secular spheres of life. Kuyper's answer, based on the Calvinist tradition he so notably expounded, was to found not a theological seminary to defend the Christian faith, but a university of the mind to claim all areas of life for their proper place in the divinely created order.[1]

In a small New Zeeland (or, as they spell it, Zealand) town in 1934 a retired Presbyterian minister gave me his copy of Kuyper's Stone Lectures, long before I had heard of new religious movements or could see the significance of his words. Now in re-reading Kuyper I find statements that are quite remarkable when placed in relation to the *de rigueur* blaming of the apartheid of the races in South Africa on the Calvinism of the Afrikaner churches. I have written elsewhere on the influence of Kuyper on the Afrikaners, especially through this University, and quoted his emphatic statements on "the commingling of blood as . . . the physical basis of all higher human development."[2]

This amounts to strong support for one kind of syncretism. Later Kuyper spoke of the need to bring together "all the talents hidden in our race" including the "precious treasures . . . from the old heathen civilization" as well as from the Renaissance (Kuyper, 164, 159). With this open and comprehensive Calvinistic humanism Kuyper was adopting a syncretic position in the biological, social and cultural spheres. At the same time it is equally clear that Kuyper was strongly opposed to any syncretism of the Christian religion with other religions or world views, and especially with the 'hollow piety' of the new mysticism of his day, itself a syncretistic product.

Since Kuyper's time this new religion has developed further and more recently has been revivified by mystic and occult influences from the East and is known publicly chiefly through certain of the "sects and cults" of the Sai Baba or other guru types. Since the 1970's it has added the amorphous and more variegated and elusive forms of the so-called 'New Age' movement, and neo-pagan revivals from earlier European history. It is in the midst of this religious mish-mash that the Christian Gospel has to identify itself. Kuyper would recognise these later developments from the syncretistic mysticism of his own day and be equally concerned to face them with solid thinking in the service of a public truth about nature, man and God.

I clearly have the authority of the founder of this university for distinguishing between general bio-socio-cultural syncretism and a syncretism of the Christian Gospel with any other faith, especially that of a new religious movement that is itself syncretic, and for regarding our relationship with this alternative religion as the chief missiological concern in Western Europe. Since the understanding of religion associated with these developments dominates the public life of Europe and infects much of the

---

1 Abraham Kuyper, *Calvinism – Six Stone-Lectures* (Amsterdam/Pretoria 1899): 47f., 58f.

2 See H. Turner, "Afrikaner Church Needs Critical Solidarity," *The Christian Century* 29 (1987): 645-46.

Christianity of our time it is difficult for us who are so involved in it to distinguish ourselves from it and to work out our duties towards it.

1. New Interaction Movements with Primal religions

I therefore turn from the Western world to another set of new religious movements, arising in the interaction between the primal religions of the tribal cultures and the Christian faith, and exhibiting both the socio-cultural and the religious forms of syncretism. By examining the latter in this non-Western context, we may discover both what syncretism can tell us about the movements themselves and, more importantly for this occasion, what these movements may reveal about syncretism itself.

The system that I have developed for classifying and analysing the vast range of these new religious movements (henceforth referred to as *PRINERMS*) envisages the various degrees and forms of interaction between the partner faiths as forming a spectrum or continuum ranging from the original primal religion to the new Christian religion. The intermediate forms between these two poles may be called firstly, 'neo-primal' (revising the old faith with some changes), then 'synthetist' (deliberate selection from both religions to form a new system), then 'Hebraist' (similar to the classic religion of Israel), and finally 'independent church' (with a recognizable Christology).[3] This is a spectrum of religious content as movements pass through various degrees of syncretism towards some identifiably Christian position. It is accompanied, however, by another process, a change in world view from the unitary, closed, ontocratic cosmos associated with primal religions to the complex, open, theocratic cosmos associated with the Semitic faiths. This process has its own syncretic aspects but has to be analysed in a quite different way and its forms cannot be correlated with the above four forms of religious content, however much they are necessarily interwoven with these.[4]

The syncretism associated with *PRINERMS* therefore embodies a complex, elusive and polymorphous process, to be examined more fully at a later point. Here we must recognise a yet further aspect of the subject. In syncretism between two primal religions (as when one adds rites borrowed from another) or between two polytheistic religions (as when one borrows from another to add to its pantheon) there is no disturbance to or distortion of the basic religious system of either faith. Where,

---

[3] See my "A New Mission Task: Worldwide and Waiting," *Missiology* 13 (1985): 5-21; *Mission-Focus* (September 1981): 45-55; "A Further Frontier for Missions: A General Introduction to New Religious Movements in Primal Society," *Missionalia* 11 (1983): 103-12.

[4] See my "African Independent Churches and Economic Development," *World Development* 8 (1980): 523-33.

however, a religion depends on a historical founder and his unique work, syncretism with another faith but without distortion of the historical element becomes more difficult.

This is clearly so for the Christian Gospel which testifies to the historical events of the life, death and bodily resurrection of Jesus and to their objective truth for mankind. This, the essential religious content of the Gospel, has an all-or-nothing quality; once Jesus is syncretized into another religion as a prophet, or some of his ideas or teaching are borrowed into another faith, the Gospel as history has vanished. With this Kuyper would agree. The Gospel cannot be related to other religious systems syncretistically, by degrees or in various elements, any more than there can be a syncretism between the views of the earth as a sphere or as a flat disk. Yet paradoxically, this is what seems to occur across the spectrum of *PRINERMS*. If conversion to Christ involves something like a quantum leap from other religious positions, is it possible to regard *PRINERMS* as a series of minor mutations forming part of the process of conversion?

2. Intermediate Syncretic Religious Forms

We shall examine this question first in relation to my spectrum of religious content. A common feature of the 'least Christian' or neo-primal form is the adoption of one single supreme god in place of a range of divinities or multitude of lesser spirits, together with the rejection of magic in favour of a faith relationship with the divine. Even if the one god is only the 'God of Africa' (as with Godianism in Eastern Nigeria) and not yet a universal deity, it is difficult not to welcome this as a result of Christian influence, or as akin to what happened among the early Hebrews, or as a step in the right direction accompanied by a great reform in religious practice.

Similarly, two stages further along the spectrum, movements such as the Ringatu and Ratana religions among New Zealand Maoris are classified as Hebraist because they have repudiated the old *tohunga* Maori religion and seem to have moved into the world of the Hebrew Scriptures, but to remain somewhat uncertain about the place of Jesus Christ. They correspond to the prophetic religion of Israel with one supreme creator God who has come to save his people, who now see themselves as historically descended from the lost tribes of Israel. These developments have occurred under biblical influence and again it is difficult not to welcome them as an advance towards the truth of the Gospel and (despite the qualities of Maori primal religion) as a step forward in religious faith and practice.

At the next stage in the spectrum lie those movements that seem to have some recognizable christology and so may be regarded as independent Christian churches in their essential religious content, while exhibiting commendable syncretism in their socio-cultural dimensions. There are notable examples in the Pacific (e.g., in Fiji the Congregation of the Poor and the Daku community, in the Solomon Islands the Christian Fellowship Church) and in Black Africa the independent churches are well known. Increasingly such movements are accepted into Christian councils at both the national and the world levels and not dismissed as regrettable religious syncretisms.

That the intermediate forms may be regarded as stages in a process rather than as terminal systems is attested by their mobility. Since they are relatively new movements, they are not yet tied to firm traditions or strong institutions and remain free to develop further through ongoing interaction with Christian influences or the emergence of new leaders from within. Thus the Kimbanguist movement in Zaire, which earlier seemed likely to elevate Simon Kimbangu into a Black Messiah rivalling Jesus Christ, and which lacked any eucharistic sacrament, by the 1970's had clarified its christology and adopted the sacrament. Cargo cults in Papua, New Guinea seem to be giving way to revival movements that may be, at least potentially, closer to the Christian position. Within the Maori Ringatu movement there are now sections which use the New Testament as well as the Old, and are moving towards a Christology. Something similar is occuring in sections of the Peyote and Shaker new religions among North American Indians.

There are, however, movements in the opposite direction, as is the case with the Bayudaya in Uganda. Originally a consciously Christian movement, they later deliberately identified with Judaism, like our Hebraist form. There are also sections of the Cherubim and Seraphim in Nigeria, and doubtless among other bodies classifiable as independent churches, that have lost any Christian identity and are probably to be seen as 'synthetist.' Overall, however, the general direction seems to be from the primal towards the Christian position. There are several factors at work here. The most obvious is continuing Christian influence, and especially that of the Scriptures in the vernacular. Modernization processes also lead away from primal world views. On the other hand there are those forms of new African theologies which glorify the African cultural and religious past and so depart from the biblical model wherein Israel confesses its sins as a people before praising God for what he has nevertheless done in their history. Primal forms have also been enhanced where African governments or elites have tried to bolster their authenticity by a chauvinist revival of tribal religions, but these artificial efforts have all proved short-lived.

In all these processes embodying various forms and degrees of syncretism, the fact of intention may be more important than the nature of the particular stage achieved at the moment. In some cases the intention is simply to confirm the new religious form as something completely given by revelation to the founder; this suggests immunity to any further Christian influence (as with the Maori Ratana movement by 1970) and an immobility which presents its own missiological problem. In some regions, especially in Africa, the common intention is to become a Christian church, even if the present achievement is unconsciously syncretic. A missionary approach may then take the form of a 'guided syncretism' and may also recognise the value of home-grown heresies as a people wrestle their way towards Christian truth. Indeed the whole process may be seen in terms of apprehending a series of 'indispensible truths,' each really true as far as it goes and contributing to further apprehension, but none as yet adequate to present the Christian Gospel. Something like this seems to have been operating in the dealings of the English Anglican mission with the Hallelujah religion among the Akawaio Indians in Guyana. In this view of the process syncretisms may play a part in the dynamics of conversion, but may also present a new obstacle to further change.

3. Syncretistic Processes in Changing World Views

We must now turn to the other process of change from a primal world view to one at least compatible with the Christian faith. In a basic sense the primal and the Christian religions already share what I call a 'web-complex' world view in which each reality is constituted by a network of relationships with other realities — an ontological view for which Christians find their final basis in the trinitarian view of God as Three-in-One. Whatever be the view of the divine or spirit world in a primal religion, relationships with these powers are taken seriously, and this concern with relationships is also seen at the social level in the kinship systems and ordered life of tribal peoples. All life is relational, and this ontology is not shared with cultures built on the 'ocean' view where all is ultimately One and our present relationships with the gods or with one another have no ultimate status in the realm of Being. At this basic level the question of syncretism scarcely arises since these shared world views represent an affinity between Christianity and the primals that helps to explain why all the major cultural-geographical expansions of Christianity have been in the areas of the primal religions, and why the vast majority of *PRINERMS* have occurred in the interactions between Christianity and the tribal peoples. It would, for instance, be impossible to imagine the hundreds of cargo and other cults that have appeared in Melanesia had it been Buddhism rather than Christianity that arrived in strength in this area.

It is at the secondary or cosmological level of world views that differences appear in the *way* the divine is related to the cosmos or universe. For the primal faiths the whole universe is usually a closed unitary system which includes nature, man, and the gods, and wherein all is sacred and each must play its part if the whole is to function smoothly. The Christian view sees God as distinct from the non-sacral universe he has created, which has not a necessary but a contingent relation to him, and where there is freedom for both parties. It is not so easy to see the transference from the one cosmology to the other as a process with intermediate stages which might represent various degrees or forms of syncretism between the two.

The possibilities of such syncretisms will emerge if we examine the transference in terms of five particular changes that are involved. The first of these is to discover the universe as a de-sacralized realm standing in a contingent relation to the sacred or the divine. This means abandoning a cosmology in which, for example, the heavens (the moon), humanity (blood, female menstruation) and the earth (red iron ore) are so necessarily interrelated that a blacksmith's work is limited to a few days after the full moon; or where certain areas of land cannot be farmed or roaded because of the spirits dwelling there. Some *PRINERMS* abandon such taboos under the influence of a biblical world-view — examples occured with Prophet Harris adopting a seven-day week with six days of work, or Zambian movements abandoning the farming taboos. On the other hand syncretism may exist when the new forms are interpreted in the old ways, as when the plain meeting-hall type of church building becomes a new sacred place in which one sleeps in order to incubate a revelatory dream by being closer to God.

The second form of change concerns the access to or control of power, whether through manipulative magic and occult knowledge coupled with repetitive religious ritual, or through scientific knowledge and technology coupled with hard work, religious faith, and prayer. The replacement of magic and traditional rituals by faith and prayer, and of secret knowledge by public secular information is a striking feature of some *PRINERMS,* especially those which develop their own schools or exhibit considerable entrepreneurship in the development of new farming or trading methods or small-scale industries. And yet there is also evidence that new rites involving the use of holy water for healings and purifications may retain the old meanings, or that the Christian faith and the Bible itself are treated as new sources for secret and powerful spiritual knowledge. Syncretism therefore does also occur in dealing with power, but whether as prolegomenon or obstacle to conversion would have to be examined in each case.[5]

[5] See my "The Hidden Power of the Whites: The Secret Religion Withheld from the Primal Peoples," *Archives de Sciences Sociales des Religions* 46 (1978):41-55.

A third area of change relates to the view of time. This involves discovering the historical dimension, with a forward-looking linear perspective allowing for real innovation in addition to the existing mythical outlook with its essentially conservative and backward-looking, repetitive and cyclical views. New millennial movements and messianic figures commonly assist this change and transfer Paradise from the past to the future. The main influence, however, is the fact of a historical founder in comparatively recent times and the great desire to know and preserve his story and that of the subsequent development of the new movement. Some produce their own histories with legendary accretions, but do not mythologize their founders. In this process of adding a further way of dealing with time there is probably less possibility of syncretic stages, and some movements have clearly demoted their biological-cultural ancestors in favour of their new spiritual-historical ancestors who may lead back to Israel.

The fourth basic change involves movement from a society that tends to be particular, closed, unitary, and sacral towards a more universal human society that is open, pluralist, and de-sacralized, and in which individual selfhood and responsibility are discovered. *PRINERMS,* as voluntary societies chosen by individuals, and usually as one among a plurality of religious options, make a massive contribution to this process. Their own founders are not divinized and there is frequent criticism when modern politics re-sacralizes the state as an absolute authority. It is true that movements may be highly authoritarian and hierarchical with the leader modelled on the traditional chief, and in this and other ways our fourth process may also incorporate syncretistic forms within what is overall a quantum leap.

The fifth and last is a moral change concerning the nature and location of evil. In primal religions evil is characteristically located externally in malevolent powers or spirits, and in sorcerers and witches; evil in the individual is more likely to be seen as ritual pollution or social offence. These views result in suspicion of strangers, a fatalistic blaming of one's troubles on others, and a feeling of social shame. *PRINERMS* which offer a new divine power and so release people from the power of lesser evil forces are replacing this ready excuse for failures by a sense of individual responsibility before God, and these are seen more in terms of sin or moral guilt. A notable example exists in Albert Atcho, a Harrist prophet-healer in the Ivory Coast, who encouraged distressed people to find the source of their troubles more in themselves. Evil forces still exist, but the individual depends increasingly on his own spiritual life. In the transference from one of these views to the other, there are no doubt both larger sudden insights, and graded steps which reveal somewhat syncretic features. Here we can do no more than suggest that the practice of exorcism and the legalistic ethic commonly found in *PRINERMS* could be seen as two signs of this syncretism.

4. Conclusion

In this survey we have not been able to discuss the various types of syncretism that occur in these transition processes. In some cases there will be the minimal form, co-existence, with different functions allocated to the two systems or their parts and a plural belonging which alternates between them. In other instances there will be borrowings and retentions in which there is reinterpretation in terms of one system or the other. Then again there will be amalgams forming what is really a new third religion, drawing perhaps on several religious sources as with Umbanda in Brazil and Cao Dai in Viet Nam. Here we have to be content with identifying syncretistic forms of any kind in the interaction processes between the contents of two different religions, or between the basic features of two different world views or cosmologies. Although individuals and perhaps small groups are capable of the quantum leap that represents conversion from a primal religion to the Christian faith, the majority exhibit the smaller mutations or syncretisms that serve either as stages to full conversion or as terminal forms that present new obstacles to the Gospel. *PRINERMS* have a special value in laying bare situations that are masked in the Christianity of their surroundings. While we plead for a positive understanding of these forms we can do so with confidence because what is syncretistic appears only to those who possess a clear grasp of the Gospel that provides their vantage point. I think Kuyper would have approved.

Chapter 9

Syncretism and Healing: A Pastoral Dilemma in Southern Africa

Matthew Schoffeleers

Christian missionaries by and large find it impossible to become so syncretistic as to share with their parishioners beliefs in witchcraft and other mystical forces causing sickness and assorted forms of misfortune. Consequently, (former) mission churches have been unable to develop an effective healing ministry. This is a disadvantage insofar as it forces mission Christians to seek help elsewhere. But it also has its positive side since it allows churches to engage in effective social criticism to a degree to which the healing churches seem unable. Hence, if a healing ministry is to be developed in the former missionary churches, it is recommended that measures be taken to safeguard their potential for social criticism.

1. Introduction

Critics often make it appear as though all missionaries were heartless barbarians. True enough, there are those, mainly of the fundamentalist type, who —unhampered by excessive familiarity with the topic— routinely condemn African religions as immoral, superstitious, or even as the work of the devil. On the other hand, from the very beginning there have also been missionaries who not only did their utmost to acquire an often impressive knowledge of local religions, but who were also able to appreciate the many positive elements in those religions. Although such missionaries have always formed a distinct minority, they have been influential beyond their number because of their publications, and because many of them also used to serve as instructors of newcomers to the mission field. One thinks particularly of people like Edwin Smith, Placide Tempels, and John Taylor — but there have been many more. Their merit has been that they were among the first to demonstrate convincingly and in terms understandable for Westerners that African religions contain ideas and values which may be a potential enrichment to Christianity. It is thanks to these studies that we can now speak of a flourishing African Theology.

2. The aetiological system

Understandably, not all their colleagues felt able to agree with these innovators. To quite a few, the main obstacle was the African belief in witches, evil spirits, and *nganga* or medicine persons —briefly, the entire aetiological and therapeutic system— which they found unacceptable (Bucher 1980, Hammond-Tooke 1986). In view of this, it is interesting to note that people such as Smith, Tempels, and Taylor discuss witchcraft and related beliefs only as side issues, as if they were of little more than secondary importance. Much the same can be said about African Theology, which hardly ever discusses these topics. Indeed, African Theology owes part of its attractiveness —particularly in the eyes of Westerners— to the fact that it carefully avoids such issues. But the price African Theology had to pay for this is that it has been unable to develop a theory of sin and evil (Schoffeleers). It therefore seems correct to conclude that as far as the mainstream churches are concerned, dialogue in the sense of a willingness to accept the reasonableness of the alternative viewpoint is possible only on condition that the African aetiological and therapeutical system is left out of consideration.

3. Healing Churches and *ngangas*.

That conclusion, however, does not apply to the leaders of the healing churches, also known as African Zionist Churches (Sundkler). One of the attractions of these churches is precisely that they share the kind of aetiological thinking of those who come to them for help, but at the same time, they have developed diagnostic and therapeutic techniques of their own which, in their eyes and those of their clients, are 'safer,' because less tainted with witchcraft. The workshop on Christian Independency at the Harare Conference of the International Association for Mission Studies (IAMS) issued a report in which it states that:

> Generally speaking it is possible to effect truly genuine and lasting healing within the African context only if this fundamental cause of evil [*i.e.* witchcraft] is taken very seriously and dealt with adequately. Most mission churches and some African Independent Churches simply reject, repudiate and then ignore witchcraft, forcing people to live schizophrenically in two different worlds. It must be stated that this constitutes an entirely deficient response to witchcraft. Witchcraft, sorcery and wizardry might well be useful as a paradigm of the Devil, a fruitful point of contact for the development of a meaningful doctrine of sin and evil. (IAMS, 79)

Just how 'schizophrenic' the life of mission Christians is I am unable to say, but judging from studies by Murphree, Kuper, and others, one would be inclined to think that most people do not find it difficult to combine Christianity with traditional religion (Murphree, 150-51; A. Kuper, 77-96). Whatever the truth, it is important to note that the established churches apparently prefer to leave that part of their pastoral task which concerns the evil perpetrated by witches and malevolent spirits to the *ngangas* and the healing prophets, rather than engage in it themselves. It is the price they are prepared to pay for keeping themselves free of syncretism.

4. Milingo's Healing Ministry

Yet from the early "sixties onwards, when the liberation struggle in Africa reached its zenith and mission churches were busy africanizing their cadres, voices were being raised to plead for a healing ministry in the mainstream churches."[1] One of the best known representatives of this movement is undoubtedly Emmanuel Milingo, the former Catholic Archbishop of Lusaka.[2] The facts about this man are generally known. Having begun his healing ministry in 1973, he was forced in July 1983 to offer his resignation as Archbishop after a protracted conflict with his own clergy, his fellow bishops, and the Vatican. Exiled to Rome, where he holds a post in the papal commission for the pastorate among migrants and tourists, he is nevertheless allowed —though not wholeheartedly— to continue his healing ministry on a more or less regular basis. It is not altogether clear what the Vatican holds against him, since a formal charge has never been made public, but Mona MacMillan, who edited and published a selection from Milingo's writings, suggests in her introduction that among other things Rome was afraid of a schism. Fear was also expressed that the public might in the end regard Milingo as one of the many *ngangas,* "perhaps more powerful and certainly cheaper than the rest" (Milingo, 5). That he saw himself as replacing the traditional *ngangas* is clear from what he wrote in a private letter:

> There are a thousand and one African doctors who claim to have mysterious powers. They charge a lot of money and they cannot stand that I have the people they would have had. (Milingo, 5)

Aylward Shorter, missionary, anthropologist and, prolific writer on matters concerning African Christianity further accuses Milingo of imposing "a fundamentalist demonological theory on African spirit mediumship, which has more in common with the *Malleus Maleficarum* of fifteenth-century Europe than with any tradition to be found in Africa" (Shorter, 190).

---

[1] See among others L. Lagerwerf, 1-62, which contains a chronological survey of colloquia and documents.

[2] For a summary of Milingo's ideas, see E. Milingo.

It is to be hoped that Shorter does not really mean it, when he says that Milingo's ideas have little to do with African religious tradition, for it is clear that those very ideas are shared by literally thousands of prophet healers in the Independent Churches of whom there can be no doubt that they stand fully in the African tradition.

The charge against Milingo is therefore fundamentally that his ministry is a threat to Christian orthodoxy and to ecclesiastical unity. The first charge seems not that serious, since he is allowed to continue his healing ministry outside Africa. The real charge is likely to be the second. The Vatican was probably afraid that Milingo's enormous success might lead to similar movements elsewhere in Africa and possibly to serious schisms.[3] By way of conclusion we may therefore note that the dialogue between Western-style Christianity and traditional religion seems to have reached its critical point in the likes of Milingo, and once again it is clear that the dialogue founders on the subject of African aetiology.

5. Social criticism

One might regard what happened to Milingo as yet another instance of Vatican meddlesomeness and leave it at that. The point, however, is that Milingo's healing ministry, like most healing ministries, raises a problem of a different kind, which is that it is, socially speaking, extremely conservative. Time and again one notices that churches and movements which are heavily involved in ritual healing seem to lose their capability of engaging in social criticism and activism. By that phrase we are referring to the capability of a church to protest openly by word and deed against oppressive structures and institutions. One of the most striking illustrations of this law —if we may call it that— is the Zion Christian Church (ZCC), which is the largest African Independent Church in southern Africa with an estimated membership of several million.

On Easter Sunday, April 7, 1985, the ZCC invited State President P. W. Botha to its headquarters on the occasion of its 75th anniversary.[4] The President was given an opportunity to address the enormous congregation, and Bishop Lekganyane, the head of the church, presented him with a scroll conferring on him the first-ever honorary citizenship of Moria, "in appreciation of his efforts to spread peace and love, and to prove the high esteem in which he is held." The President returned the compliment by giving the bishop a leather-bound Afrikaans (!) Bible. In his speech, which was frequently interrupted by applause, Botha warned his audience

---

3 See Shorter, 191, for a Tanzanian case of a Catholic priest-healer.

4 I am indebted to Ms. I. Vegter for passing on to me a set of newspaper clippings on the ZCC and for allowing me to make use of her unpublished M. A. thesis for the Department of Anthropology at the Free University, Amsterdam.

against "the powers of darkness and the messengers of evil," terms which were interpreted by sections of the press (April 8, 1985) as referring to the African National Congress and its supposed communist supporters. Citing St. Paul's Letter to the Romans, he declared,

> ...every man is subject to civil authorities. There is no authority except that which is willed by God. Good behaviour is not afraid of magistrates; only wrongdoers have anything to fear. If man lives honestly, authority will approve of him. The state is there to serve God for your own benefit.

Coming in the wake of the Uitenhage shooting and countrywide civil unrest, with the attendant international outrage, the chance to be seen addressing such a massive gathering of Africans provided Botha a heaven-sent opportunity to recoup some lost political ground and to ensure the neutrality of ZCC members in defiant townships. The latter point was alluded to by Bishop Lekganyane who, preaching on I Corinthians 13, said that love and not violence was the key to the solution of all problems: "We have love and this has enabled our church to take the word of God to so many people" (SA OORSIG, May 24, 1985).

The event was widely covered by the mass media, both nationally and internationally. Reports of the event impressed even the *New York Times* (April 8, 1985), which gave it front-page coverage. Most expressed surprise at the warm reception which Botha received at Moria, but there was cynical comment as well. Thus the *Sowetan* (April 12, 1985) noted that, while the South African Government was in the habit of accusing church leaders such as Tutu and Boesak of meddling in politics, the man at its helm was apparently free to address a church gathering on a political subject. The paper further noted that Botha's 'political pilgrimage' to Moria City had caused considerable anger among organisations such as the United Democratic Front (UDF), Azania's People's Organisation (AZAPO), Azanian Students' Movement (AZASM), the African National Congress (ANC), and the South African Council of Churches (SACC). Dr. Beyers Naudé, general secretary of the SACC, for his part reminded the public that this was not an isolated case, but that the government had been trying to build up good relationships with the ZCC over a number of years (Vegter, 11). Although Botha was the highest ranking, he was not the first government official to pay a visit to the ZCC's Easter Celebration. Daan de Wet Nel, minister of Bantu Administration and Development, had preceded him in 1960, and in 1980, on the occasion of its seventieth anniversary, the church's leadership had invited such political figures as 'Mayor' David Thebehali, chairman of the Soweto Community Council, Cedric Phatudi, Chief Minister of Lebowa, and Piet Koornhof, minister of co-operation and development. Bishop Lekganyane had on that occasion called on his followers to support the government's homeland policy and to abide by the laws of the country. That speech too had been sharply criticised by African churchmen and political leaders, but the ZCC leadership apparently had felt confident enough to ignore such criticism.

Although the case of the ZCC is an extreme one, it by no means stands alone, and the experts are unanimous in stating that healing churches avoid oppositional political commitment (Kretzschmar, 52-55; Adam & Moodley, 201-202). Kaja Finkler, an anthropologist who carried out research among a popular Christian healing movement in Mexico, found that this conservative attitude is found even in movements which are critical of the social structures to which they are subject. According to Finkler, ritual healing illustrates in the clearest possible way the contradiction in the healing process, which is directed at the well-being of the individual, but which at the same time supports the social structure which is directly or indirectly responsible for his or her illness (Finkler, 627-42). Her conclusion is therefore that to change social structures or to effect a significant social transformation one needs personalities which stand outside healing movements, a thesis which seems perfectly illustrated by the situation in South Africa, where ecclesiastical protest against apartheid is a matter for churches without a healing tradition.

Finkler explains the correlation between healing and social conservatism in terms of the emphasis placed on the interaction between the healer and the supernatural, the vertical dimension of life being considered more important than the horizontal. Put differently, the charismatic healer tends to lose sight of social reality because of his or her extraordinarily strong relationship with the supernatural. That same relationship could lead to increased individualism on the part of the healers so that people engaged in ritual healing are less likely to form a common front against their oppressors.

The weakness of Finkler's explanation seems to lie in its *ad hoc* character. It is difficult to see why a strong relationship with the supernatural should prevent one from militating against social injustice or why it should lead to an increase of individualism. Rather, I would maintain in line with some of Horton's thinking that healing pertains to a person's microcosmic social structure (Horton); that is to say, his or her day-to-day relationships with neighbours and kinsmen. It is there that witches and harmful spirits operate, and it is at this small personal world that the attention of the healer and the patient is directed, and it is thus that attention is deflected from wider concerns.

6. Conclusion

Despite these reservations about religious healing, we would plead for the recognition of a healing ministry in the African Christian communities. Our reason for saying so is that religious healing undeniably has a potential, which other forms of healing do not possess. Having said this, we can think of two ways of saving the healing ministry:

I. The mainline churches could acknowledge the value of the healing pastorate, but prefer to leave it in the hands of traditional healers and healing prophets. This is not as fantastic as it sounds, for it is precisely this which happens from one end of sub-Saharan Africa to the other. It would imply, however, that the mainstream churches would have to recognize those healers and prophets as their equals. This would leave those churches available for the struggle against social injustice, which is what we see happening in South Africa.

II. A second possibility would be to have the mainstream churches organize a dual ministry, consisting of the present ministry of Word and Sacrament alongside a ministry of Healing. The former would take care of issues concerning social justice among other things, while the second would take care of the suffering individual. The advantage in this case would be that the church would be in a position —at least in theory— to discourage syncretism, but the question is how to carry this out in actual practice.

Bibliography

Adam, H. and K. Moodley. *South Africa Without Apartheid: Dismantling Racial Domination.* Los Angeles/London: University of California Press, 1986, pp. 201-202.

Bucher, H. *Spirits and Power.* Cape Town, 1980.

Finkler, K. "The Social Consequence of Wellness: A View of Healing Outcomes from Micro and Macro Perspectives." *International Journal of Health Services* 16 (1986): 627-42.

Hammond-Tooke, W. D. "The Aetiology of Spirit in Southern Africa." *African Studies* 45 (1986): 157-70.

Horton, R. "On the Rationality of Conversion." *Africa* 45 (1975): 219-35, 373-98.

IAMS, *Christian Mission and Human Transformation: Mission Studies* 2, no. 1 (1985).

Kretzschmar, L. *The Voice of Black Theology in South Africa.* Johannesburg: Ravan Press, 1986, pp. 52-55.

Kuper, A. "The Magician and the Missionary." In *The Liberal Dilemma in South Africa.* Ed. P. L. van den Berghe. London: Travistock, 1979, pp. 77-96.

Lagerwerf, L. "Witchcraft, Sorcery and Spirit Possession: Pastoral Responses in Africa." *Exchange* 14, no. 41 (1985): 1-62.

Milingo, E. *The World in Between: Christian Healing and the Struggle for Spiritual Survival.* Ed. with Introduction, Commentary, and Epilogue by Mona MacMillan. New York: Orbis Books, 1984.

Murphree, M. W. *Christianity and the Shona.* London: The Athlone Press, 1969, pp. 150-51.

SA OORSIG. Inligtings-Nuusbrief, Bijvoegsel tot SA OORSIG. Pretoria: Departement van Buitelandse Sake, May 24, 1985.

Schoffeleers, M. "Black Theology and African Theology in Southern Africa: An Old Controversy Re-examined." *Journal of Religion in Africa* 18, no. 2 (1988); forthcoming.

Shorter, A. *Jesus and the Witch Doctor: An Approach to Healing and Wholeness.* New York: Orbis Books, 1985.

Smith, E. W., ed. *African Ideas of God.* 1950; rev. edn. London: Edinburgh House Press, 1960.

Sundkler, B. *Bantu Prophets in South Africa.* London: Oxford University Press, 1961.

Taylor, J. V. *The Primal Vision.* London: SCM Press, 1963.

Tempels, P. *La Philosophie Bantoue.* Elisabethville, 1945.

Vegter, I. "Waar Olifanten Vechten Groeit het Gras Niet: Apartheid and the Zion Christian Church." Unpublished M.A. thesis, 1988, 99 pp.

Chapter 10

John B. Cobb, Jr., and the Encounter with Buddhism

Tilmann Vetter

This paper concerns itself with the present dialogue between Christianity and Buddhism, and its likely result of syncretism on the side of Christianity, whether it be valued positively or negatively. Taking as my point of departure André Droogers' definition, I have given a clarification of my own use of the term syncretism. The second section of this article is devoted to John Cobb's *Beyond Dialogue, Toward a Mutual Transformation of Christianity and Buddhism* (hereafter simply "p."). His proposals for incorporating the accomplishments of Buddhism into Christianity are presented in a philological way, preferably employing his own words. His proposals are not syncretic in the narrow sense, but they are in the sense in which I apply the term. The third section contains some remarks on theoretical and practical problems which might arise in following Cobb's lead. At the end, mention is made of a less syncretic alternative.

1. Syncretism

I want to support a definition of syncretism which is as objective as possible, but it may then become difficult to use it meaningfully in respect of religious movements, since nearly all are characterized by what that term objectively indicates. A contrast is then necessary to make it a relative term. 'Reformation' seems suited to this purpose.[1] I therefore assume that all movements which are subsumed under such a definition have been criticized, or could feasibly be criticized in the future, as deviations from the original purity of a movement. This criticism comes from religious specialists and/or lay people who find strength in clinging to simple —or less syncretic— beliefs and practices, which are usually viewed as representing the original condition of the movement.

[1] In *Christentum und Weltreligionen*, Hans Küng speaks of a "synkretistisches" and "reformerisches" paradigm with regard to movements within Buddhism (p. 589).

I appreciate the approach to the phenomenon of religion used in social science which André Droogers indicates (Chapter 1), because important aspects come to light here to which I usually do not pay attention. I particularly value the distinction he makes between an objective and a subjective meaning and would like to concur with his definition of syncretism, which is said to be based (eclectically) on the functionalist, marxist, and symbolical models of social science. I myself, however, focus on the self-understanding of revered religious individuals, taking it more seriously than these models seem to allow.

According to Drooger's definition (p. 20-21) syncretism is religious interpenetration, either taken for granted, or subject to debate. Pursuing this articulation, which I would extend to include cultural interpenetration, I would like to understand 'taken for granted' in two ways. First, it describes a quality of the belief of the people being discussed of which they are almost unconscious. In such cases, religious interpenetration, must be observed, in my opinion, not only by students of religion, but also by religious persons themselves. It must at least be possible to imagine that adherents of more simple beliefs and practices will, at some place or time, contest this as a breach of —a supposed original— purity.

Second, 'taken for granted' comprises conscious attempts by theologians to adopt alien beliefs, including philosophical theories, and practices. Such attempts may not really be contested (or may be contested only by a minority which has no influence or power), but theologians, aware of possible complaints, feel obliged to reflect theoretically on them. In the first centuries of Christianity, some theologians justified adopting elements from Greek culture with the idea that the Logos —itself already a borrowed concept?— had enabled Greek writers to grasp fragments of the truth, or had even made them an instrument of preparation for the gospel (p. 5). The hermeneutical terms, *chrêsis* or *usus iustus* (Hacker, 348, 356, 797, 800) can be found, in this connection, with reference to the seeds of the Logos in pagan writings. Such attempts and reflections were constitutive for the Christian culture of the Middle Ages and were employed in the concept of natural theology. Later, however, even though they had not always been completely 'taken for granted,' they were rejected by influential reformers, who were inspired by the idea of the original purity of Christian faith. Such attempts and reflections would therefore fall under syncretism as defined above, even though the term may not have been employed by those who rejected them.

The same holds true of modern theologies which have prepared the way for the acceptance of religious (and secular) dialogue, and/or which try to defend interpenetration resulting from this acceptance. At the moment, such theologies are not officially called syncretic. The Roman Catholic church which in the sense of the above definition represents a strong syncretic tradition cannot, at any rate, be expected to use this term too readily since it includes an echo of abuse in religious circles.[2] Not even the World Council of Churches, the heir of the reformist movements, expressly repudiates such theologies as syncretic. It did, however, show its anxiety by warning against a kind of syncretism which it defined as "conscious or unconscious attempts to create a new religion composed of elements of different religions" (Nairobi: 1975; Cobb, p. 20).

2. John Cobb's proposals

John Cobb's book can be seen as part of the tradition of theological reflection on, and commendation of, the adoption of selected theories which are foreign to Christianity and to a lesser extent practices. He is strongly convinced that all religions are involved in an on-going process of change throughout history, and that those win and survive in this competition who adjust to new situations, assimilating appropriately from others (p. 40). However, he wants to avoid the kind of syncretism the World Council of Churches warned against.

Our contemporary situation is characterized by the widespread acceptance of dialogue between religions. For some people this fact itself represents a distortion of their belief, even if it leads only to peaceful coexistence. For most participants, however, and for some church leaders as well, dialogue means more than coexistence. It implies a readiness to receive enrichment and enlargement (p. 21), and to take the risk of being more impressed and altered by the other side than was anticipated when reading their texts.

The situation is now more difficult for theological reflection on such dialogue than it was in the first centuries of Christianity. The Jews who believed that the promises of God were fulfilled in Jesus (and the Church Fathers who followed in their footsteps) were convinced that they had a distinctive message of supreme importance, and could therefore borrow freely from Gentile culture, especially philosophy, without any threat to their own identity (p. 2). But the modern acceptance of a dialogical relation to other religions strains the concept of superiority.

Cobb speaks (p. vii-viii) of "a widespread sense that our choice is either to continue our belief in Christian superiority and to act upon it or to see Jesus as one savior among others." He remarks (p. viii) that neither the Roman Catholic church nor the World Council of Churches has accepted either horn of this dilemma, that both are working painfully toward a Christology which avoids imperialism and relativism, and that his own book is set in this context.

---

[2] See Droogers, however, p. 13, who mentions a Catholic theologian who recently did so.

Cobb wants to "go beyond the antithesis of all religious traditions moving toward Christianity or each making its permanent separate contribution to the history of salvation" (p. 52). Others too want to do this. They mostly seek a common denominator. Such a synthesis, however, is unconvincing because it loses too much of the concreteness of the elements which it purports to unite and also tends towards syncretism as condemned by the World Council of Churches (see p. 38, with regard to John Hick and Wilfred Cantwell Smith). Cobb wants to preserve and strengthen the life of religious movements, or at least that of Christianity, by adopting from others as much as is possible without distortion.

His method of doing this consists of "passing over" and "coming back" (p. 68). First one passes over, i.e. uses all the clues one can to gain an imaginative identification. After that, one comes back to one's own world with the extension of imaginative experience. The best means for passing over is dialogue between religious representatives who are capable of exacting textual study and who speak out of the experience to which the texts point (p. 69). Coming back from such a dialogue may result in attempts to appropriate what has been learned.

Cobb hopes that dialogue will lead to incorporation of insights and attitudes on both sides, an incorporation that is not only a matter of a doctrinal adjustment, but which includes the transformation of their respective historical memories (p. 49). This will, in his opinion, not obliterate the difference between them, but provide a new basis for fresh dialogue and fresh transformation. "The lines that now sharply divide us will increasingly blur" (p. 52).

He presents, in chapter six, some interesting ideas about what Buddhists could appropriate from Christianity (e.g. that they must learn to see Amida as Christ).[3] But I must impose restrictions on myself and will have to be content with sketching only his proposals for the incorporation of Buddhist achievements into Christianity.

In chapter four, Cobb shows how he passes over to Buddhism, and in chapter five, how he comes back to Christianity, trying to integrate what he thinks to be of value. Through dialogue with a few Japanese Buddhists, mostly Zen, but some of the Pure Land tradition, combined with modest study of some texts in English translation and of secondary literature (p. 75), he has apparently acquired the above-mentioned imaginative identification. On this basis, he assesses Buddhist ideas and suggests appropriations.

He concentrates on Nirvana because for him this is the center of Buddhist wisdom. Though Nirvana is actually only one of two centers of the Mahayana Buddhism with which he is familiar (the other being compassion or, from another point of view, Samsara; cf. Masao Abe, 1985), his

---

[3] Cf. H. Küng, p. 609-10. The most interesting recent development in this field seems to be the suggestion of incorporating "degree Christology" into Nichiren Buddhism by Makoto Ozaki, in his paper, "Towards a Future Theology: Buddha and Christ in Perspective."

observations on this theme,[4] expressed partly in the concepts of Whitehead's philosophy, are brilliant here and there, and the consequences which he proposes for Christian thinking are impressive.

His passing over to this modern kind of Buddhism has resulted in the understanding that Nirvana is 1) the cessation of all clinging, 2) the extinction of the self, 3) ultimate reality as Emptiness, and 4) the immediacy of momentary being (Cobb, p. 76).

Cobb's passing over is intended to be more than philology, but it is not a practice in which one experiences Nirvana as envisaged above, and then perhaps loses all interest in the central themes of Christian faith. Cobb wants to come back, and he wants to come back enriched. Though accepting this vision of liberation seems to involve repudiation of Christian doctrines, he hopes that he can convert apparent contradictions into complementary contrasts and possibilities for enlarging these doctrines (pp. 97-99).

He must now answer four questions in accordance with the fourfold understanding of Nirvana mentioned above. First, is it possible and commendable to try to integrate the aim of cessation of all clinging with the experience of Christian faith, which would seem to entail some form of attachment to God and Christ? In his view it is. He is impressed by the combination of faith and cessation of clinging as it exists in the Pure Land tradition of Shinran and he reminds us that in the Christian tradition a similar position can be found. Luther realized that as long as his salvation depended on a right mental and spiritual attitude on his own part it would forever remain uncertain. Cobb concludes that perfect faith is complete letting go, not holding fast. Even its hope is the hope given by God in the moment rather than a hope nursed and nourished by the self and then grounded in God (p. 104). In this respect he is now very close to Pure Land Buddhism, but there the accent seems to fall on a state of being or consciousness rather than on an interpersonal relation (p. 103).

Secondly, is it possible and commendable to integrate the dissolution of the self or, more accurately, the realization that there has never been a self, where Christianity seems to depend on a self that never abandons responsibility for its actions? The Buddhist vision of reality recognizes only momentary human experience which is an instance of dependent

[4] One must bear in mind that Cobb is concerned with this part of Buddhism, and not, as his use of the word 'Buddhism' too often suggests, with the whole of Buddhism. Although he says that it would be absurd to claim that the understanding of Nirvana that comes to expression here is *the* Buddhist understanding, he immediately forgets this, continually speaking of Buddhism, and sometimes comparing it typologically to Christianity and Hinduism (pp. 83-84). I will not dwell on the Buddhologist's (and perhaps other specialists') irritation at this presentation, and will overlook the possible impediment this forms to the dialogue with other Buddhists (e.g. Cobb never mentions the idea of never being reborn which occurs to many Buddhists upon hearing the word Nirvana).

origination, that is, as Cobb translates it into Whiteheadian terminology, of objects coalescing into a subject (p. 105). In Christian and humanistic Western thought the self as agent and patient has usually been distinguished from the flux of action and events and has generally been conceived substantially. Though it is not necessesary to read the Bible in such a way, Christians cannot adopt the Buddhist vision, which is perhaps more in harmony with modern thinking, without answering the question whether an instance of dependent origination involves an element of responsible freedom. The philosophy of Whitehead seems to offer a solution to this problem which has been generally neglected by Buddhists (they simply presuppose some freedom). Decision is a matter of selection from among significant possibilities, which must be elements in the coalescence. The presence of possibilities would mean that the coalescence is not a mere product of the actual world. And the decision to actualize a possibility expresses some immanent intention guiding the coalescence. If one abandons a substantialist view, then one can see the Christian self as the decision-making element in the coalescence (pp. 106-107). Accepting this explanation, one can perhaps agree with Cobb's description of the aim of (modern) Buddhists as wanting the present instance of dependent origination to be free from bondage to past personal experience, and perhaps also agree with a contrasting observation on his part that Christians must be open to the new possibilities that are given by Christ; they must not simply give up past purposes, but allow them to be transformed by Christ (pp. 107-108).[5] Cobb also hopes, that another of the achievements claimed by his dialogue partners can be incorporated in some way without sacrificing such a nonsubstantial self: to become open to the whole world. For the Christian, it can not be a direct openness resulting from a total dissolution of the self; it must occur by way of analogy. According to Whitehead, each self comes into being moment by moment as a coalescence of elements which include other people as well as one's personal past. The personal past may dominate the coalescence, but the mode of relationship that one such instance of dependent origination bears to instances of its own personal past is not different in kind from the mode of relationship which it bears to other instances of a different provenance. If one presently has almost perfect empathy for one's own immediate past, one can increase the degree of empathy one has for others.

Third, can Christians appropriate the vision of ultimate reality as Emptiness without weakening their belief in God? For Cobb, it is possible. He distinguishes between the ultimate reality which is Emptiness and the ultimate actuality which is God. Thus he neither *reduces* God to Emptiness nor *subordinates* God to Emptiness (as would be the case, if he called God a 'manifestation' of ultimate reality, or used the distinction between

5 This is not an exclusively Christian idea. It may be compared to the description of the constitution of a Buddha's qualities in some Buddhist texts (Schmithausen, p. 169).

Godhead and God which occasionally made its appearance in Christian theology; p. 111). This implies that God must be conceived of as wholly lacking substantiality. He is the one, cosmic, everlasting actualization of ultimate reality on whom all ephemeral actualizations depend. And as such he is just as ultimate as Emptiness is (pp. 112-13). To think of God in this way is in tension with most Western theologies, but Cobb hopes that Christians will in time find that such a Buddhized vision of God resonates better with the meaning of God which they have come to know through Jesus Christ than does the identification of God as 'being' or Supreme Being. Theoretical acknowledgement of the complementarity of God and Emptiness may also provide a context in which faith in God and the realization of Emptiness can mutually enrich one another in living human experience (pp. 113-14).

Fourth, should Christians appropriate the immediacy of momentary being which is an aspect of Nirvana, as proclaimed by Cobb's dialogue partners? It might imply too great a loss of orientation for a faith which is focussed so strongly on the future, and, in recent times, has also been deeply transformed by the scholarly study of history and by the scientific study of nature. Though Christians also recognize the relativity of meaning frames, they know that adequate frames remain necessary for the time being. Theoretically, they could accept the immediacy of momentary being inasmuch as past and present are introduced into the coalescence itself. The elements witness here-now to their occurrence there-then; the not-yet, as claim and hope, is also an ingredient in the coalescence (pp. 115-16). However, there seems to be some need to go beyond this. The idea of pure immediacy of experience can be employed as a vision of what is hoped for. The expectation of the kingdom has been diminished in its forcefulness partly because Christians have found it increasingly difficult to believe in a condition of fulfilled immediacy. The encounter with Nirvana provides a new way of conceiving the immediacy of blessedness, for which time is no longer important. If the realization of a Christianized Nirvana is the future for which Christians hope, then they can presently allow themselves the joy of pure immersion in the moment as a part of their orientation to that future for all people. Insofar as they do not remain there, they resemble the Bodhisattva who refuses to enter Nirvana fully until all (or at least many) sentient beings have been saved (pp. 117-18).

3. Some remarks

I am personally impressed by these proposals and their background in process theology. I have chosen to present these ideas to this symposium in order to make them more widely known and discussed. I know of few Christian visions with such appeal for cultured people. Appreciation, however, does not prevent me from reflecting on the problems in this approach. Two of which in particular are its methodological foundation and the practical limitations to appropriation of foreign beliefs.

In terms of the methodological foundation, let me first repeat that Cobb is no syncretist in the narrow sense of the word, even though he can expect criticism by adherents of traditional forms of belief and their corresponding theologies for his openness. In conformity with the reformist movements, he orients himself to the Biblical heritage, not to later accretions. He opposes the search for a common denominator in all religions, because its abstractness leads to impoverishment of the biblical heritage. He sees possibilities, however, for strengthening this heritage and for adapting it to our cultural situation by assimilating the achievements of Buddhism (and similarly those of other religions and of science). In this sense he is no reformer, but a syncretist and a modern representative of *chrêsis.*

This is also the only way, in his opinion, to fulfil the missionary aim in our time —an aim which belongs to the Biblical heritage— with regard to members of other religions. The Biblical heritage must now be presented to others as encompassing what is important to them. One can learn what is important to them through dialogue, and they must be inspired by the dialogue to incorporate what is essential to Christianity. The object of Christian mission is no longer the members of other religions, but the religions as such. This aim should not prevent Christians from winning for the church those millions which are cut off from the wisdom of the world's great religious traditions, and who participate in no community with serious purpose (p. xi-xii).

Cobb anticipates that the religions themselves will be transformed by dialogue, but only when Christianity is also transformed by it. The other religions will not lose their identity, but will gradually be enriched just as Christianity will be enriched. They must survive in order to be able to contribute to this development, which, by the way, presupposes much work by 'theologians' in eliminating apparent contradictions and in cultivating a sense for complementarity (see below). At the end of this process, Christianity may have assimilated all that is of value in all religions and cultures and become the heir to the entire history of the human race, as Cobb says in a more recent publication (1985: 160). Cobb can even hope that the other religions, which have evolved in the same direction, will no longer have any need to preserve their identity, and will be merged into Christianity.

Let us assume that this were possible. What would then exist, however, would not consist only of the essentials of Christianity, but also of the essentials of other religions. Intellectuals will demand that this be no mere addition of elements, but that the elements be structured and organized by a central idea. They will expect a theologian who appeals so strongly to intellectual capacities on many other scores to consider this question, and if such an entity represents the fulfillment of the missionary aim of Christianity, it should be dominated by a Christian principle, and not be Christian only in name.

Christianity has a great disadvantage in such theoretical questions, however, for its strength lies in the relative concreteness of its essentials. These can never subsume, as Cobb himself concedes (1985: 155), the exceedingly subtle principles of Buddhism (again restricting ourselves to this religion), while Buddhism seems to be able to do this with other religions, judging from a most interesting article by Masao Abe (1987: 163-90), addressed largely to Cobb. Abe sees Emptiness, conceived of as pure openness and receptivity as the dynamic principle that could be the foundation of a future world theology (as we will call it here). If Cobb does not want to follow Abe, the only remaining solution for this theoretical problem is the assumption of double-centeredness, or multi-centeredness, for such an enriched religious organism. The old idea of the universality of Jesus Christ could thereby be at least partly saved.

This solution is actually already present in Cobb's above mentioned idea of the complementarity of two ultimate principles: ultimate reality and ultimate actuality, the first being Emptiness, the latter being God as revealed by Jesus Christ. Abe thinks that one needs a third position to be able to speak of complementarity. Such a position could perhaps be found in a kind of metaphysics, which, however, he rejects, just as Cobb does. Instead he proposes a dynamism through which "the relativity of various religions and the ultimacy of each religion can be realized as dynamically nondual" (Abe 1987: 175). He calls this a positionless position and refers to a mode of speaking in the Perfection of Insight texts. But since this 'position' is explicated by an adapted interpretation of Emptiness, one of the two centers to be reconciled, and by employing the metaphysical category of manifestation (Abe 1987: 189), subordinating God to Emptiness, Cobb may be justified in not pursuing this proposal.

To defend himself against Abe, he could utilize another mode of speaking widely accepted in Buddhism, and evolved from the same Perfection of Insight texts: the mode of paradoxical juxtaposition (Vetter, 506). It is stating two principles which seem to exclude each other, but are both felt to be of the utmost importance. Through direct juxtaposition it conveys the awareness that the wisdom of the intellect is inadequate for describing the complexity of reality. This was the way in which ancient Mahayana Buddhism generally insisted on two principles: perfection of insight (which includes the unreality of all living beings), and compassion towards all living beings. Symbolically this is expressed by the famous Mantra "*Om maṇi-padme hūm*": both jewel and lotus (the *e* in *padme* is a nominative dual ending, not a locative singular) are to be aimed at. Christianity too, though not in the paradoxical sense, has two main principles: love of God and love of one's neighbour (Matthew 22:36-40). Few theologians have been able to keep these balanced.

The modern Kyoto school of Philosophy, to which Abe belongs, is more inclined to suggest synthetical dialectical solutions for such problems. They claim that the great self and selflessness issue forth from the highest realization of non-self. This is less appealing to me than the old paradox, just as the idea that one has to love people because they all are the children of the same Heavenly father is less convincing to me than a stark imperative lacking any kind of sanction. Cobb's problem, however, is not only a problem of opposite intentions. It also seems to contain a logical contradiction, insofar as one expects only one ultimate principle in the theoretical realm. But Cobb denies that we have any such handle on real ultimacy (1985: 157). People can operate in terms of different interests in approaching ultimacy, and he has found a way of convincingly demonstrating the complementarity of Emptiness and God. Emptiness, he says, is the ultimate answer to the question *what* one is and *what* all things are; but if I were to ask: 'Why is there an ordered world at all?,' 'To what do I owe what is good in my life?,' or 'Where should I place my trust?,' then answers in terms of the God of the Bible seem eminently appropriate (1985: 158-59).

The second problem involves the practical limitations to appropriating foreign beliefs and practices. One often hears that theology has a theoretical and an apologetical function. Yet it cannot be denied that it also has some impact on everyday religious life. One could imagine that what Cobb has said about faith without clinging would have such an impact. However, this would imply losing other forms of belief, such as 'clinging' to images, which are perhaps not of the same high intellectual level, but which do give some persons much more firmness. Individuals cannot have it both ways at the same time. In this context, however, Cobb reactivated one of the possibilities of the Christian tradition, viz. Luther. Within the framework proposed by Cobb, non-Christian possibilities (from science and other religions) can also be activated (compare the above-mentioned ideas about a nonsubstantial self). Though it is true that one can incorporate many things in everyday practice, there are limits. In the history of Buddhism, we see that the Japanese Tendai, for instance, had incorporated nearly everything that could be called Buddhist at one time. The reactions to this system, especially in the Kamakura period, were such as to allow us the conclusion that it no longer satisfied practical needs, but rather impeded them. One might assume that in such a system, comparable to what happens within the Roman Catholic Church, one observes some basic demands, and for the rest selects the practices one likes. For many people this works, but not for all. It is therefore safe to assume that the proposed architecture of enrichment will also repel some people. This is to be expected all the more since it could never be as strongly oriented to Jesus Christ as Roman Catholicism, whereas for many Christians such an orientation represents not only a theoretical demand, but the very way to salvation.

The alternative would then be not —or only slightly— to become enriched by the interreligious dialogue, and to use it, in addition to discovering that others are not natural enemies, only as a means of stimulating one's own way, or perhaps of substituting one way for that of another. Such a 'reformist' alternative, however, could better renounce proselytizing adherents of other religions —Cobb's is perhaps the best proposal of our time for this aim— and at least partly accept what J. van Baal suggests at the end of *Man's Quest for Partnership*: "Man's real and effective home is, of old, not on the market but in the small group, socially as well as spiritually" (p. 317).

Small groups can, of course, also be syncretic, but even if a small group wants to avoid syncretism, we may nevertheless, in our times, expect it to be aware of the pluralistic situation in which we live. In order to temper their strong inclination toward feeling themselves to be the only possessors of truth, I would suggest that such a group deliberately embrace an attitude characteristic of many religions, particularly in earlier days, namely the attitude of henotheism, at least as defined by Norbert Lohfink, in his attempt to account for the fact that monotheism cannot be found in the earlier strata of the Bible (Lohfink, 144-51). With respect to our problem, this would mean that one does not deny the existence of other gods and principles, and one is in this sense able to engage in dialogue with others, but in the act of worship or meditation, one knows and experiences that there is only one god or principle. This god or principle may well be experienced at that moment as the origin or essence of everything. Thereafter, other gods and principles might be interpreted as aspects of the same reality.

Bibliography

Abe, Masao. Review of *Beyond Dialogue,* by John Cobb. *Eastern Buddhist* 18, no. 1 (1985): 131-37.

——. 1987. "A Dynamic Unity in Religious Pluralism: A Proposal from the Buddhist Point of View." In *The Experience of Religious Diversity.* Eds. John Hick and Hasan Askari. Avebury Series in Philosophy, 1985; rpt., pp. 163-90.

Baal, J. van. *Man's Quest for Partnership.* Assen, 1981.

Cobb, John. *Beyond Dialogue: Toward a Mutual Transformation of Christianity and Buddhism.* Philadelphia: Fortress Press, 1982.

——. 1987. "Christian Witness in a Pluralistic World." In *The Experience of Religious Diversity.* Eds. John Hick and Hasan Askari. Avebury Series in Philosophy, 1985; rpt. pp. 144-62.

Hacker, Paul. *Kleine Schriften.* Ed. L. Schmithausen. Wiesbaden: Franz Steiner Verlag, 1978.

Küng, Hans. *Christentum und Weltreligionen.* Munich/Zürich, 1968.

Lohfink, Norbert. "Zur Aussage des Alten Testaments über 'Offenbarung,' " In *Offenbaring: Geistige Realität des Menschen.* Ed. Gerhard Oberhammer. Vienna, 1974, pp. 135-51.

Ozaki, Makoto. "Towards a Future Theology: Buddha and Christ in Perspective." Paper presented at the 3rd International Conference on Buddhism and Christianity: Toward the Human Future, held conjointly at the University of California and the Graduate Theological Union, Berkeley, Aug. 10-15, 1987.

Schmithausen, Lambert. "Ich und Erlösung im Buddhismus." *Zeitschrift für Missionswissenschaft und Religionswissenschaft* 53 (1969): 157-170.

Vetter, T. E. "A Comparison between the Mysticism of the Older Prajñā-Pāramitā Literature and the Mysticism of the Mūla-Madhyamaka-Kārikās of Nāgārjuna." *Acta Indologica* 6 (1984): 495-512.

Chapter 11

The Religion of Japan: Syncretism or Religious Phenomenalism?

Jacques H. Kamstra

Japanese religion is seen as a classic example of syncretism by most Western scholars of religion and —in their footsteps— various Japanese scholars. Whence comes this view? Does it stem from Western scholars or from Japanese religion? Do not many Western prejudices form a tremendous impediment to seeing Japanese religion as it really is? How do Japanese scholars and religious leaders see the reality of Japanese religion? This paper attempts to examine these questions. It pauses to consider a number of Western prejudices, and endeavours to characterize Japanese religion not as syncretism, but as religious phenomenalism. These answers are assessed in relation to a bodhisattva and a Shinto god: Jizō and Inari.

In many publications it is almost customary to point to the religion of Japan as a classic case of syncretism. I have done so myself in several publications.[1] I have serious doubts of a methodological nature, however, concerning the use of this word as a suitable classification for all kinds of religions. Where does the use of this word come from? Is syncretism as such not much more likely to be a matter of the subject (the Western scientist) than of the object (the non-Western religion being studied)? What about the opinions of the believers of Japanese religion themselves?

In these lines I hope to clarify two points: the role of Western prejudices in the study of Japanese religion and the opinions of the Japanese believers themselves about what we term syncretism. A good understanding of Japanese religion is often very seriously hampered by a whole set of Western and Christian prejudices. I will therefore first

[1] Jacques H. Kamstra 1967: 468-9; 1982: 199 ff.; 1970: 20-22.

consider these prejudices prior to looking at Japanese religious phenomenalism in general, as well as two instances of it, Inari and Jizō in particular.

1. The Western approach to Japanese Religion

Many of our Western prejudices originate in our own culture and language, and are primarily the results of our way of life, which is in many ways the opposite of the Japanese mind. Here I will confine myself to what I consider the main prejudices impeding a good understanding of Japanese religion. I would like to distinguish four sets of preconceptions.

1.1 The first group concerns the theological distinction between faith and superstition. Many scholars are still inclined to look at Japanese religion from this point of view. Thus, W. Gundert looks at some important aspects of Japan's folk religion as 'Vulgarreligion und Aberglaube' (1935: 139-40). Even some Japanese agencies and scholars in folk religion follow these patterns of their Western colleagues. They not only distinguish between religion and superstition, but they also confuse religious elements with superstition. In 1952, Japan's Department of Education, which statistically lists all the existing religions and denominations, issued the results of field research by the 'Committee of Japanese Superstitions' based on questionnaires under the heading of *Nihon no zoku-shin.* This should have been translated as 'Common beliefs of Japan,' but was rendered as 'Superstitions and Common beliefs.' In 1961, a member of this research committee wrote: *Gendai no meishin,* translated by Hoti as 'Contemporary superstitions.' Here the idea of superstition has been put on the same footing as magic and common belief. The Japanese language is rich in several words for 'superstitions' (Hori, 47). These words have quite different meanings however. The word *majinai* is sometimes translated as 'magic.' Its real meaning is *ayashii okonai de hito o noroi gai o kuwaeru koto,* 'curse and harm people with awful acts' (Kanno, 325), but also 'to pray to gods and spirits in order to avoid all kinds of dangers, and to cure sickness,' in other words, as what I am accustomed to describing as the religion of the common man (Ikkyosuke, 1714; Matsuoka, 1150; Kamstra 1986). *Meishin* is also used for superstition. Its real meaning is 'heresy, mistaken belief.' *Zoku-shin,* or popular belief, is put on a par with superstitions by Hori when he writes: "Superstition or popular beliefs are like weeds in a wilderness" (Hori, 47), and,

> Therefore, all religious leaders who have a sense of vocation to enlighten the common people, regardless of their religious affiliation, share an urgent responsibility. They should lead people from folk beliefs into a high level of religious experience, or from popular superstitions into right faith, as well as from magic to metaphysic, if we may borrow Max Weber's term. (Hori, 47)

I wonder why so many missiologists up until the present have not taken the concrete mind of the common man seriously, instead of replacing it by their abstract mind. Why must we confuse folk religion with superstition and black magic? Why is it necessary to assert that the religion of the common man has to be raised to the level of intellectuals and the higher clergy, who have been his oppressors in former times? It goes without saying that this set of prejudices has to be set aside.

1.2 A second set of Western prejudices stems from some deeply rooted prudish Western feelings which consider non-sexual symbols to be real religion, and sexual symbols to be magical aberration. In Europe, crude peasant realities were accordingly not allowed to be dealt with. It is worth quoting the Belgian born Japanologist de Vos in this respect:

> Modern literate urban-oriented Japanese are not comfortable with the phallic tradition of agricultural Japan.... A straining, socially pretentious bourgeoisie prefers hypocritical coverup to the acknowledgment of a peasant past as part of its heritage. In Europe, the fountain statues that streamed water out of female breasts have all had their plumbing cut off, A singular exception, Mannukin–pis, still performs in a nook of central Brussels as a quaint throwback to a more honest avowal of natural functions that was much more in evidence prior to the social triumph of the urban bourgeoisie throughout Europe. (p. 15)

It has been due to these and to prudish American feelings that many hundreds of phallic symbols alongside rice fields and roads, especially the crossroads, have been removed and repressed since World War II. The complex of the sexual fertility of men, animals, and plants is an essential part of the religion of the common man in Japan, and is harmoniously interwoven with other religious phenomena, being "a source or well spring in human religious beliefs" (de Vos, 14, 44). Without this source, the cults of Inari and Jizō are impracticable.

1.3 A third complex of biases is based on ideas which take root in Western feelings of cultural, theological, and philosophical superiority: it is the need for Western classifications, critical analyses, and a logic based on the principle of non-contradiction. By following the impetus of this bias, Japanese religion is torn apart in pieces in order to make it correspond to Western topics such as true and false, logical and illogical, rational and irrational, while the true, logical, and rational is limited to Japanese sect Buddhism, and the false, illogical, and irrational to Shinto and Folk religion. Here it is also worth noting de Vos' remarks:

> Japanese thought is considered 'illogical,' 'artistic,' and 'intuitive,' even 'feminine' by some opposed to the 'clean,' noncontaminatory categorization savored by a Western-trained 'masculine' philosophical mind. A heritage of Judaic as well as Aristotelian logic is trained into Western thought so thoroughly and at such a young age, that to find oneself without it threatens one's sense of reality —or better still, one's sense of control over reality— so violently as to be equated with uncontrollable insanity. (pp. 14, 15)

I have pointed out on other occasions that some religious or psychological universals can by no means be forced on Japanese religions. Thus, the Japanese concept of *oku,* the inner core, cannot be reconciled with M. Eliade's idea of *axis mundi.*[2] The logic and language of our Western study of religion thus have to be carefully reconsidered before applying them to Japanese religion.

1.4 This also holds for our concepts of syncretism and dialogue. These could constitute enormous barriers to the understanding of Japanese religion. In this respect I agree with Carmen Blacker, the English scholar of Japanese religion, who writes of Shinto and Japanese sect-Buddhism:

> The large area of religious practice common to the two, in which the worshipper is scarcely aware whether the deity he is addressing is a Shinto *kami* or a bodhisattva, has been either ignored or relegated to various snail patches with pejorative labels such as superstition, syncretism, or magic. (Blacker, 33)

The problem of syncretism as such exists mainly in the minds of Western intellectuals. This is particularly the case with theologians' minds and —though in a different sense— with the minds of scholars of comparative religion. In the minds of common people all over the world, however, it constitutes no problem at all. In the minds of theologians, the problem arises out of the distinction between true and false religion and revelation. In this they are led by faith as their prevailing standard. In the event that a theologian has a positive, or —to put it in more modern phraseology— 'contextual' approach to other religions, he might distinguish 'sparks' of truth and elements of falsity in other religions.[3] The task of the scholar of comparative religion, however, is not primarily and methodologically, to observe syncretic phenomena in other religions. For the object of his study is the faith of the believer, no matter whether he himself regards this faith to be true or false. From a secondary view, taking into consideration his knowledge of (the history of) other religions, he might be able to distinguish between the historically original form of this religion and forms derived from other religions. Hence I agree with Baird that syncretism is a reflexive and secondary observation only.[4] As such, syncretism is therefore a problem which originated in Western dichotomies within religion, such as: true and false in theology, sacred and profane in comparative religion, and culture and nature in cultural

---

2 With respect to the religion of the common man, I have my doubts about other such universals as: transcendency, monotheism, liberation, salvation, etc. (Kamstra 1986: 53-58).

3 I dealt with this approach in more detail in "Kathina, een Boeddhistische Gemeenschapsviering van Boven en van Beneden Bekeken" (Kamstra 1985a: 31-33).

4 I consider syncretism to be an analytic tool only, needed by the Western scientist of religion for the division of the holistic faith of the common man into parts. As is the case with vivisection, the tool might kill the faith (Baird, 151; Kamstra 1985b: 215-16).

anthropology. The problem of syncretism will have to be solved by those who invented it, not by some tenets in Japanese religion. For the organizing principles of this religion are,

> ... not to be found by laying its corpus of beliefs on Levi-Strauss' procrustean binary bed and reducing the complexities of human mythology to the pairing of opposites. For the Japanese do not conceptually oppose 'the raw and the cooked' or 'culture and nature.' They embrace them as inseparable unities of experience to be tasted and savored together.
> (de Vos, 353)

Japanese believers live in an undivided unified religion which is neither Shinto nor Buddhist. Even the founders of Buddhist sects are inclusive in their views on other religions. Thus Saichō (767–822) and Kūkai (774–835) established not only the Tendai and Shingon sects respectively, but they also put their sects under the protection of tutelary Shinto deities. This leads me to my second point.

2. The Religion of the Japanese: Massive syncretism or religious phenomenalism?

The Japanese way of thinking and acting is almost antipodal to many of our Western prejudices and our way of thinking. In Japanese religion, synthesis is emphasized more than analysis, and holistic philosophy is preferred to a piecemeal approach. Following in the footsteps of Nakamura Hajime, Japan's famous Buddhist scholar, I prefer to scrap the concept of syncretism and to use the word phenomenalism instead. This '-ism,' however, does not imply some kind of false ideology. Nor is it a mixture or an osmosis of several abstract ideas. It is the best characterization of the religious mind of the Japanese I know. What it means is eloquently formulated by Japan's great Zen-master Dōgen:

> The real aspect (i.e. Buddha nature) is all things. All things are this aspect, this character, this body, this mind, this world, this wind and this rain, this sequence of daily going, living, sitting, and lying down, this series of melancholy, joy, action, and inaction, this stick and wand, this Buddha's smile, this transmission and reception of the doctrine, this study and practice, this evergreen pine and ever unbreakable bamboo.
> (Nakamura, 352)

Dōgen formulates this phenomenalism in one concise phrase: "There is not the one mind apart from all things, and there are not all things apart from the one mind" (Nakamura, 353). With this comment, he blocks any idealistic interpretation of the following phrase in the Chinese *Hua-yen-chiao* (the *Avataṃsaka-sūtra*): "In all three worlds, there is only one mind" (Nakamura, 353). It is well known in Shinto that god *(kami)* is intimately connected with all phenomena of nature. So in the religion of the Japanese, neither the idea of *kami,* nor that of Buddha nature, will allow any detachment from the phenomenal world. This is testified to in

Buddhism in a modern ballad (*jōruri*): "The grass, trees, and soils all become Buddhas" (Nakamura, 360).[5] In Shinto on the other hand, the old myths of the *Kojiki* and the *Nihonshoki* describe the formation of this world, and particularly of the world of the Japanese, as a creation of gods out of the bodies of Izanami and Izanagi. Unlike the Christian idea of God, the concept of *kami* is not abstract and alien, but very concrete: *kami* is a part of this world. A God who is not materialized in an active and visible symbol is supposed not to exist at all. Hence the Christian idea of God cannot by any means be reconciled with the Japanese concept of Buddha or *kami*. This is confirmed by the *Shakubuku kyōten,* i.e. the official manual of the Sokagakkai, which has been re-edited and re-written many times under the authority of Daisaku Ikeda, one of the Japanese champions at dialogue and peace. It rebuts Christian doctrines with explicit Japanese arguments which are rooted in Japanese phenomenalism:

> God is spirit. This is also wrong. For all beings all and sundry possess one life body and soul. A spirit separated from matter does not exist really. A real being which is almighty and all-knowing is therefore not conceivable, (Sokagakkai, 344)

and further:

> Christianity separates in its ideas: matter and life, spirit, body, and life. Therefore, it gets to nothing, for this view being the fruit of the assumption of the existence of a spirit is obviously false. (Sokagakkai, 350)

Hence in Japan the ultimate values of religion, in Shinto as well as in Buddhism, are within grasping distance among the phenomena of this world: they are the fundamental nutshell of our own world.

This phenomenalism implies that in Japan it is wrong to distinguish between various religions: Shinto, Buddhism, Taoism, or Confucianism as separate entities. Scholars on Japanese religion prefer the use of the word religion (in the singular) to describe the whole range of religious phenomena in Japan, and to look at Shinto, Buddhism, Folk religion, etc., as mere aspects of one and the same religion. Division of this religion into several independent compartments bespeaks a misunderstanding of the holistic 'system' of Japanese religious phenomenalism. There are several arguments in favour of this statement.

---

[5] Many Buddhist sects in Japan on the other hand emphasize that the basic principle of the universe and hence of mankind consists in *issai mina kū*, the Emptiness of all phenomena. It is worth noticing that the word Emptiness is identical to Buddha nature (Sanron sect). The Kegon sect holds that *nirvāna* is this world or that the whole world and *nirvāna* are present in every speck of dust. This is profoundly laid down in its principle of *jijimugeengi*, all forms in the phenomenal world blend with each other without impediment by the law of causation. The Tendai sect sees in *en*, harmony, the unifying principle of the enormous mass of phenomena in this world. Kūkai, founder of the Shingon sect, stresses the identity of *ri* and *ji*, of the internalized aspect of this world and of the externalized understanding of this same world. I have described the phenomenality of Japanese religion in "Een Fenomenale Godsdienst: De Japanse Religie" (1988).

2.1 Both Buddhism and Shinto developed close ties right from the outset of their encounter, which made them complementary to each other. No matter what kind of disaster hit the nation, everyone always sought their recourse in Buddhist temples and Shinto shrines. Whenever the country was struck by typhoons, the emperors immediately had special offerings made to the *kaze no kami,* the gods of wind, and at the same time, they ordered that Buddhist sutras be copied or that hundreds of people enter into monastic life, for the same reason. This phenomenon is called *shimbutsu-shugo,* the aggregation of *kami* and Buddhas. This *shimbutsu-shugo* is the core of Japanese religion. Anyone who dares to destroy this core is taking grave risks. A special decree was enacted in 1868 to separate Buddhism and Shinto: *shimbutsu-shinri,* the decree of the separation of *kami* and Buddhas. The outcome of this decree is described by Umehara. It led to rebellions in the North of the country. Many authors agree that it caused the collapse of Japanese religion: *shukyō no hakyoku* (Kamstra 1967, 460-61, note 1). When this decree was lifted in 1945, the *shimbutsu no shinjin,* the belief in *kami* and Buddhas combined, led to an explosive growth of new religions. In terms of syncretism and dialogue, this *shimbutsu-shugo* "creates for every religion which enters Japan and wishes to remain true to its principles a dilemma between either isolation or total absorption in the Japanese religion" (Ibid).

2.2 The principle of *shimbutsu-shugo* of Japanese folk religion gave special assignments to both Shinto and Buddhism. Shinto is thus committed to taking care of all the ritual milestones of life from birth to death. After death, however, the recitation of sutras at fixed dates by Buddhist priests for the dead, called *hotoke,* i.e. Buddha, is believed to change these dead ancestors (not into Buddhas! but) into *kami.* Shinto (and with it Taoism too, with its huge variety of practices, adopted by Shinto) thus functions together with Buddhism in the life- (and death-) span of every Japanese person.

2.3 All this is also confirmed by the statistics issued every year by the Japanese Department of Education, which administers the 'religion of Japan.' The figures for 1984, based on Western distinctions between religions, rather oddly divides the total population of about 120 million as follows: Shinto adherents: 112,107,000; Buddhists: 88,965,000; Christians: 1,656,000; other religions: 14,378,000. It estimates the total population of believers at 226,022,000, almost twice the population of the entire country! The latest polls estimate the number of believers at about 35% of the population. So according to these statistics, every Japanese believer should adhere to at least 5 religions.[6]

[6] According to the 1981 survey of the NHK (the national broadcasting system of Japan) entitled: "The Religious Consciousness of the Japanese," 65.2% of the Japanese claim to have no personal religious affiliation at all. On the other hand, 72% of the

2.4 The principle of *shimbutsu-shugo* has been modified in the course of time by competing Buddhist and Shinto specialists, who have yielded several theories, emphasizing their own aspects of Japanese religion. Both sides bring the affinities of Shinto *kami* into contact with Buddhas and Bodhisattvas. The Buddhist theory is called: *Honji-suijaku-setsu,* i.e., the 'true nature — trace manifestation theory.' In Shinto, it is called the *Yui-itsu-shinto,* the 'One and only Shinto,' or *Ryōbu-shinto,* the 'Shinto of the two (Shingon) maṇḍalas.'

A. Matsunaga describes the *Honji-suijaku-setsu* in detail. I need only to refer to her excellent work. This theory is as old as Buddhism itself. Its essence has been explained by the Chinese Buddhist monk Seng-chao (374–414) in his commentary to the *Vimalakirtinirdesa sūtra*:

> In terms of essence, Buddhism is non-duality. All these doctrines are the origin (*pen,* Jap.: *hon*) of the unthinkable.... Without the origin there is no manifestation (*chi,* Jap.: *ji*)...without the manifestation there is no origin. Origin and manifestation are different but unthinkable oneness. (Matsunaga, 47)

Chih-i (538–596), the Chinese founder of the T'ien-tai (Jap.: Tendai) sect, divides the *Lotus sūtra,* the main source of Tendai-Buddhism, into two parts: the first part of it was designated as *chi-men* (Jap.: *jaku-mon*), gate of manifestion. The second part was termed *pen-men* (Jap.: *hon-mon*), gate of origin. In the first part of the *Lotus sūtra* Śakyamuni, as a historical manifestation of the eternal Śakyamuni, preached a kind of Buddhism more suited to the weak minds in his audience. In the gate of origin, however, the real nature of the first gate, the gate of manifestation, becomes apparent. It is a gate of 'trace-manifestation,' the opposite of the real or true gate, which reveals the true nature of Buddha since it is eternal and original. This theory was used in Japan to formulate more precisely the merger of Shinto gods with Buddhas and Bodhisattvas. Vairocana, Buddha of the eternal light, symbolized in the Great Buddha statue of Nara, the summit of Buddhism prior to this in Japanese literature —mostly of a Tendai origin— became linked to the headquarters of Shinto in Ise, and particularly to its main goddess Amaterasu. At the same time, *jinguji,* i.e., shrine–temples, were constructed in honour of *kami* and Buddhas and Bodhisattvas combined. Vairocana (*honji*), the true nature, figures at the apex of religion in Japan and equaled Amaterasu, who was his Japanese manifestation (*suijaku*). Nowadays there are no Buddhas or Bodhisattvas in Japan who are not equated with the *kami.* Sometimes one figure is identified with many others. Thus, the 32 gods described in the *Kojiki's* "Descent from Heaven" were equated with the divine Buddhist entities occurring on the Vajradhātu-maṇḍala of the Shingon sect (Sadao, 220).

---

respondents declared that religion is needed in certain circumstances (Swyngedouw, 2-3).

Kiyohara Sadao describes the Shinto theories. Yoshida Kanetomo (1435–1511) tried to link Shingon Tantrism with Shinto. He ascribed this brand of Shinto to four great masters of the Tendai and the Shingon sects. He emphasizes the uniqueness of Shinto in this theory, Shinto being the original form and the basis of Buddhism, Confucianism, and Taoism. This kind of Shinto later received its name from Yoshida's book: *Yui-itsu shintō myōhōyoshu*. *Ryōbu-shintō* attached Shinto to the two principle maṇḍalas of the Shingon sect. These maṇḍalas should become apparent in the two shrines of Ise: the outer shrine of Toyouke and the inner shrine of Amaterasu (Matsunaga, 193).

3. Two Symbols of Japanese Phenomenalism: Inari and Jizō

There are two trends nowadays in modern Japan which are symptoms of problems with religious implications. They touch life (=Shinto) and death (=Buddhism). The symptoms are the enormous economic growth of many companies, and a whole set of psychological problems concerning life after death. Since 1970 Japan has been undergoing its second wave of new religions since the second world war: the *shin shin shukyō,* the new new-religions. These religions, amounting to a few dozen, are trying to cope with these problems.[7] Alongside of this wave, however, most of the Japanese fall back on the more than 30,000 Inari shrines, or to the tens of thousands of Jizō-statues lining many streets and cemeteries.

The god Inari, generally depicted as a white fox, is believed to foster national and economic welfare; the bodhisattva Jizō, represented as a bald headed monk holding a sistrum or staff in one hand and a gem in the other as symbols of benevolence, is credited with being able to deal with the unavoidable problem of death, which also implies the millions of abortions with which people must cope (Dale Saunders, 181, 186). Most business shops in Japan have a small Inari shrine somewhere on the premises, and, in the case of department stores, even have one on the roof. Now almost 40% of Japanese firms have taken this god as their titulary deity, as do Mitsubishi, Yokohama rubber, Takenaka, Daido, and many others (Swyngedouw, 6-7). Inari can fulfill many purposes, being the guardian deity of prosperity, of money, of business, and of the geisha.

Jizō, on the other hand, is believed to rule human destiny after death. He informs shamans of the whereabouts of the deceased, and is responsible for all kinds of rebirth. He is represented in many ways: as a solitary monk; in a row of six Jizō statues, which refer to the six destinies after death; in groups of a hundred, or even piles of thousands,

[7] Some of these religions, such as the Mahikari (the True Light) religion, and the Agonshu (the Āgama-religion), have an enormous rate of conversions, amounting to a few hundred thousand people (Swyngedouw, 13).

of Jizō statues; roughly carved in phallic stones or other flat stones in rows arranged in cemeteries; dressed up like a doll, and sometimes with a hat on his head to protect him from rain and heat of sun.

Both these divine beings are situated on the margins of Shinto and Buddhism by scholars of Japanese religion; they are, however, the focus of Japan's folk religion and stand flatly opposed to the Western prejudices mentioned above. I have described these figures in more detail elsewhere on another occasion.[8] Here I will briefly present them vis à vis the topics dealt with in this paper.

1.1 *Folk religion and superstition*: Both Inari and Jizō are on the margin of what are considered to be Japan's official religions: Shinto and Buddhism. Many scholars consequently do not pay much, if any, attention to these divine entities, although they are the focus of folk religion.[9]

1.2 *Sexuality*: In origin, Inari was the divine spirit of rice who took care of the fertility of rice. The fox holds sexual symbols in his jaws and in his tail, as tokens of all kinds of fertility: crops in agriculture, products in industries, etc. The fertility of the human race is linked to Jizō. That is the reason why his figure is hewn in the top of phallus stones, or is represented kissing a female partner: the kissing Jizō.

1.3 *Logic and rationality*: The 'idea' of a rice-goddess turned into a heavenly white fox, which in turn even became a bodhisattva, is contrary to Western concepts of logic and rationality. So is the figure of Jizō with its many disguises.

1.4 *Syncretism*: Both figures are a challenge to Western scholars of religion who believe that syncretism exists. Inari was originally a Korean or Chinese goddess of rice. Inari stems from *ine-nari*: what becomes rice. The cult was inaugurated on a mountain southeastward of Kyoto. Fusion of this goddess with the ancestor-gods of the mountain and with nine other Shinto gods into the one god Inari made him adaptable to many purposes. Kūkai (774–835) linked the Inari goddess to the Hindu goddess Dakini, who occurs on one of the maṇḍalas of his Shingon-sect. In many shrines, Inari was later depicted riding on a fox, there being a white heavenly fox in Taoism. Yet later people started to prefer the mount to the rider. Replacing Dakini, the fox himself became a bodhisattva and the object of Buddhist worship, despite his 'Shinto' origin.

The worship of Jizō is also complicated. He is originally supposed to have been a Hindu deity: Kṣitigarbha, 'treasure of the earth.' In the third

[8] Kamstra 1987: 95-111. A more extensive article will be published in 1989 in a Festschrift in honour of prof. Dr. Bruno Lewin (Bochum). An article on Jizō will also be published this year. Excellent publications are de Visser 1908; 1914.

[9] Hori (1974) makes no mention of Inari. Examples could be multiplied.

century A.D., we find him in China as Ti-tsang (Jap.: Jizō). Here he developed into the leader of the ten Taoistic rulers of hell, who decide the fate of people after death. He became as popular as Kuan-yin and Amitābha. In Japan, the cult of Jizō as guardian of a good birth reached its peak during the Edo period (1603–1868). He is now very popular again, in relation to the modern problem of abortion. He is believed to have 'the same body' (Jap.: *dōtai*) as Yama, but also as Amida, Kannon, and Roshana (Vairocana).

2. *Phenomenalism and shimbutsu shugo*: Both Inari and Jizō are believed to be present in this world. Their statues are believed to be their *shintai*: their divine bodies. People are thus in contact with these divine bodies as if they really are Inari and Jizō. *Miko* (female shamans) and *yamabushi* (mountain ascetics) can evoke them at whim. The theories of *Yui-itsu-shinto* and *honji-suijaku* linked both Inari and Jizō to many Buddhist and Shinto divine entities respectively. Jizō not only became *dōtai,* of 'the same body' as many other Buddhas and Bodhisattvas, but also became, "One of the most popular *honji* of many of the native Japanese gods" (Matsunaga, 237). Matsunaga lists 25 of them. To me these figures are a kind of Zen koan. I have not yet reached satori. The religion of the common man remains a difficult choice!

Bibliography

Anesaki, M. *A History of Japanese Religion: Unity and Diversity.* Encino, Calif, 1974. And many others volumes.

Baird, Robert D. *Category Formation and the History of Religions.* The Hague, 1971.

Blacker, C. *The Catalpa Bow: A Study of Shamanistic Practices in Japan.* London, 1975.

Gundert, W. *Japanische Religionsgeschichte.* Tokyo/Stuttgart, 1935.

Hori, I. *Folk Religion in Japan.* Chicago, 1968.

Ikkyosuke, Kanda. *Jikai.* Tokyo, 1957, p. 1714, s.v. *majinai.*

Kamstra, J. H. *Encounter or Syncretism: The Initial Growth of Japanese Buddhism.* Leiden, 1967.

——. 1970. *Synkretisme: Op de grens tussen Theologie en Godsdienstwetenschap.* Leiden.

——. 1982. "Het Spinneweb." In *Antwoord: Gestalten van Geloof in de Wereld van Nu.* Ed. J. Sperna Weiland. 1975; rpt. Amsterdam: Meulenhoff.

——. 1983. "Between Inwardness and Axis Mundi: Analysis of Some Japanese Rituals and their Background." *Nederlands Theologisch Tijdschrift* 37, 230-41.

——. 1985. "Religie en Syncretisme: Oecumene en Dialoog." In D. Hoens et al, *Inleiding.*

——. 1985. "Kathina: Een Boeddhistische Gemeenschapsviering van Boven en van Beneden Bekeken." In *Religies in Nieuw Perpectief.* Ed. D. C. Mulder. Kampen.

——. 1986. *Een Moeilijke Keuze: De Godsdienst van Gewone Mensen.* Bolsward, 1986. See for a general specification of the religion of common men.

——. 1987. "Who Was First: The Fox or the Lady? The God of Fushimi Inari in Kyoto." In *Effigies Dei.* Ed. D. van der Plas. Leiden, pp. 95-111.

——. 1988. *De Japanse Religie: Een Fenomale Godsdienst.* Hilversum.

Kanno, Michiaki. *Jigen.* Tokyo, 1956.

Kiyohara, Sadao. *Shintoshi.* Tokyo, 1942.

Matsunaga, A. *The Buddhist Philosophy of Assimilation.* Tokyo, 1942.

Nakamura, Hajime. *Ways of Thinking of Eastern Peoples.* Honolulu, 1981.

Saunders, E. Dale. *Mūdra.* London, 1960.

Matsuoka, Shizukao. *Nihonkogodaijiten.* [Dictionary of Old Japanese.] Tokyo, 1947, p. 1150, s.v. *majinai.*

Sokagakkai, Kyōgakubu. *Shakubuku Kyōten.* Tokyo, 1954.

Swyngedouw, J. "Religion in Contemporary Japanese Society." *The Japan Foundation Newsletter* 13 (January, 1986): 2-3.

Visser, M. W. de. *The Bodhisattva Ti-tsang (Jizō) in China and Japan.* Berlin, 1914.

——. "The Fox and the Badger in Japanese Folklore." *Transactions of the Asiatics Society of Japan* 36, part 3 (1908): 1-159.

Vos, G. de. Foreword in *Gods of Myth and Stone.* Ed. M. Czaya. New York/ Tokyo, 1974.

Chapter 12

Panikkar's Encounter with Hinduism

Walter Strolz

Starting point of this contribution is today's context of universal history and the interdependence between different cultures and religions. The repercussion of this for Raimundo Panikkar is the Christian obligation to interreligious dialogue. In Panikkar's case this dialogue is realized primarily in the Christian encounter with Hinduism. He is guided in this by his *cosmotheandric* vision: an all-embracing experience of the Whole which allows of no dualism between God and man, cosmos and history, mythos and logos. The religious heritage of Hinduism —which his vision encounters existentially— is interpreted within the light of the universal message of Jesus Christ.

What remains to be discussed within this bold concept is the fact that the problem of theodicy is overlooked, as well as the fact that human finitude is scarcely articulated.

Already a decade before the beginning of the Second Vatican Council, Raimundo Panikkar undertook Christian dialogue with Hinduism. Such dialogue transpires in a world-historical context, a fact which stood out clearly to him. It is taking place on account of the merging of cultures and religions brought about by science and technology, and the possibilities for universal communication which issue from this. Panikkar was profoundly impressed by the experience that we are living at a historical juncture, and that this historical rupture encompasses all religions as well. The time of mutual aloofness and isolation between religions is irrevocably past. No religion can now afford to continue existing as an adversary to others. The question as to the credibility of the message of salvation which they brought in the past has never been more acute, particularly when we pause to think that the imminent danger of mankind's self-annihilation from the face of the earth belongs to the signs of the times in which we live. What forces can religions mobilize in their struggle? If they do not fulfill their prophetic commission of pointing a way towards a peaceful existence for man, then they have become superfluous.

For Panikkar, the interreligious encounter could never be animated by some standard religion. Its heart must lie in the retention of the concrete diversity which exists. This acknowledged richness of perspectives excludes the absolutizing of one religion.

> We dare not say what man is, while overlooking other perspectives. No culture and no religion can tell us a priori what man is, since this question concerns the subject, man (and not just man as object), and may not be answered until the faintest voice and most distant people have been heard. What man is, is not a matter of natural science, since man himself is the one who questions, and therefore no questioning person —nor his answers— may be left out of consideration. (Panikkar 1985: 167)*

Panikkar has left no doubt that the inspiration of his encounter with Hinduism was Indian, even though the instigation for dialogue came from the side of Christianity. Guided by the maxim: "Religion is existential and not objectifiable" (Panikkar 1986: 30), he set out on the audacious venture of living in more than one culture and religion, and describes his experience as follows:

> It is not that I arbitarily regard myself as Indian and European, Hindu and Christian, or that I artificially declare myself a religious and a secular person. It is rather that, by birth, education, commitment, and by my actual life, I *am* a person who lives in terms of the Western, Christian, and secular tradition as well as the Indian, Hindu, and Buddhist tradition. (Panikkar 1978: 200)

We must now show with what method and in what spirit Panikkar carried out his dialogue program, and what questions are raised by such East-West encounter. Is the road taken here to bring Christianity and Hinduism closer to each other a syncretic experiment, a missionary experiment, or neither? When Panikkar declares what his interreligious and intercultural encounter do not wish to be, he makes it clear where this basically leads: It had no missionary design, and it did not arise from a comparative religions approach. Nor does theological reflection in the sense of conceptual thougt serve as a measure, even though this is indispensable for mutual understanding. As a consequence, the Christian-Hindu encounter goes far beyond the scope of what can be grasped doctrinally, without however steering clear of it altogether. The concern is for an *encounter of fountainhead to fountainhead* in the religious spirit.

> Religions meet each other in a common origin, not in the similarities of ideas and ideals, but in their inmost depths. (Panikkar 1986: 50)

The methods and perceptions in the study of comparative religions can never attain this, since only those who commit themselves with their entire existence can participate in the religious depth-experience (Panikkar 1956: 27-54). Panikkar sketches this occurrence as a 'mystical act of

* All quotes in this article have been translated from the German [tr.].

faith.' And as far as Christianity is concerned in this perspective, there is no insurmountable opposition with Hinduism.

> Although Christ is a specifically Christian phenomenon, as the incarnate son of God, the presence and reality of the Spirit is a significant element both in Hinduism and in Christianity. (Panikkar 1986: 63)

With these references, the *existential* drift of Panikkar's position has already been determined. There is certainly a holistic Indian inheritance operating here, which points back to the experiential unity of thought and contemplation, of philosophy and religion, of God and the world, of speaking and keeping silence.

> The greatness of the Indian spirit lies in the power of its synthesis, in its awareness of the whole, in the insight into relations and coherence, while discrete facts are seen from a another —higher— perspective. Unity, oneness, and community, are loftier values for Indians than are distinction, duality, and the particular. (Panikkar 1963: 42)

This insight is realized in *worship.* It is the connecting link between the cosmos and human existence. If one separates creation and salvation, one is lost. For the Indian, this belonging together holds just as strictly as it does in the worship of the Jewish-Christian tradition. Man and the cosmos form a unity. In sacrifice, in prayer, and in worship, a ritual appreciation of creatureliness takes place. The offerings are the human response to the creation as an offering of God, since he foregoes being omnipotent over it, allowing the Other to exist, calling the Other into being, preserving him and destining him for return. In worship, man is embedded in a divine-cosmic process from which he cannot be excepted, and from which he cannot retreat. Panikkar pointed out the philosophical implications of this awesome cosmic bond of humanity, which in Christianity is related to the faithful creator. It is not the restless 'why' questions which correspond to man's existential constitution. These ultimately always founder *on that, which has always already been,* and which transforms questioning reflection into reverence.

> Can anyone actually question why God is there, or why reality is there, the *way* it is, without contradicting God and reality? If there is a God, then no one can give to him a transcendental why. Every why is shattered in God. Any ground or any why outside of God and reality would then be the true God and true reality. It isn't that the ultimate why must somehow remain unanswered or must justify itself: such a why makes no sense. There is no such a final why, just as there can be no square circle. The question for a why always posits a because, and that is simply impossible in this instance. If man were God, then he certainly would not ask for any why. If he does ask for a why, he is, in the final analysis, asking for God —who is the final because— and furthermore, expresses thereby that he himself (the questioner) is not God. (Panikkar 1963: 79)

The *question* of God proves to be a preliminary stage of verbally conditioned thought. While for Christianity the tradition of negative theology is a shield protecting the incomparability of God (Is. 40:25; 46:5;

von Balthazar, p. 13-31), the *Buddhist* encounter with the Absolute is more radical, inasmuch as it abandons the concept of being altogether, allowing no 'is' predication, neither of Being, nor of Nothing, nor of their interplay. Where this is renounced, a definitive silence reigns. For Buddhism does not, according to Panikkar, claim

> ... that the Absolute is nothingness, that there is *no* such a thing at all, but rather that no being can be ascribed to that something, that there is nothing 'behind' it, that there is no 'is.' It would be a thorough disclaiming of Buddhism to have it assert that one ought to think of the Absolute as nothingness; no —the Absolute must simply not be thought, for when one does, one is compelled to think of it as a being or a non-being, whereas it is neither. (Panikkar 1967: 100)

Whoever occupies himself persistently with Panikkar's writings, will acknowledge that thinker and religious person form a seldom seen unity in his case. We will now discuss, inasmuch as such a short contribution allows, his main ideas, viz. the 'cosmo-theandric contemplation' of all things (Panikkar 1985: 183). If it is true, Panikkar asks, that Jesus Christ is the Light who enlightens every man who comes into this world (John 1:9), then God is present in all religions. And when Christian faith confesses the definitive revelation of God in the dogma of the trinity, neither the metaphysics of substance nor that of subjectivity is the thought corresponding to this revealed Word. Theological reflection on the trinitarian divinity demands an extensive alteration of language. Father, Son, and Holy Ghost are 'together among' each other, they are not 'in themselves,' but are essentially Relation.

> The Son is the mediator, the *summus pontifex* of the creation, redemption, and exaltation or transformation of the world. Beings *are*, inasmuch as they participate in the Son, are *his*, are *with* him, and are *by* him. All being is Christophany, else it *is*n't. (Panikkar 1967: 126)

In cosmo-theandric contemplation, the divine, human, and cosmic are united. It is an unfathomable All-Oneness experience, which illumines every being by the Light of the divine-human mystery of Being, and by which all religions are related on the pilgrimage to ultimate reality. In pursuit of the 'unknown Christ in Hinduism,' Panikkar is therefore able to compare texts from the Upanishads with like texts from the Bible, without mixing them together. The independence of religious traditions is maintained, while at the same time precluding the danger of a dualist opposition. The problem of mediating between the inarticulable One and the multiplicity of the world is resolved with the image of Iṣvāra on the part of Hindus, and with Christology on part of Christians— inasmuch as man's limited powers of cognition allow.

We are living in a changing world within an open, uncompleted cosmos. Since the final end has not yet been reached, the religions will continue to exist from generation to generation, the promises will remain in effect, the struggle for overcoming ignorance about the true condition of mankind will continue.

> The mystery of reality is not static; it is expansive; the spiral extends itself; the adventure of reality, of cosmo-theandric destiny, of trinitarian life, is not something which takes place only in an unreal time, so that all things have always been from eternity. The life of the trinity, to which mankind belongs, is rather radical newness. (Panikkar 1985: 186)

The experience of man's finitude, with its concomitant openness of meaning, always provides occasion for Panikkar to recall the *mythical-symbolical* dimension of our existence. As exponent of synthetis thought, he thereby relates himself *undividedly* to religion and to the secular world. In the performance of liturgy, logos, myth, parable, action, and contemplation meet. Man, needful of salvation, speaks and offers in his symbols and gifts. In liturgy, everything points beyond itself, and nevertheless, it remains true to earthly things, since it consecrates these by its sacrificial offers, its thanksgiving, and its praise. While mythos and logos are still unified in the performance of liturgy, they become separated in the age of secularism. The objective mind of modern science grasps in a vacuum, however, when it forgets the *basic mythical presupposition* on which human cognition fundamentally remains dependent (Panikkar 1986; Dürr; Heidegger 1954: 45-70.). Panikkar steadfastly maintains this in his writings with amazing consistency, since it presents the possibility of thinking through the relationship between science and religion anew, and of leading us out of the unholy dualism of knowledge and faith. What considerations of this kind teach us, appears from the following passage:

> They tell us that no single intellectual paradigm will ever suffice to explain reality, ultimately, because reality is irreducible to paradigm. They tell us, further that our situation is just another moment in the adventure of reality. They make us aware that consciousness, not even absolute consciousness, is all that there is 'in' reality. Furthermore, they may help us to overcome the dialectical impasse of our time in religion as well as theology and science, by making us aware that the problem of truth and of reality can never be totally solved because we are necessarily a part of it. We may objectify part of reality. We cannot objectify totally. We would eliminate ourselves. (Panikkar 1987: 256)

Does Panikkar's encounter with Hinduism show traces of *syncretism*? There is, even if these were to be present, no basis for an a priori negative appraisal of such traces, particularly considering that every religion adopts and assimilates *intercultural* influences in some way. The historical process by which a religion emerges, and the later process of cultivating its own tradition are events which are entirely unthinkable without the operation of some foreign elements. It will suffice here to refer to the *interpretatio israelitica* of the Babylonian myth of the creation of man and of the flood by Judaism. The mythic-cultic elements which were modified and introduced into the Christian celebration of such holidays as Christmas and Easter have also long since been elucidated. As far as the present is concerned, we will only take note of the possibility of a syncretic synthesis through the Christian appropriation of Zen-Buddhist meditation methods. Whether this involves an earnest and enduring effort cannot yet be determined (Panikkar 1978: 256; Waldenfels). In our conception, Panikkar himself, in his unabating endeavour for a theological interpretation of an intercultural conception of man, is an advocate of syncretism, inasmuch as this is an essential feature of human communication which enriches one's *own* tradition (Panikkar 1975: 47-52). His thought displays the courage to take the Biblical revelation at its word, meaning that the efficacy of its *universal* announcement of salvation has also been testified to in Hinduism by virtue of its own, unique legacy. Weightier questions arise where aspects crucial to Christianity are missing from this encounter. There is the problem of *theodicy,* and its pressing question as to the origin of evil and its continuing power in history. This experience relates back to the Christian understanding of salvation, which is essentially distinct from the Hindu one (Strolz 1986). Controversy also remains on the point of the *finitude of man,* and about the historicity of truth, which is the result of this *conditio humana.* Along with Heidegger, we wonder whether Indian thought hasn't a 'dehumanizing' trait, insofar as it postulates the attainment of pure, naked Being via the atman-Brahman-identity. The 'finitude of man,' according to Heidegger,

> ...consists in the fact that he cannot experience the presence of the whole of Being, of that which has passed and is still to come, in an immediately present Presence as Being in a *nunc stans.* This is reserved for God in Christian thought. Christian mysticism did not want anything else either. (All Indian 'meditation' wants nothing else than to reach this experience of *nunc stans,* the culmination of this ascent into this *nunc stans,* in which Past and Future have been overcome in a unitary, unchangeable Present.) (Heidegger 1987: 224)

Directing these questions to Panikkar entails renewed reflection on the *mystery of the Incarnation* (John 1:14). Creation and Redemption, time and history, mythos and logos, finitude and transcendence, they belong together (Strolz 1983: 98-126). And if, in accordance with Christian faith, God himself has irrevocably entered into this tension of existence in His own Son, then the *human faithfulness to the contingent* is the free answer of the creature to the condescension of God.

Bibliography

Balthasar, H. U. von. "Bibel und negative Theologie." In *Sein und Nichts in der Abendländischen Mystik.* Ed. W. Strolz. Freiburg, 1984, pp. 13-31.
Dürr, H. P., ed. *Physik und Transzendenz.* Bern, 1986.
Heidegger, M. "Wissenschaft und Besinnung." *Vorträge und Aufsätze.* Pfullingen, 1954.
——. 1987. *Zollikoner Seminare.* Ed. Medard Boss. Frankfurt am Main.

Panikkar, Raimundo
——. 1956. "Die existentientielle Phänomenologie der Wahrheit." In *Philosophisches Jahrbuch der Görresgesellschaft* 64.
——. 1963. *Kultmysterium in Hinduismus und Christentum: Ein Beitrag zur vergleichenden Religionstheologie.* Freiburg.
——. 1967. *Kerygma und Indien: Zur heilsgeschichtlichen Problematik der christlichen Begegnung mit Indien.* Hamburg/Bergstedt.
——. 1975. "Some Notes on Syncretism and Eclecticism Related to the Growth of Human Consciousness." In *Religious Syncretism in Antiquity: Essays in Conversation with Geo Widengren,* I. Missoula, Montana.
——. 1978. "Gedankenfreie Meditation oder seinserfüllte Gelassenheit." In *Festschrift für H. M. Enomiya-Lasalle.* Ed. G. Stachel. Mainz.
——. 1978. *Philosophers on Their Own Work,* IV. Bern.
——. 1985. "Der Mensch: in trinitarisches Mysterium." In *Die Verantwortung des Menschen für eine bewohnbare Welt im Christentum, Hinduismus, und Buddhismus.* Eds. R. Panikkar and W. Strolz. Freiburg.
——. 1986. *Der unbekannte Christus im Hinduismus.* Mainz.
——. 1986. *Rückkehr zum Mythos.* Frankfurt am Main.
——. 1987. "Theomythia and Theology: Mythos and Logos." In *Festschrift für Walter Strolz.* Freiburg.

Strolz, W. "Das Schöpfungswort im Anfang (Gen 1:1-31) und das fleischgewordene Wort (Joh 1:14)." In *Christliche Grundlagen des Dialogs mit den Welt religionen.* Eds. W. Strolz and H. Waldenfels. Freiburg, 1983, pp. 98-126.
——. 1986. *Heilswege der Weltreligionen,* II: *Christliche Begegnung mit Hinduismus, Buddhismus und Taoismus.* Freiburg.
Waldenfels, H. and Th. Immoos, eds. *Fernöstliche Weisheit und christlicher Glaube.* Festgabe für Heinrich Dumoulin S.J. zur Vollendung seines 80 Lebensjahres. Mainz, 1985.

Chapter 13

Jesus and the Avatāra

Richard De Smet

The purpose of this contribution is fourfold:
First, to situate the *Bhagavad-gītā* within its historical context and to thus characterize the literary nature of this fictional dialogue between Arjuna and Krishna.
Second, to set forth the original conception of the Krishna-***avatāra*** and to analyze it.
Third, to determine the *Gītā-Sāṅkhya* ontology of the Krishna-***avatāra*** as implied in the *Bhagavad-gītā* and as interpreted by three classical commentators.
Fourth, to present the chief similarities and differences between the Hindu conception of ***avatāra*** and the Christian conception of incarnation.

The Hindu conception of *avatāra* and the Christian conception of incarnation have often been brought into parallel, but so far the Christians in India have not seriously been tempted to turn this into syncretism. Many Hindus, on the contrary, simply equate the two distinct conceptions and speak of or revere Jesus as another *avatāra.*

My aim is to help dispel this rather widespread syncretism by shedding some light, principally on the notion of *avatāra.* (I shall presuppose that you have a better understanding of the Christian incarnation.) I think it will appear historically and contextually situated; deeply religious; prolific within Vaishnavism; and seminal for several Indian religions; a key-theme for inter-religious dialogue; and of great value for Christians, for it can bring a new vigour and perspicacity to their study of Christology.

1. The conception of *Avatāra*

Avatāra 'descent' means here a divine descent of the absolute God into the world and history of man. This conception, without the same name, appears without any real antecedents in the *Bhagavad-gītā,* 4:4-9, probably around 200 B.C. The Bhagavad-gītā itself is, again probably, an insertion into the fabric of the epic *Mahābhārata,* as then extant. It quickly became well-integrated by the bards, and was even emulated in the further development of the epic. Why was it thus inserted?

a) The origin of the Gītā

The answer is: for definite socio-religious reasons which had to do with the crisis through which the Indian people were passing at that time. Buddhism, not to mention Jainism, was spreading vigorously. The religious minds were presented with opposite options: should they choose the path of non-violence and the pursuit of the pacifying virtues with the promise of ultimate salvation (*nirvāṇa*), or should they remain faithful to Brahmanism with its caste-duties and its normative value, *dharma* (right conduct and reputation), which sanctioned the active virtues, including violence in sacrifices or in just wars? Should they opt for action or for renunciation in monastic mendicancy? Should they abide by the hoary religion of their ancestors which tied together the very sinews of their society of unequal classes, or take their refuge in a supra-social pursuit of a nebulous salvation which bypassed the differences between classes, disrupted the continuity of the hereditary vocations, and had been started only recently by a mere man, though a prestigious teacher and a model of humane virtues?

Beyond the failing accommodations and compromises of some *dharma* specialists, a man of genius (probably a Bhārgava Brahmin or perhaps a Kṣatriya) conceived a bridge-teaching which would resolve the dilemma by adequately merging the ideals and virtues of the old and the new religions. But he needed a herald of this teaching, a teacher of *dharma* both in the sense of normative teaching of an assured way to salvation and of a norm for traditional society. He had to be as human and humane, as wise and discerning as the Buddha, but more, a proclaimer of a new *dharma* which would yet remain a revived form of the old one, the announcer of a promise of salvation for all, but better authorized, and of a salvation more positive and attractive than *nirvāṇa*. And a medium of communication would be needed which was more widely diffused and more captivating than the preachings of Buddhist monks.

He found this medium in the *Mahābhārata*: he would create a new episode of the epic and entrust it to the bards. As herald he picked out Krishna, the charioteer, and thus the predestined guide of Arjuna. He endowed him with the manly excellences of *kṣatriya* warriors, the wisdom of Brahmins, and the benevolence, compassion, and disinterestedness so central to Buddhism. And to make him authoritative in his own right, he made him divine, a descent of the supreme Lord himself.

b) The Krishna *Avatāra*

It is in the early course of this highly creative piece of literary fiction, a dialogue of Krishna and Arjuna, that the conception of *avatāra* is formulated in a definitive way:

> [You tell me that the same eternal *yoga* (duty *cum* renunciation) which you have just been teaching me was proclaimed by you to Manu Vivasvat, the first of our human race, but surely] later is your birth, earlier Vivasvat's; how should I understand your word that in the beginning you did proclaim it:

Śrī Bhagavān said:

> Many a birth have I passed through, and you too, Arjuna: I know them all, but you do not.
>
> Unborn am I, changeless is my Self, of beings I am the Lord. Yet by my creative energy (*ātma-māyayā*) I consort with *prakṛti* [natura simul naturans et naturata] —which is mine— and come to be (*sambhavāmi*).
>
> For whenever the Law of righteousness (*dharma*) withers away and lawlessness (*adharma*) arises, then do I generate myself (*ātmānam sṛjāmy-aham*).
>
> For the protection of the good, for the destruction of evil-doers, for the setting up of *dharma*, I come into being age after age (*sambhavāmi yuge yuge*).
>
> Who knows my godly birth and work, thus as they really are, he, his body left behind, is never born again: he comes to me (Bhagavad-gītā 4:5-9).

We find the essential components of the conception of *avatāra* clearly enunciated here.

i) Krishna proclaims *the fact* of his present and his many past *births*. The term 'birth' is to be taken literally: *sambhavāmi, sṛjāmi*.

ii) He also proclaims the *fact that he knows them all,* whereas Arjuna, like every ordinary man, knows none of his previous births. Originally the Buddha was said to have known only his last seven births. The concrete mode of Krishna's 'godly' birth is not mentioned and the pre-Gītā epic had not said much about the life of this ally of the Pāṇḍavas either. This lack later creates pressure for further fictional elaboration in the later enlarging of the *Mahābhārata,* then in the *Harivaṁśa* and much later in another genre of writings, the *Purāṇas* (Legends), namely, extensively in the *Vishnu-* and the *Bhāgavata-Purāṇa.* These developments would deviate rather a lot from the noble simplicity of the Gītā itself, and would modify the concept of *avatāra* in ways which we will not be able to consider here. How many times had Krishna been born and in which creaturely forms also goes unmentioned. The *Purāṇas* were to describe ten births in either animal, semi-human, or human forms; and Hinduism still described many more, for the elasticity of the concept lent itself to much variation.

iii) He then proclaims the simultaneous but transcendent *fact that as God he remains unborn and changeless*: What is this God, as explained in the rest of the Gītā?

He is the *Creator of the universe*: the source and seed, father and mother and grandsire, the ordainer and sustainer, the one of infinite strength, of limitless and matchless power, the basis supporting 'great Brahman' (i.e. the double *prakṛti* comprising the whole universe, bodies, and spirits), the unmanifest by whom all this was spun out and apart from whom no being can exist, yet one detached, indifferent, none of whose works can limit or bind him.

He is the *one, changeless, transcendent, supreme Brahman-Ātman*: he is the one Brahman out of which the diversity of beings radiates and in which it abides, the highest Brahman, the goal, receiver, and rewarder of every sacrifice (even if wrongly addressed by the ignorant). He is the supreme Ātman or Self, knowing no beginning, change, defilement, or passing away, yet standing in the heart of all beings, illumining and ruling them —even those who hate him— yet immune to the vicissitudes of action. He is the imperishable, the changeless: when all things fall to ruin, he is not destroyed.

He transcends all contingent beings, the all-highest and far beyond nature and its three constituents: "In me subsist all beings; I do not subsist in them. And [yet] beings do not subsist in me: my Self sustains beings, it does not subsist in them; it causes them to be-and-grow" (Bhagavad-gītā 9:4-5).

He is *all-knowing*: by his Self, he knows himself; he is the universal witness, he knows all beings, past, present, and yet to come; he is the founder and guardian of the eternal law, the teacher of the world. He is the illuminator of all minds and their inner ruler, but above all, he is the One-to-be-known for "finite is the reward of men of little knowledge . . . but my worshippers come to me" (Bhagavad-gītā 7:23-25).

He is *unmanifest but partially manifestable*: creatively, he manifests himself in "whatever being shows wide power, prosperity, or strength" (Bhagavad-gītā 10:41); in Ch. XI, he gives Arjuna a 'divine eye' so that Arjuna may witness the tremendous theophany which displays his widespread and multiform power. But the most astonishing invention of the Gītā is to have conceived of God as generating himself in a human body, and at the end of the vision, revealing his humaneness and humility with words banishing fear and awe, and with a countenance "friendly-and-kind" (11:51), or, as at other times, "faintly smiling" (2:10). But the Gītā is unacquainted with what Christ was to reveal: that the incarnate God is better seen in the humblest and most despised.

Above all, he is *the supreme Person, the utmost Puruṣa, and the bountiful sharer (Bhagavān)* of his superabundant being, goodness, knowledge, and love.

The term *puruṣa* 'male,' 'man,' 'entity,' 'monadic life-principle or ātman in living bodies,' 'intellectual principle,' 'spirit' belongs to the register of Upanishadic, Gītā, and later *Sāṅkhya* philosophy. When used of God in the Gītā with an adjective like 'highest and supreme' (*para, parama, uttama*), 'primeval' (*sanātana*), 'divine,' (*divya*), 'eternal' (*śāśvata*), or 'abiding' (*avyava*) it designates God himself as perfect Spirit, knowing and loving Subject, and thus we may say as Person in the most elevated sense of the term. He is indeed addressed by and addressing Arjuna as the supreme 'Thou,' and his *avatāra* is a highly personal 'descent.'

In his dealings with men, he is the *Bhagavat,* the active distributor of all good gifts, and of the salvific *jñāna* and *yoga,* knowledge, and practice. He is indeed the *way* to salvation. This *yoga* is primarily 'skill-in-works' (*karmasu kauśalam*; 2:50), i.e., performance of class and individual duties and even of every action without regard for the fruits (*niṣkkāma karma*) accruing from them for oneself, but only with regard for the cosmic end intended by God's activity: *loka-samgraha,* the maintenance in *dharma*-cohesion of the three worlds and human society. This means acting as a mere instrument (*nimitta mātram*) of the Lord (11:33). In itself, this 'renunciation in action' is hard, but it becomes 'easy' if one is invaded by *bhakti,* the love of loyal service to the *Bhagavān* (8:14). Then, constantly 'intent' on him, 'trusting-and-loving him,' 'winning him by a *bhakti* directed to none other,' one overcomes all selfish desires and wins him.

He is the way because he "gives this knowledge-yoga by which one may draw near to him. . . . Out of compassion for those same men, I, standing (within them) in my mode-of-being as their Ātman (*ātma-bhava-stha*), dispel with the shining lamp of wisdom the darkness born from ignorance" (10:10-11).

The result of this grace of illumination is not the cosmic order, and not only God's accompanying grace and love (*bhajāmi*: 'I return their love'; 4:11), but blissful salvation: "they are not lost to me" (6:30), "they come to me, to my own mode-of-being" (4:10), "he is dear to me" (7:17), "through his *bhakti* he comes to know me as I am . . . and enters me forthwith" (18:55).

iv) Krishna further proclaims the *sovereign freedom of his births in time.*

They are not due to the unceasing metamorphoses of *prakṛti* as blind nature haphazardly causing a new form according to the momentary predominance of one of its three 'inner tensors' (*guṇa*). Neither are they due to the law of *karma* like the births of Arjuna and every other living being. They are directly produced by his own free initiative and his own creative energy (*māyā,* not as denoting illusion, but rather, uncommon power, at most with a connotation of mysteriousness). He wields his *māyā* in this, by masterfully consorting with (*adhiṣṭāya*) *prakṛti* which is not independent, but is 'his' as, we may venture to conjecture, the conjoined quasi-instrument of his *māyā*.

Since the present formulation and indeed the whole Gītā anthropology is *Sāṅkhya*, a most important question ought to be posed here: How human is the individual *avatār* Krishna?

(1) His bodily individuality is not a flimsy concatenation of successive mini-events in Buddhist fashion, because *Sāṅkhya* is realistic.

(2) It is not a mental form like the vision of the theophany of Ch. XI, because the *vikṛtis* or metamorphic emanations of *prakṛti* are material, though they can be either gross or subtle.

(3) It must, therefore, be a *sāṅkhya* human nature. What does this mean?

What is common to all *sāṅkhyas* is the dualistic coexistence-in-heterogeneity of material nature and the consciousness-centres, the dynamic sphere of activity and the passive consciousness-monads, the one *prakṛti* and the countless *puruṣas*. *Prakṛti* evolves living bodies on two distinct but continuous levels: gross and subtle. The gross perishable bodies are made from the material elements; the subtle transmigrating bodies comprise the senses of action, perception, and the three inner senses. Any aggregate of gross and subtle bodies is of itself unconscious, although it performs the computing operations of knowing; but by being near to its own *puruṣa*, it is illuminated by his light, which it in turn reflects in the form of conscious sensations, judgments, etc., known to this *puruṣa*. The Gītā says:

> *Prakṛti* ... is the cause of cause, effect, and agency; *puruṣa* is ... the cause in the experience of pleasure and pain.
>
> For *puruṣa* is lodged in *prakṛti*, experiencing the guṇas that arise from it; because he attaches himself to these he experiences its good and bad births. (13:20-21; cf. 15:16-17)

However, the Gītā is monotheistic, and therefore adds:

> [And yet another there is who,] surveying and approving, supports and experiences [the *guṇas* of prakṛti.] He is the mighty Lord: 'Higher Self' some call Him, the 'Highest *Puruṣa*' in this body. (13:22)

We may now ask: Are there two *puruṣas* in Krishna, as in every other man, both lodged in his dual 'gross and subtle' body?

But in that case, his lower and properly human *puruṣa* would be ignorant like theirs, attributing to himself the births and the pleasures and pains of his adjoined body. He would then also be in need of salvation.

Besides, like them, he would have to say: "I am a man, ignorant and sinful, I am not God." But what Krishna says exactly, is: "I am the Lord"; his I-statements are the Lord's utterances, some purely human and others divine.

Is he not theandric? The answer depends on understanding the *Sāṅkhya* conception of man well. In *sāṅkhya*, there is no union, substantial or instrumental, between *puruṣa* and body; but only close nearness, irradiation by the *puruṣa* and reflection by the body via its 'intellect' (*buddhi*) and by false appropriation of the body by the *puruṣa*. Since the dualism is strict, they are not integrated into one unitary human nature. And since there is no such human nature, we cannot say that the Lord took up a human nature with consequences which extend to the whole human genus.

What the Lord took up (or gave himself by his *māyā* ruling over his *prakṛti*) is a human body uniquely generated (independent of any *karma*). His union with it is not hypostatic, but manifestative, or at most instrumental. And he has truly remained unborn and changeless. Besides, his body does not transmigrate, though it is born and dies (in a later addition, at least).

v) Krishna proclaims *the disinterested motive of his periodic birth.* It is *dharma-saṃsthāpana.* This means, in the Brahmanic sense, the resetting up of the primordial law of order, and particularly of the four-class system which "he himself generated" (4:13) as "arising from the nature of things as they are" (18:41). This implies the kingly function of "protecting the good and destroying the evil-doers." In the Buddhist sense, it means the firm doctrine of salvation. We have described above how his doctrine (both theory and practice) leads by way of selfless action and *bhakti* to final union of the 'good,' the devotees, with him. As to the unbelieving and wicked ones:

> Birth after birth in this revolving round, these vilest among men, strangers to [all] good, obsessed with hate and cruel, I ever hurl into devilish wombs.
>
> Caught up in devilish wombs, birth after birth, deluded, they never attain to me:
>
> Desire – Anger – Greed: this is the triple gate of hell, destruction of the self. (16:19-21 and see 9:11-12)

vi) Finally, he proclaims even more clearly the *salvific effect of the recognition in faith and practice* of his godly birth and work as establisher of *dharma.* This is a deliverance: never to be born again, and a blissful fulfillment: to come to Him.

2. Classical Interpretations of *Avatāra*

There is no searching 'Krishnology' parallel to Christology. But the great theologians of Vedānta did not fail, each one in his own way, to offer interpretations of the *avatāra.* Let us briefly take stock of those based on the *Bhagavad-gītā* rather than on the late *Bhāgavata-Purāṇa* (circa 10th century).

a) ***Śaṅkara***

He is clear about the fictional character of the Bhagavad-gītā: it is *smṛti,* a human literary production, and not *śruti,* eternal revelation. It is useful because it conforms with *śruti.* It is not history, but a didactic device. It commends selfless action which, even though non-salvific, can purify the mind, incline it to complete renunciation, and thus equip it for the realization of the transcendent *Brahman-Ātman.* The latter alone is Real in the supreme sense of the term (*paramārthataḥ*). The rest, including the human body of Krishṇa, is un-Real. This truth is upper-most in Krishna's teaching, which thus coincides with the *Vidyā* (Knowledge) of *śruti.* He is free of the common Nescience (*aVidyā*). When he discloses that his Self is the supreme *Ātman,* he makes the transcendental condition of every embodied being clear.

Just as in causing being the transcendent Brahman is not really embodied in its effect, though its ruling presence is innermost, so also in its *avatāra* it is not really embodied in Krishna, but only 'as if' (*iva*). That does not mean that Krishna's body is a mental vision, an illusion, but that it has no more ultimate Reality than other living bodies. This is non-dualism, not docetism. *Śaṅkara* rejects the idea that the Brahman would be transformed into Krishna's limited individuality. But just as any effected being is manifestative of Brahman "in the manner of a part" (*aṁśatvena*), so the *avatāra* manifests it partially.

b) ***Rāmānuja***

Rāmānuja's theology is anthropomorphic in a refined way. Using the *Sāṅkhya* body-*ātman* analogy, he views God as Vishnu, the perfect *Ātman,* with infinite auspicious qualities and having an eternal glorious body and paradise. As Creator, Vishnu produces contingent bodies of his own: the creatures and the intermediary bodies of his accessibility such as the *avatāras.* 'Body' is defined as: whatever a conscious *ātman* supports, controls, and uses to his own purpose. "He assumed bodily form, overwhelmed by his affection for those who seek refuge in him" (On the Bhagavad-gītā, Introduction). In these *avatāras,* he displays his entrancing beauty.

Like the creatures, the *avatāra*-form is eternally distinct from the divine *Ātman,* but its constituent union with him is not marred by selfish *karma,* sin, and bondage. Furthermore, Krishna does not appear to have a distinct human *ātman* or *puruṣa,* but his sole *Ātman* is the Lord's. His compassionate embodiments are very real nevertheless: he has assumed animal and human forms so as to "conform to different generic structures of various creatures" (On the Bhagavad-gītā, Introduction). And while remaining ever ontologically transcendent, he has become love-dependent on his devotees, just as they are on him. Such relations add much to the creational relation of Self-body which unites them.

This conception is genuinely *Sāṅkhya.* God is perfect Soul-Body. Through his creative energy (*māyā*), via self-modification (*parināma*) of his Body, he evolves the creatures as his contingent bodies. By the same *māyā*, he generates his unique *avatāra*-bodies to reveal and realize his loving accessibility. They are free of moral imperfection, and he uses them as perfect instruments of his salvific purposes.

c) *Madhva*

Madhva is a realist, dualist theist for whom God, the ever free (*sva-tanta*), has organized beings out of beginningless unconscious *prakṛti* and conscious *puruṣas.* Their destiny is to become totally obedient (*para-tantra*) to his will. But they face such obstacles as ignorance and sinful *karma.* The *avatāra* is no ordinary creation, but a unique 'manifestation' of his paramount will by which he descends in a body unrestrictedly obedient to his salvific will. Though made out of *prakṛti,* this body is not subject to the imperfections its normally imports. *Śaṅkara* had said that Brahman creates freely, out of 'play' (*līlā*). *Madhva* employs this metaphor especially of God's descent. It takes place not out of necessity, but out of sheer play; yet the play is the compassionate and most potent play of salvation.

3. *Avatāra* and Incarnation: Similarities and Differences

To all Vaiṣṇavas, *avatāra* is central. To sympathetic Christians, it is fascinating as the closest *pre-figuration* in another religion of the *incarnation* central to their own religion. Let us compare them briefly.

(a) Vishnu as Krishna many times assumes a creaturely body which does not seem to require a creaturely *ātman.* The Logos as Jesus takes a body animated by a human soul once and for all. On the one hand, it is complete (gross and subtle) *Sāṅkhya* body; on the other, a complete human nature. Both are generated by a free initiative of divine power.

(b) Whether fictional or historical, the human life they lead is conformed with other men's lives (birth, growth, professional work, teaching, extraordinary 'signs,' and even death), save for religious ignorance and sin (though in later Bhagavatism, Krishna behaves 'immorally' at times).

(c) In both, the motive is God's wise and potent compassion. The purpose is the salvation of man, either only through teaching, helpful grace, and love (Krishna), or through teaching, transforming grace and love, and suffering (Christ).

(d) These teachings, etc., are addressed to all, regardless of class and sex. But Krishna's efficacy reaches only his devotees; that of Christ even his enemies.

(e) Both convey us to high faith, hope, love, and instrumental selfless work with the Lord "for the welfare of the world": but Christ teaches that the service of the Lord cannot be true apart from love for one's (even inimical) neighbour.

(f) The reward of this service is salvation — *from* either ignorance, *karma,* and rebirth (Krishna), or from ignorance, sin, and death (Christ), and *for* blissful union with the glorious Lord.

(g) Krishna dies, but does not rise in a glorious humanity. Christ does rise from the dead in a glorious body, a living promise of our own glorious resurrection in him.

(h) In Krishna, the union of God and man is only manifestative and instrumental. In Christ, it is not only manifestative and instrumental, but also theandric and hypostatic. The integration occurs not only at the human level, but is also closer knit at the God-man level.

(i) In both cases, God remains transcendent and 'unborn'; the human body or nature remains distinct from the divine as creaturely.

Chapter 14

Salvation in the World A Hindu–Christian Dialogue on Hope and Liberation

David J. Krieger

Today irresistible pressures are forcing every people and all religions into a global melting pot, shattering carefully balanced cultural and religious 'ecologies' and destroying many traditions, if not through suppression and assimilation then by compelling them to assume a militant and apologetic stance. These are the forces of syncretism which could be consciously appropriated as a possibility for dialogue. Dialogical existence in the global situation requires a rethinking of the meaning of hope and liberation, so that these are no longer based upon the supposed righteousness of what can only be partial truths, but upon the righteousness of the *way* we give witness for what we believe. Advaita Vedānta and Gandhi offer Western Christian thought a vision of liberation as *being-the-whole* which can lead to an understanding of history more adequate to the problems of our global situation.

In the final chapter of the *Bhagavadgītā* Krishna must once again remind the reluctant Arjuna that though he take it into his head not to fight in the great fratricidal war between the Pāndavas and the Kauravas, he will nevertheless be constrained to do so by the force of events as it were. Krishna tells him: "That which you do not wish to do, that you will do, like one who is under the control of another." And this because the Lord himself "who is sitting in the heart of all beings moves them round like puppets by means of his *māyā*."[1]

If this indeed be the case, namely, if it is so that we are mere puppets in the divine (or demonic?) game of history, why does the Lord go to such great effort to make us aware of this fact? Does the puppet maker, out of some strange vanity, require that his play things admire

[1] *Bhagavadgītā*, Chapter 18, verses 59-61. (My translation, [DJ].)

the art which produces, sustains, and finally casts them away? Or does the *knowledge* which the puppet gains of his condition so change the nature of the game that fate becomes freedom and blind compulsion becomes a task to be consciously and freely appropriated such that it is no longer only *one* who pulls the strings but *all*?

I believe the latter is what Krishna wishes to teach us about the world-historical events taking place upon the *kurukṣetra.* But we must remember that the *kurukṣetra* is also the *dharmakṣetra,* the field of *dharma,* that is, the stage upon which the spiritual struggle for justice, truth, and meaning is enacted. In this sense every age and every people has its *dharmakṣetra.* Ours is no exception to this rule, though it is distinguished by the fact that for us the field of *dharma* is truly of global proportions. In the second half of the 20th century we no longer need historical perspicacity to see that we are witnessing and, whether we like it or not, contributing to the emergence of a global culture.

What is peculiar to our situation is that within the global horizon every religion, world view, ideology, or way of life has as much right to claim universal validity as every other. The reliable and very useful distinctions between friend and foe, saved and damned, and even real and unreal have become meaningless. For what criteria do we possess which could arbitrate between conflicting interpretations of reality, truth, and meaning itself? What counts as a rational argument, a just cause, a revealed truth when the criteria of rationality, justice and truth are themselves in dispute? The peculiar lesson which our historical situation seems to contain is that the moment the field of *dharma* becomes universal, *dharma* itself becomes particular and pluralistic. And since particular and conflicting *dharma* is as good as no *dharma* at all, everything we had held to be true and substantial begins to totter, shimmer, and reel in a vortex of illusions. The field of *dharma* turns out to be *māyā* indeed!

Arjuna must have had an intimation of this as he stood upon the *kurukṣsetra* and refused to fight a battle in which there was no *dharma.* For in his view, although he was fighting for a just cause, justice itself forbade him slay cousins, teachers, and friends who stood in the opposing ranks. No matter what he did, there seemed to be only particular interests at stake and no universal order, no vision of the *whole.*

But neither Arjuna nor we have much choice in this matter. Just as he did for Arjuna, so today the Lord seems to lead us out into a no-man's land between the battle lines of opposing claims and bid us take stock of what is happening, not so we may choose to do otherwise than the course of events determines us to do, but so we may do it freely and thereby do it right.

Today irresistible pressures are forcing every people into a global melting pot, shattering carefully balanced cultural and religious ecologies and destroying many traditions, if not through suppression or assimilation then by compelling them to assume for purposes of self defense a militant, apologetic and therefore distortingly ideological stance. These are the forces of syncretism. If we speak of an ecological catastrophe on the biological level in which practically every day entire species are being lost, it is also possible to speak of a similar danger on the level of 'cultural ecology.' What is left, for example, of the invaluable traditions of many African, Asian, and American cultures? What insights, abilities, values, and possibilities of human existence will continue to be threatened with distortion and even extinction if we allow the gigantomachia of brute political and economic power to determine what is truth and justice for the entire human community? We may not be able to resist the pressures of syncretism, but we can appropriate them as a possibility for dialogue.

In the global situation syncretism seems to be our historical destiny. It is what is happening and will happen to us whether we like it or not. In this respect we are indeed being moved about like puppets. Dialogue is what we do when we come to *know* that this is what is happening and therefore are no longer victims of a blind fate, no longer fatally identified with our particular views, but are able to ride the wave of *māyā,* as it were, and use its power to participate in the whole. From this point of view syncretism and dialogue may be thought of as models for a global future: one fatalistic, the other hopeful. Again, there may be 'nothing' we can do, but *that* at least is something we can do right.

Nevertheless, if Arjuna had to fight, so do we. There can be no alternative to giving witness in word and deed to that which we believe to be true and right.[2] Still, if we wish to avoid a dangerous polemic and a blind and ideologically distorting apologetic we must step back from our beliefs far enough to allow the other to be heard and perhaps ultimately for him or her to convince us of the truth he or she stands for. On the field of ultimate convictions, which is the place where religions meet, this can only mean opening ourselves for the possibility of *conversion.*[3]

Religious conversion is an eschatological experience. For it is here and nowhere else that human beings are lead out of the 'old world' of illusion, suffering, sin, and death into that 'new heaven and new earth' which is the promised land of peace, justice, and truth. In Christian theology this is the content of hope. And insofar as hope is not merely one virtue among others but a constitutive moment of faith, salvation, which is attained through faith, cannot be separated from the concrete historical struggle for liberation which is motivated and guided by hope.

---

[2] For this reason the ideal of a purely secular world has proven to be an illusion. A fully de-divinized world is one in which human beings can find no meaning whatsoever, and the attempt to create such a world ends, as modern secularism has seen, in the re-divinization of man.

[3] See the methodological foundation for these remarks in Krieger 1986.

If history has any meaning at all, it is only to the extent that it is the place in which and through which the eschatological event occurs.[4]

Western secularism and Christian theology have understood the connection between hope, history, and liberation in different ways. For secularism, the world and history belong to man and not to God. Liberation is either immanent within the world process, a matter of fulfillment of what is already there (Hegel, Marx), or it is beyond this limited and corrupt world and can never be a part of it. In this case, there is only hope *against* and *despite* the world (Bloch), whereas in the first case hope is hope *in* the world and what it will progressively become. As Hegel put it, there is reason in history and this is the true theodicy, the justification of God, whereas for Bloch, there can be no justification for the God of this world, there can only be hope in an open future.

Protestant theology bases its understanding of hope and history on the doctrine of justification by faith, that is, grace alone. This world stands under judgement. The new heaven and earth of the Kingdom of God comes entirely from without and apart from whatever struggle for liberation humans may undertake. The world and history are God's and not man's. If we ask what is left for human beings to do, the answer is that there is nothing we can do *for ourselves,* but we can do everything *for God.* Hope makes an 'eschatological reservation' (Moltmann) with regard to all human achievements and places us without reservation into the hands of God, who comes toward us out of the openness of His inscrutable future.

Catholic theology can accept neither a future without God nor a future which is God's alone, completely apart from human responsibility and participation. If hope is to have meaning and serve to guide human action, then it must have a concrete content drawn from the presence of salvation, albeit anticipatorily, in this world. For action must have a goal which lends it direction, otherwise we must embrace a meaningless and potentially nihilistic affirmation of *change* for its own sake. Therefore it is not sufficient to know that liberation is *not yet* realized in this world, we must also know that it has, at least in principle, *already now* been granted us, and we must have some idea of what it is. The old world must have in it the seeds of the new, else it is impossible for human beings to act in service of the world to come. A purely open future is as good as no future at all. Furthermore, we must know that what we hope for is God's will and not merely human projection, else we cannot speak

[4] This is the conclusion of the recent discussion concerning a 'theology of hope,' and, as I shall argue, a thesis not incompatible with Indian thought. See Kerstiens, Moltmann, Schaeffler.

of a specifically *Christian* hope distinct from the atheistic hope of secularism.[5]

In summary, the secular view of history represented by Bloch says that humans in fact do only wrong, but paradoxically can and will do everything right in a future belonging exclusively to humanity.[6] Christian versions of history leave the future up to God in faith and hope and differ only with regard to the role humans play in God's future, whether it be more a negative one of deconstructing, as it were, the barriers human pride has erected to God's will so as to keep the future open for God, or a more constructive cooperation in the coming of the Kingdom.[7]

It is important to see that what is common to all these views is the concern for legitimating human action in history. Both secular and Christian 'theologies' of hope are first of all theories of political and social *praxis*.[8] The eschatological reservation with regard to the status quo, whatever it may be, is intended to rouse us, on the one hand, from a conservative acceptance of our situation, and on the other, from a quietism which despairs of this temporal world altogether and relinquishes it to the powers that be in the ineffectual hope that all will somehow be made right in heaven. If, as for Protestantism, we know God is the Lord of history and that his revelation to us harbors the promise of the Kingdom, then we are responsible to keep the future open to Him through continuous effort to change the world. And if, as for Catholicism, since it is not enough merely to know what the Kingdom is *not* in order to act (since action must have a positive goal toward which it moves, if it is to avoid nihilism), we must look for indications and foreshadowings of the Kingdom in creation, and assume our co-responsibility with God for the coming of God's reign. In either case there is a latent or explicit *dualism* at work which polemically distinguishes this world of bondage and those who represent it from the kingdom of freedom and peace. This indeed provides motivation for praxis and gives it a clear and definite goal, but only at the price of buying into gnostic ideologies.[9]

---

[5] This is made very clear in the criticism of the Protestant theology of hope in Kerstiens; and also in the excellent discussion in Schaeffler.

[6] The great dialectical paradox at the origin of so much modern secular thinking is that we *are* free, but at the same time *are not*.

[7] This latter being based upon the natural law tradition in Christian thought as well as an emphasis upon the doctrines of creation and incarnation.

[8] This represents a decisive break with the traditional, that is, Augustinian theology of history which rejects all forms of eschatological immanentism.

[9] See the discussion of gnosticism as lying at the basis of modern political movements in Voegelin 1952. Voegelin writes: "Gnostic speculation overcame the uncertainty of faith by receding from transcendence and endowing man and his intramundane range of action with the meaning of eschatological fulfillment. In the measure in which this immanentization progressed experientially, civilizational activity became a mystical work of self-salvation" (p. 129). And again: "The Gnostic revolutionary ... interprets the coming of the realm as an event that requires his military co-operation" (p. 145).

Western thought, it seems, has come to the conclusion that hope and human action in history requires us to believe that we are not of this world and that therefore God is on our side (or we on His), or, in the case of secularism, that there is no God and we may for that reason set our own goals absolutely. The *Bhagavadgītā*, however, tells us that there is no real difference between God and the world and that therefore the Lord is on everybody's side.[10] To assume the absolute truth of any particular vision of the Kingdom of God would amount to placing liberation within the realm of opposites and thus inevitably mistaking one's partial understanding of salvation for the whole truth.[11] For this reason Hinduism has declared that it does not matter whether one wins or loses in history but only *how* one plays the game. From Indian thought we might learn that the presence of salvation in the world, of liberation in the midst of bondage, manifests itself not in the righteousness of the causes we may fight for —since in fact we can never know whether they are really just or not, and even if we could, that would not exclude the equal validity of our opponents goals— but in the *way* we fight for them.

As we move into a global culture the partial and therefore illusory character of every historically and culturally determined interpretation of reality, that is, of every religion and world view, becomes embarrassingly manifest. Our world has broken up into many little worlds. Our heretofore taken-for-granted convictions about the world and ourselves have turned out to be not much better than subjective opinions, while the 'objective' truth about reality escapes any particular system of thought. Human consciousness has become irrevocably pluralistic. But at the same time it has become holistic in a way which Western historical consciousness cannot grasp. For history has turned out to be more ambiguous than relativism and historicism ever dreamed. As Troeltsch had seen, we are indeed unable to grasp the whole; the 'end' of history is not a datum within history. But contrary to historicism, since we are no longer able to naively identify ourselves with one culture and its history as Troeltsch could still do, the 'subject' of history has all but disappeared. 'Whose' history we are 'in' has become an open question and it has thus become increasingly difficult and also irrelevant to base our actions upon the assumptions about a linear origin and goal which constitute historical consciousness.[12]

---

[10] See *Bhagavadgītā* 15:12-15; 9:4-6; 7:7-11. This, of course, is the *advaita* interpretation.

[11] See Michael von Brück, "Wer die Fülle (*purna*) des *ātman/brahman* erfährt, erlangt *moksa*, Befreiung. *Moksa* ist reine Nicht-Dualität. Denn stünde der Befreiung noch der Zwang eines Bereichs von Nicht-Befreiung entgegen, wäre sie nicht absolute Befreiung und man käme zu einer neuen Dualität. Dieses Paradoxon ist die tiefste Intuition der Indischen Philosophie. Sie ist das Mysterium der Einheit von Sein und Nichts, Gut und Boese, Befreiung und Verstrickung, *brahman* und *sunya*" (p. 63).

[12] It was the discovery of a "plurality of centers of meaning" which caused Eric Voegelin to abandon his project of reconstructing historical consciousness in his

Instead of asking how the present relates to the future and the past, it is increasingly necessary to ask how the part relates to the whole. Global consciousness seems to exist more in the a-historical tension between the whole and the part —a whole which is fully present but hidden by ignorance— than in the historical tension between origin and goal. It is a situation which is significantly similar to what the Indian tradition has called *māyā.*[13] To exist in this situation is to exist in the tension of simultaneously knowing *that* we are the whole and yet not knowing *what* it is. *What* we may know is always only a partial view. The danger here, as with *māyā,* is that we may forget we know and mistake our dreams for reality.

It is hard to lay one's life down for what one believes to be true while knowing all the time that it is at best one interpretation among others. In fact the general effect of this insight into the nature of history is paralysis, for it makes all action meaningless and futile. Arjuna was well aware of the paralyzing effect of the knowledge of *māyā,* an effect which contemporary Western thought, as we saw, seems able to avoid only at the cost of a dangerous and polemical dualism. But the important thing is that the Lord's counsel to Arjuna in the *Gītā* was not to desert the battle field and lead the life of a mendicant renunciate. Rather he is told to renounce *and* to fight.

If a renunciate fights at all, then not for the realization of his goals. There is nothing for him to achieve, or more correctly, whatever a human being may achieve is really nothing, for God alone is the one who 'acts.'[14] Since a renunciate has nothing to fight for, the only relevant question is *how* does a renunciate fight.

Here it is Mahatma Gandhi who has most to tell us about the *Gītā,* for Gandhi, in opposition to traditional interpretations, understood the battle upon the *kurukṣetra* as a symbol for the spiritual battle we all must fight against the demons of self-righteousness and pride which deceive us into identifying our goals with the truth itself and to thus legitimate any

monumental study *Order and History.* For historical consciousness is based upon the articulation of an origin and a goal around one center of meaning. See the Introduction to *The Ecumenical Age.*

13 For a thorough discussion of the Advaita Vedānta theory of illusion upon which I am here relying see Swami Satprakashananda 1974: 124-140. In the Introduction to his commentary on the Brahmasutras, Shankara defines illusion (*adhyāsa*) as "the apprehension of something as something else." Here this means apprehending our own world view as the whole of reality, that is, mistaking the part for the whole. In the *advaita* tradition *māyā* is ultimately responsible for the apparent multiplicity of reality. First by means of 'covering over' (*viksepa*) and then by 'projection' (*āvarana*). On the level of human perception it is called *avidyā* or *ajñāna.* See also the excellent description of the 'cosmic' world view of Hinduism in Francis X. D'Sa, *Gott: Der Dreieine und der All-Ganze.*

14 *Bhagavadgītā,* Chapter 3, Verses 22-25. See also the discussion in "Zur Heilslehre in Hinduismus und Christentum." (In Krieger, Braun 1986: 59-74.)

and all means we may employ to achieve them.[15] The renunciate, for Gandhi, is he who has seen through the veil of *māyā*, which leads him to mistake his or her own beliefs for God's truth, but who has not for that reason abandoned the world and human history as an illusory realm of meaningless suffering. Gandhi's intention was, therefore, not merely to develop new techniques for strategic action which could serve the realization of particular interests, but rather to develop a method of resolving the conflict of interpretations on the level of universalistic claims such that a mutual *conversion* to an ever more complete truth might occur.

What separates Gandhi from all utopian fanatics is his thoroughly realistic appraisal of the ability of men and women to know absolute truth. He writes: "... we will never all think alike and we shall always see Truth in fragment and from different angles of vision" (Iyer, 246). What we can know, however, is *that* there is truth. It is *what* this truth may be that cannot be the private property of any person or group, but only the goal of all. This is the reason why non-violence must be the method, the means, since it alone can realize this goal in and through human action. For if we force our view of the truth upon others, we inevitably raise a partial truth to an absolute status and thus prevent a dialogical exchange of views which alone could give us the complete truth. Insofar as we prohibit all correction of our position by means of violence we remain bound to our partial truth and cut ourselves off from the whole which alone is true and real.

After fifty years experience of ideological conflicts Gandhi was convinced that the only way that an ideological absolutization of a particular world view could be broken was by means of *solidarity with the enemy*. What else could *tat tvam asi* ('That art thou') mean on the level of practical human concerns? This in turn led him to see the importance of *voluntary self-suffering*. In every ideological conflict each party takes the resistance of the other to be a confirmation of their previous condemnation of the other's position.[16] This then legitimates suspension of communication and the use of coercion of one sort or another. But if one of the parties does not answer violence in kind, and nonetheless continues to resist, then, according to Gandhi, no one can remain secure within his prejudices. The one who uses violence will be compelled to ask himself where his opponent obtains the courage and the moral force necessary in order to resist non-violently. He will be forced to admit that his opponent does have some truth after all. At this point he has already placed his own ideology in question and the walls of non-communication have been broken through.

---

[15] For Gandhi's interpretation of the *Bhagavadgītā* see *Discourses on the Gītā*.

[16] Cases in point are the 'resistance' of the patient in psychoanalysis as well as political and social resistance in Marxism.

When the aggressor sees that his opponent takes the suffering arising from the conflict upon himself and does not answer with violence, then his own fear and mistrust are overcome and an open and sincere dialogue becomes possible.[17] In this way we might say non-violence becomes a *sādhana*, that is, a means for *moksa*, liberation. Or we may think of it as a form of dialogical *upāsana*, meditation by which the *oneness* of the truth is realized not only in the certainty *that* it is, but also in the explicit and concrete knowledge of *what* it is.[18]

Gandhi saw conflicts as necessary for the purification, we would say development, of society, indeed, for the development of the entire cosmos. The course of history and all social change is therefore inevitably bound up with suffering. For out of every conflict there arises a certain amount of suffering.[19] The task and privilege of humans who are by nature 'identical' with the absolute and thus co-responsible for the perfection of creation is to accept this suffering, take it voluntarily upon themselves, and to thus transfigure it into a creative rather than a destructive force

> If love or non-violence be not the law of our being, the whole of my argument falls to pieces, and there is no escape from a periodical recrudescence of war. . . . I know that it cannot be proved by argument. It shall be proved by persons living it in their lives in utter disregard of consequences to themselves. There is no real gain without sacrifice.
>
> (Iyer, 194)

Most men and women, however, because they have falsely identified themselves with finite things are *ignorant* of this their true nature, and in a conflict situation they react automatically with fear. They attempt to avoid the suffering which accompanies the conflict by pushing it off onto others. It is this so-called 'natural' reaction which, according to Gandhi, is the source of violence. In fact violence is nothing other than the attempt to escape the suffering which arises when false identifications with partial truths create a conflict by thrusting the suffering onto the other party in the dispute. Non-violence, on the other hand, consists

---

[17] This is the reason why Gandhi had no use for Marxist theories of violent revolution. He writes: "Violence interrupts the process and prolongs the real revolution of the whole social structure" (Iyer, 247).

[18] In classical Advaita Vedānta it can only be known *that* the *one* (*ekam*) is and not also and with equal validity *what* it is, since the *vyāvahārika* standpoint, from which alone being is determined with regard to *what* it is (i.e. name and form), has no final ontological or epistemological validity. Gandhi's interpretation of the *Gītā* could be seen as a corrective to this 'world denying' tendency. For if the *pāramārthika* or absolute standpoint is to give knowledge of the *whole*, it cannot simply leave out the variety and richness of the world as well as the relations constitutive of personal being. This is the point of M. von Brück's interpretation of *a-dvaita* as 'integration' rather than 'identity.'

[19] Suffering is not a mere feeling which overcomes a man or a woman, but a metaphysical force which human beings are responsible for and must learn to deal with constructively. Thus does mere pain (*duhkham*) become *tapas*.

precisely in acting out of solidarity with the whole, and thus voluntarily taking as much of this suffering upon oneself as possible.[20]

Still, we may ask, if fear and violence are to a certain extent natural reactions, how can we overcome them? The answer which Gandhi gave to this question is *karma yoga.* The Indo-European root of the Sanskrit word '*yoga*' (*yuj*) means "the act of yoking, joining, attaching, harnessing." In the Hindu tradition, *yoga* has come to have the general meaning of spiritual 'discipline' or, as we may say with reference to its original meaning, of 'attachment' to the divine. In order to harness oneself to the divine, however, it is necessary to 'loosen' or 'unbind' oneself from all that is not godly, that is, from all that is less than the whole. In the tradition which influenced Gandhi this meant all that a man or woman undertook to satisfy his or her own interests. *Karma* implies an inseparable bond between the action and the result of the action, identical to that between cause and effect. The renunciation of the result breaks the bond which ties action to specific goals and interests, and thus empowers it to incarnate solidarity with the whole of reality. *Yoga,* then, is what frees us from identification with the limited and finite, and in so doing leads to a 'knowledge' (*jñānam*) which is liberating inasmuch as it 'identifies' us with the whole. If this is what Krishna would have us *know,* then we may see how knowledge can make us free and how freedom can transform a situation.

Nowhere does this become more apparent than in Gandhi's understanding of *yoga.* For what was atypical of Gandhi's *yoga* was its political and social *engagement.* This amounted to an important renewal, if not 'reformation,' of Hinduism, into which Western Christian ideals of social justice and an appreciation of history as a *history of salvation* have been integrated. Gandhi's *yoga* was anything but a world-denying asceticism. It was a *yoga* of action. The Sanskrit term for action is *karma.*[21] The *Bhagavadgītā* was so important for Gandhi —he called it his 'lexicon'— because it was a book about action (*karma*) understood as *yoga,* as praxis in service of the divine. The concept of *karma yoga* was not new with Gandhi, but he gave it a new dimension, namely, ritual praxis and fulfillment of religious law (*dharma*) understood as political and social praxis. For him, there was no distinction between religion and politics, between private and public. This, according to Gandhi, was the teaching of the *Gītā* and the very meaning of non-duality (*advaita*).

---

[20] The implication is that an 'imperative' ethics which prescribes rules of action, regardless of what sort, inevitably bases action upon a partial truth and is therefore always violent, for there are no rules which could apply to all possible situations and thus be truly rooted in the whole.

[21] Karma has many meanings. In the *Bhagavadgītā* it often has the meaning of 'ritual or cultic works.' For a relatively complete list, see the Sanskrit Concordance in Kees W. Bolle, *The Bhagavadgītā: A New Translation.*

From this point of view it may be said that the struggle for material security which has been placed at the root of human action in modern secular theories of society from Hobbes to Habermas —as well as the 'political theologies' based upon them— are incapable of founding human community. A one-sided over-valuation of the productive aspect of human action understood, for example, as *labor,* and the technical or instrumental rationality accompanying it, has the effect of identifying us with limited goals and of detaching us from that solidarity with the whole which grounds all true community.[22] Despite claims to act in God's name, we become hopelessly closed in upon ourselves in little worlds constituted by our own ideologies. *Karma yoga,* the discipline of renunciation in action, frees us from self-interested action sufficiently to break these bonds and stave off the reaction of fear which tends to come when our interests are threatened in an ideological conflict. We at least have the chance to know ourselves as instruments (puppets?) of the divine and therefore also of giving a practical content to the symbols of the cross and the resurrection by transforming a conflict through self-suffering into a free and creative opportunity for advancement of the entire community.

No matter how different and seemingly exclusive of each other world views are, they can be included in a universal dialogue only when the conflict of interpretations is fought out on that common ground, that ultimate unity (*ekam*) which non-violence discloses. Non-violent resistance allows us to remain faithful to our own beliefs while at the same time realizing that these are not the absolute truth, but only an interpretation — an interpretation which, because of the *way* we give witness to it, participates in That One (*tat ekam*) which is God.

22 "The more fervently all human energies are thrown into the great enterprise of salvation through world-immanent action, the farther the human beings who engage in this enterprise move away from the life of the spirit. And since the life of the spirit is the source of order in man and society, the very success of a Gnostic civilization is the cause of its decline" (Voegelin, 131).

Bibliography

Bolle, Kees W. *The Bhagavadgītā: A New Translation.* Berkeley, 1979.
Brück, Michael von. *Einheit der Wirklichkeit: Gott, Gotteserfahrung und Meditation im hinduistisch-christlichen Dialog.* Munich, 1986.
D'Sa, Francis X. *Gott: Der Dreieine und der All-Ganze.* Düsseldorf, 1987.
Gandhi, M. *Discourses on the Gītā.* Tr. V. G. Desai, Ahmedabad, 1960.
Iyer, Raghavan. *Moral and Political Thought of Mahatma Gandhi.* Oxford, 1973.
Kerstiens, Ferdinand. *Die Hoffnungsstruktur des Glaubens.* Mainz, 1969.
Krieger, David J. and Hans-Jürg Braun, eds. *Indische Religionen und das Christentum im Dialog.* Zürich, 1986.
Krieger, David J. *Das Interreligöse Gespräch: Methodologische Grundlagen der Theologie der Religionen.* Zürich, 1986.
Moltmann, Jürgen. *Theology of Hope.* Tr. J. W. Leitch, New York, 1975.
Satprakashananda, Swami. *Methods of Knowledge According to Advaita Vedānta.* Calcutta, 1974.
Schaeffler, Richard. *Was Dürfen wir Hoffen?.* Darmstadt, 1979.
Voegelin, Eric. *The Ecumenical Age.* Baton Rouge, 1974.
——. 1952. *The New Science of Politics.* Chicago.

Chapter 15

Christianity and Reincarnation

Reender Kranenborg

The notion of reincarnation has never been sanctioned by the Christian church. The church has always resisted it because it found it to be incompatible with Christian faith.
The idea of reincarnation, familiar primarily via Hinduism, has had recurrent resurgences in the West. Again and again there are Christians who believe that Christianity and reincarnation can be joined. Two examples, more or less inspired by Theosophy, are given here. Are Christianity and reincarnation indeed permanently opposed?
Even though much of the work of both authors is consistent with classical church doctrine, and even though their idea of reincarnation differs from that of Hinduism, tensions continue to exist.

1. Introduction

In every encounter between religions, an exchange takes place. Even when the meeting of two religions results in dissociation and the adoption of a harsher stance toward each other, it is possible that certain elements are adopted. When religions meet one another, believers may perceive objectionable and repulsive aspects in the other religion, but may also find attractive ones. If some aspect is interesting, one will try to integrate it into one's own system of belief, and if its introduction does not entail conflict with other central religious perceptions, that religion may be enriched.

But if the introduction of this element elicits conflict with other religious convictions, it can be rejected, or retained as a non-integrated element. In this respect I subscribe to Droogers' definition of syncretism: syncretism is "contested religious interpenetration." In my article I will examine a specific subject: the phenomenon of Christians trying to introduce an element hitherto unknown in their own belief system, namely, the idea of reincarnation.

In the current religious encounters it seems that many Christians are attracted to the notion of reincarnation which occurs in some other religions. They therefore try to relate this notion to their own Christian conviction. The question which then arises is: Is this relationship free of problems, or does the introduction of the notion of reincarnation into Christianity elicit a fundamental conflict with other Christian convictions? We will treat this question in three sections:

- the role of reincarnation in the early Christian church and in gnosticism.
- the role of reincarnation in the 19th century (theosophy).
- the role of reincarnation in the thought of two modern Christian theologians.

By the term 'reincarnation' I mean the conviction that an imperishable principle exists in every human being which for some reason comes back after death, usually in a new human form, on this earth. In Hinduism and Buddhism one can, it is true, reincarnate as a plant, an animal or a god in a subsequent life, but in order to attain ultimate liberation, one must be reborn at some time as a human being on this earth. The notion of having numerous human lives on earth is therefore essential to reincarnation. When former or future lives on non-earthly levels are involved, whence one arrives on the earth as a human being only once and whence one does not return to the earth in human form upon death, one can no longer speak of reincarnation (in this case we can possibly employ the term pre-existence). Such synonyms as metempsychosis, rebirth, and transmigration are included in the term reincarnation. But before we occupy ourselves with the idea of reincarnation in history, it is useful to pursue the reasons why people in our time find it acceptable to assent to this notion.

2. The background for contemporary belief in reincarnation

There are several reasons today why many people believe in reincarnation. Many find it an acceptable solution to their questions about life. We wish to start by mentioning a number of arguments and considerations which convince people that the idea reincarnation is plausible:

- one is provided with a good explanation for the why of the events which befall a person. These are not the result of God's arbitrary judgment, nor are they purely coincidental, bringing fortune to one and misfortune to another. Nay, everything which befalls a person has to do with what he has done in an earlier life. In this life, he can proceed to put right what was wrong. Things do not happen to man accidentally.
- one is provided with a solution to the problem of unrevenged injustice in this life. It is all too easy to see that there are people who have committed the most heinous crimes without being punished in any

way. It is satisfying to know that this will be requited in a subsequent life of theirs. This has nothing to do with a desire for vengeance, but with the need for this world to be ordered honestly and justly.

- many have the notion that the life which one leads here on earth is no more than a beginning. Various tasks and projects are started when life suddenly ends, even though one is by no means finished. It is a comforting thought that a person can resume his course in a subsequent life, and can proceed with what he was doing, even if he retains no memory of this life.
- many people are convinced that all of existence is involved in a process of growth and evolution. Human existence leads to something, to a higher goal. This goal can be attained through various lives. All lives, the present one included, are thus a phase, a stage to a higher goal.
- some are convinced that a person should have experienced everything in life once: being wealthy and being poor, being a man and being a woman, being strong and being weak. This is impossible in one life; it is possible only if there are numerous lives.
- some feel revulsion at the idea that a single life here and now could be all there is, and therefore decisive for all eternity. They find gruesome and inhuman the notion that one could be eternally damned, with no further opportunity for compensation, after only a few brief years here on earth. The idea of reincarnation is rather more compassionate by comparison. Then one has the opportunity to make restitution for one's mistakes, and to make progress.

The above arguments are more considerations stemming from what would be probable or attractive. To put it differently: they are the deliberations of belief. One could put them up for debate and weigh them against other beliefs.

For the proponents of reincarnation there is more than just beliefs, however. Many are convinced that reincarnation is demonstrable. The following facts play a role:

- it occurs from time to time that small children know things which they could not have learned. They know, for instance, that they lived in another town, had an accident there, and upon being brought back there, recognize everything and are able to mention minute details which they could not possibly have heard. Does this not prove that the person who died then was reincarnated in such a child?
- there are people to whom facts or information from another reality (the 'spheres') is conveyed concerning earlier lives or previous phases of world history. The name of Edgar Cacey could be mentioned here. Like Rudolf Steiner, he is able to tell much about previous lives and about the phenomenon of reincarnation and *karma*. Such things are not the

products of fancy, they say, but facts which make reincarnation probable.

– then there is the phenomenon of regression therapy. People are returned to previous lives, usually under hypnosis, and practically everyone who journeys back in hypnosis arrives at a previous life. When present in a former life, they are able to describe things with in great detail, things which they could not otherwise have known. It is often remarkable that anachronisms hardly occur. What people experience in such a former life fits the cultural situation of that time. The recollections from these lives are moreover of great importance for particular problems now. There is often a clear *karmatic* relationship.

– another remarkable point is that the phenomenon of reincarnation occurs in so many places all over the world. It is almost a universal belief, despite mutual differences. The fact that people all over the globe are acquainted with it is another proof for the fact that reincarnation is not nonsense. Such a thing cannot be imagined, it is believed.

3. Reincarnation in Hinduism

The notion of reincarnation is to be found in various religions, but it is most strikingly present in Hinduism. The contexts in which this notion can be found within Hinduism are not all alike. As an example, we will take the system of the Vedanta (Shankara); in the West this system currently serves as a model of Hinduism. Notions which we see in the Vedanta system can generally be found in older movements and scriptures as well, such as in the Upanishads. The following relations are important:

1) Creation is an emanation from God; it is part of him. Matter is nevertheless of a lower order; it is not substantial; it does not touch the core of existence.
2) God and man are basically one (*ātman* = *Brahman*). This *ātman* is the core of the human being.
3) a) The history of the world runs in a cycle of periods. Man, or rather, man's core (*ātman*), takes its own course through many lives; in a subsequent life, one can be on a higher or on a lower level.
   b) The imperishable core of man is unique and absolute; the body is not essential; that is to say, it does not belong to the core (*māyā*).
4) There is a reckoning for evil; it will be settled in a subsequent life; the absolute law of *karma,* the law of cause and effect applies here.
5) A guru (in Buddhism, a *bodhisattva*) can help a person on the way to salvation through his grace.
6) a) Man must effectuate his own salvation.

b) In this life one works to reach a higher level in a subsequent life. *Dharma* applies here, or at higher levels: the way of detached action which no longer begets *karma.*

7) Man is part of the cosmos, and participates in the course of its evolution. He can return in the form of an animal or of a god. The 'soul,' however, can ultimately be liberated only by returning in a human body on the earth.

As has already been said, differences do exist within Hinduism. Accordingly, with regard to the first point it could also be said that matter does not emanate from God, but that it is an eternal, independent principle next to the divine (we can speak of dualism here, as for instance, in the Samkhya system). In this case, the soul, identical with the divine, according to the second point, is imprisoned in the darkness of matter (and of corporality) from which it must be liberated.

4. Christianity and reincarnation in the early church and in gnosticism.

A belief like reincarnation always stands within a religious context and cannot be easily extracted from it. Some other beliefs are indissolubly connected with it. When the notion of reincarnation is introduced into a religion which is unacquainted with it, this means that other elements are also introduced. The system of this religion, therefore, is changed, for a religion is not a composite of loose beliefs, but includes relations and elements which are indissolubly connected with each other. In order to ascertain if the notion of reincarnation can exist within Christianity, it is first necessary to see which essential beliefs and relations exist within the Christian faith. In order to find these ideas we will recall the beliefs of the early church as laid down in the creeds and resolutions of synods and councils:

1) God is the creator of man and the world; this world has been created once, and is fundamentally good, but is now marked by sin and evil.
2) God and man are different. God is transcendent, personal.
3) a) God shares a history with mankind, a history of salvation. This history is linear, starting at the beginning of humanity, culminating in Jesus Christ, and going on to the coming of the Lord. In this history every human being has a place of his own, determined by God.
b) Everyone has to account for his deeds in this life. The history of one's individual life is decisive. At the end of time there is a resurrection of the body, which means that it is assumed that human beings will live again in body and soul.

4) Man commits sin, does evil, and will one day be punished by God on that account at the last judgment.
5) a) Jesus Christ has suffered vicariously for mankind and has borne their sins.
   b) In Jesus Christ, therefore, there is absolute forgiveness of sins, and absolute grace.
6) Man cannot attain salvation on his own; he cannot liberate himself. Once salvation is given to him in Christ through faith, he is obliged to live by faith (or, by the spirit, by grace).
7) Man is the crown of creation, and is placed above all other earthly creatures; he may govern all things.

In this Christian view, the way to human salvation is clear.

Although the existence of India was known in the time of the early church, we cannot speak of an encounter between 'Hinduism' and Christianity. Yet thoughts closely akin to Hinduism were not unknown. In the philosophy of the Orphians and Pythagoreans, as well as in the thought of Gnosticism, we encounter belief systems which correspond to the later Vedanta-Hinduism, systems in which the notion of reincarnation was incorporated organically, and in which a direct causal connection existed between this life and former and future lives (in Hinduism one would say *karma*). In contrast with the later Vedanta, we find dualism here, which means that matter is a prison in which the soul is bound. In some of these gnostic movements, Jesus has an important role. He is the herald of revelation to mankind, who tells him the way which he ought to go; he is the one who can help and support man. Usually he is a being of light (and not a real human being), and he can be seen as the prototype of the liberated man.

The early church rejected Gnosticism, and reincarnation along with it, as incompatible with Christian faith. The objections are many, against Gnosticism as well as against reincarnation. We will not deal with the objections against Gnosticism; we will concentrate on the objections against reincarnation. Origen, for instance, has the following objections:[1]

- the notion of reincarnation cannot be found in the Bible,
- the notion conflicts with the conviction found in Bible that the world is finite. According to Origen the world will never terminate if one believes in reincarnation, for no one can be so perfect that he can be liberated by himself.
- but suppose that a Christian could accept this notion, then it would be in conflict with the assertion that Jesus will still find people on the earth at his return. For if people can be freed through reincarnation,

[1] Origen, in his commentary on Matthew, Book XIII, § 1 and 2.

everyone would be free before Jesus' return at the end of time, in which case he would find the earth empty.
- the notion confuses what identity is. If, for instance, John the Baptist is a reincarnation of Elijah, which one is Elijah and which John?

It is striking that Origen did, after all, teach the notion of pre-existence (the soul is eternal, created by God; it descends into a human body, and returns to God via other lives on other levels). The church, in later centuries, regarded this notion as a case of syncretism between Hellenism/Neo-Platonism and biblical belief. But for Origen (and also for other early church fathers such as Justin Martyr) it is essential that an individual have only one life, as a unique person, on this earth: that is what accords with the Scriptures. The notion of a several lives on earth does not agree with Scripture. Whether someone can live on other levels or in other aeons is quite another case. For then he is still one unique soul, which has been visible in the body on earth, and which remains eternally unique. The notion of pre-existence was later condemned by the synod of Constantinople in 551.

Before I go on to the 19th century, there is one aside: the notion of reincarnation reappears from time to time in the Middle Ages in systems of belief closely related to gnosticism (Manicheism, Paulicians, Bogomils, Catharism). We can also note that the church explicitly condemned this notion, although the condemnation did not concern reincarnation as such: To the church the problem was the menace which these groups posed to the church hierarchy, the liturgy, the official theology, and the position of the church in the organization of the state in the Middle Ages.

5. Christianity and reincarnation in the nineteenth century: theosophy

In the last century the notion of reincarnation again came strongly into the fore of Western culture. The Theosophical Movement was very important in this respect; one of its aims was the unity of all world religions.
Their system of belief is as follows:

1) The world is an emanation from God; matter and the corporeal are on a lower level.
2) God and man are identical in their essences.
3) a) Man has more than one life, but in contrast to Hinduism, there is always growth, progression, and evolution in subsequent lives. To be

reborn into the body of an animal in a subsequent life, for instance, is impossible.

b) Man's core is unique and imperishable.

4) The law of cause and effect, the law of *karma*, is essential.
5) Jesus is the one who gives hope, courage, insight, and help in one's evolution. Jesus is the incarnation of the universal cosmic principle of the Christ.

Substitutional suffering, forgiveness, and atonement are explicitly denied by Blavatsky:

> We neither believe in substitutional suffering nor in the possibility of forgiveness of even the smallest sin by a god, not even by what can be called 'personal absolute' or 'infinite,' if something of that kind would exist. We believe in strict and impartial justice. Our conception of the unknown, universal god, represented by *karma*, is that it is a power which cannot fail and therefore does not know wrath or grace, but only absolute justice, through which every cause, large or small, has its inevitable effects. (Blavatsky, p. 184)

6) Man must work out his own salvation. Man himself chooses the way; *karma* is penance, retribution. Man must meet his obligations, and, consequently, love his neighbour. Man can help his fellow man to work out his *karma*; by so-doing, he is also able to work out his own *karma*.
7) Man stands within cosmic relations; in the process of evolution, man occupies the highest place; reincarnation into lower forms is impossible.

Closely related to Theosophy is Anthroposophy, of a somewhat later date. One of the differences is that the revelation of the principle of the Christ in Jesus is much more important. Another difference is that they do not believe that everything which happens to someone is caused by his own *karma*; sometimes things just happen. This will be compensated for, however, in a later life.

Compared with Hinduism and the Gnosticism of the early centuries we could say that Theosophy is closer to the Christian system of belief. There is a place for Jesus; the role of history is no longer cyclical but evolutionary; man is assigned a higher position than other creatures (incarnation in an animal is impossible).

Nevertheless, Christians in the last century repudiated Theosophy, and with it, the idea of reincarnation.
The liberal Protestant theologian Van Mourik Broekman makes the following remarks regarding reincarnation:

- there are many inconsistencies and controversies.
- the notion of *karma* is too superficial; the good and positive power of suffering is not seen.
- God is no longer the sustaining power of life; God's grace does not break through *karma*.

– the views of atonement, liberation and forgiveness are not Christian.
–the notion of reincarnation is deterministic (not fatalistic).
– the notion of reincarnation makes people passive and indolent.

When someone from the liberal camp of Christianity voices such remarks —and liberal Christianity has a positive appreciation of what is universal and valuable in other religions— one can well imagine the objections of the orthodox Christians.

6. Reincarnation in the views of two modern Christian theologians

In the course of the 20th century, and in particularly in the second half of this century, philosophers and theologians have reflected periodically on reincarnation, or tried to integrate it into their Christian system of belief. In this chapter, we will deal with two Roman Catholic theologians who are of the conviction that it is possible for a Christian to believe in reincarnation.

a) Geddes MacGregor

1) In MacGregor's view, the world has come forth from God; but not in the sense of emanation, as is the case in Hinduism, for God remains distinct from his creation. The world is energy, originating from God. We can discern between higher and lower: consciousness is on a higher level than matter, the body is on a lower level than the soul.
2) God and man are closely akin; man is a spark of the divine fire. Yet there is a difference: God is transcendent.
3) Man has more than one life on this earth and on other planets or levels. There is evolution or growth. Evolution and growth take place by living; living has a cleansing effect. MacGregor introduces the notion of purgatory in this respect: it is not a state after death, but life itself. The many lives a man has on earth are, so to speak, different levels of purgatory. This life is part of purgatory.
4) *Karma* is an absolute law: but grace can also influence it. To MacGregor the law of *karma* means that one can attain salvation through one's deeds.
5) God works in Jesus Christ. Jesus gives mankind the possibility of taking the way of evolution and growth. More strongly stated, without Jesus' grace it is not possible to walk the way of growth and evolution. "The self-emptiness of God to which the Christian is called to respond becomes, then, the way of salvation that frees us from

the imprisoning aspect of the karmic law, and enables us to use it, rather, as a springboard for release" (p. 124).

Grace is "the condition of this realization" and

> He [Jesus] liberates me from the burden of my sin, the guilt of which would block my progress. So I am enabled, being restored to health, to struggle on toward the fuller appropriation of the love of God. In short, Christ may be seen, as Christians have always seen him, as providing me with the condition of freeing myself. (pp. 172-73)

(It ought to be noted here that this view may apply to Roman Catholics, but not to the followers of Luther or Calvin.)

Moreover, MacGregor states that Jesus is not the redeemer; that he did not suffer vicariously.

6) Man has to achieve his own salvation, once he has been set on the path. Working is a condition of further growth.
7) Man is a part of the total process of the creation and development of energy; some energy may be lost.

The inclination towards Christian faith is stronger here than in Theosophy. Points 3, 4, 5 and 6 show differences with the classical Christian beliefs mentioned at the beginning of this article (and also vis à vis Hindu beliefs). Grace is more important, and so is Jesus' work; there is no difference between Jesus and the principle of Christ. Corporeality is judged more positively, and working for salvation is founded in grace.

Compared with the early church, however, big differences remain, especially with regard to redemption by Jesus and the place of grace. Reincarnation itself also remains a difference of course. The introduction of the notion of purgatory may be attractive to many Christians, but many will not feel enriched.

b) Karel Douven

In the Netherlands, the Roman Catholic theologian Karel Douven, a member of the order of the Jesuits, has recently devoted himself to combining the notion of reincarnation with the Christian faith.[2] Douven has construed a system which assigns a place to reincarnation. He regards this as possible, being a Christian himself. His system can be summarized as follows:

1) The relation of God to matter is not his primary concern. We can ascertain that there is emanation in terms of evolution. The corporeal is on a lower level: "The earthly personality is only a condensation of that higher ego, that is beyond time, which is our soul."
2) God and man are essentially one. God is alive in man. "I am God on my level, I am God in growth."

[2] The quotations are from an article in "Ons Geestelijk Leven," p. 213-22.

3) There are many lives; one life is too short to do everything; there is evolution and growth. Reincarnation is, "Coming down from the spiritual spheres to these regions of sorrow and unruliness, where we have to endure our tests, and to learn lessons, be they given or chosen."
4) *Karma* exists: "It is a universally operative cosmic law, the law of cause and effect. It operates everywhere; it is adapted to every level. At the purely material level, it is mechanical regularity, while at higher levels freedom comes into play. . . . *Karma,* therefore, is neither punishment nor fate, but a new opportunity, a challenge to do things better."
5) There is a difference between the eternal cosmic principle of the Christ and the man Jesus, in whom it was once incarnated. Man must express the Christ in himself. Jesus is not a redeemer in the sense that he suffered vicariously, thus forgiving all sins. But we can say that the power of the Christ has incarnated itself in this world, and that the whole process of evolution and reincarnation is a process of God's power in this world. In the whole of this process the Christ suffers together with people, helping them. The whole process of evolution, and also the process of spiritual growth, is an expression of God's love.
6) Man must liberate himself: "Redemption, liberation, even if it takes place in 'Christ,' cannot be anything but the continuing self-realization of man, self-determination, power toward self-redemption; these dynamics are built into the whole of creation."
7) Man has been placed within a cosmic and holistic context.

We can see, comparing Douven and MacGregor, that the former is not as closely connected to the classical Christian tradition as the latter. Douven displays more differences and fewer similarities. The structure of his thought is closer to the East. We note how well-known Christian notions have taken on another meaning. But the notion of reincarnation as a process of love in which God suffers together with mankind is new.

As far as we know, no official reactions to the views of these two theologians have been given by the Roman Catholic church.

7. Conclusions

We have seen how there have been continuous attempts to absorb reincarnation into the Christian faith. In the early church, and in the 19th century, this combination proved impossible: because of the context in which reincarnation was found, the church saw it as something incompatible with and essentially foreign to the Christian faith.

As far as we can tell, it was not vibrant in the religiosity of the common people either. In this respect, we cannot speak of syncretism. In this century there are again Christians within the churches —among them theologians— who are willing to accept this idea. We can see then, that reincarnation never comes on its own; there is always a close connection with *karma* and self-redemption (although the meanings of the terms are prone to change their content). Beliefs originating from Christian faith are modified, particularly the place of Jesus' work (substitution) — and the place of grace and forgiveness. (Quite often a distinction between Jesus and the Christ is made in this regard.) In Douven's case it is particularly evident how his views on reincarnation have changed his views on the work of Jesus Christ, on the relation God and man, on the person of Christ (or rather of the Christ and Jesus), and on man's way to redemption. We also note differences between Douven and the Hindu view we have presented: Jesus plays a role, there is a suffering of God together with mankind, there is an evolutionary-linear conception of history, and the aspect of love is important.

MacGregor, as we have already seen, is closer to the Christian tradition, cited at the beginning of this article. In Douven's case, we note that the above mentioned Christian convictions have clearly been altered. It would be possible to speak here of a syncretic Christianity (Christosophy). With regard to MacGregor, matters are more complicated. His view is more closely connected to the classical Christian beliefs (they are interpreted in a different way, but not so different that they depart from classical Christian tradition, in my view); but there are still two great points of difference:

- the work of Jesus Christ, who does not atone by substitution, and does not forgive sins. Consequently man must go it alone although there is the aid of grace.
- the place of the corporeal, and along with it, the uniqueness and non-recursiveness of the human being. Reincarnation always entails that the physical is on a lower level.

Here we must ask to what extent these essential beliefs within the Christian tradition are unalterable. At the beginning of my article, I started with the doctrine formulated by the early Christian church. But in the course of the ages, changes have occurred, for Christian doctrine is not static. There are differences between Roman Catholics and Protestants, especially with regard to the nature and scope of Jesus' grace, and to the place of Jesus. It is no accident that the two theologians cited are Roman Catholic: their thought diverges precisely in the area of grace and forgiveness.

Are Christianity and reincarnation incompatible? If we compare the views of the latter two authors to the doctrine of the early church, which has been determinative until now, we see that these beliefs are incompatible. Specific aspects of this comparison which form stumbling blocks are the views concerning Jesus' work and person (along with the role of substitutionary atonement and vicarious suffering, absolute grace, and forgiveness). By accepting the notion of reincarnation, these beliefs are either changed or take on an altered meaning; and moreover, new elements are introduced, which were unknown to the early Christian tradition (*karma*, evolution).

We are bound to note here, as an aside, that many people in the Christian tradition who more or less accept the notion of reincarnation are unaware of such theological relations and connections. To them, their belief in reincarnation stands on its own, and can be interesting and helpful, but it is not a well-considered system.

We also have to note that the notion of reincarnation can be more easily linked to some so-called heretical movements in Christian history, than to the church itself (Christian Gnosticism, Pelagianism, Alchemy).

Bibliography

"Reincarnatie: Pastorale ervaringen." *Ons Geestelijk Leven* 63 (1986): 213-222.

Blavatsky, H. P. *The Key to Theosophy*. Pasadena: Theosophical University Press Agency, 1985.

MacGregor, G. *Reincarnation in Christianity: A New Vision of the Role of Rebirth in Christian Thought*. Wheaton, Illinois, 1978.

Origen. *The Writings of Origen*. Ed. A. Mensies, tr. J. Patrick. *The Ante-Nicene Fathers*, IX. Edinburgh: T. and T. Clark, 1864; rpt. Grand Rapids: Eerdmans, 1980.

Mourik Broekman, M. C. van. *Geestelijke Stromingen in het Christelijk Cultuurbeeld*. Amsterdam: H. Meulenhoff.

Chapter 16

Religion in an Alien Context: The Approach to Hinduism in a Western Society

Corstiaan J. G. van der Burg

Traditional 'orientalist' approaches to Hinduism fail to contribute towards research on dialogue and syncretism with respect to Hinduism as a minority religion within Western society because they generally lack tools appropriate to making a serviceable analysis of such a local variety's position. Since Western Christian theology is only on the threshold of a serious encounter with Hinduism, its contribution to a better understanding of Hinduism in all its local facets is limited as yet; it must base itself too heavily on the available orientalist material. There are indications that an approach which takes into account the fact that culture is a dynamic process related to social and economic conditions, and which acknowledges the inequality of power in majority–minority relations, is more rewarding for dialogical discourse in a plural Western society. Such a 'minority approach' is sooner to be found in the social sciences, which are also capable of providing a suitable conceptual framework.

1. Introduction

Although European culture has experienced a marginal but growing influence from Indian religions for centuries, it is only in the last decennia that the presence of the adherents of some of these religions is taken seriously by official institutions in European countries, particularly in the United Kingdom and the Netherlands.

The arrival of Hindu migrants and refugees from Suriname in the seventies greatly contributed to the establishment of Hindu religious institutions in the Netherlands.[1] Moreover, it not only added to the already

[1] The mere fact that Hindu religious institutions could be established in the Netherlands gives rise to more fundamental questions about the nature of Hinduism itself. How is this religion capable of surviving in an alien cultural context, apparently without giving up much of its identity? In other words, what makes Hinduism survive, and what kind of Hinduism will eventually survive in the Netherlands? However relevant

existing minority problem, but it also confronted Christianity once more with the presence of another world religion on its own ground. The main concern of this paper is therefore not the Hindu side to this confrontation, but rather the Christian side. Its purpose is to frame some practical and conceptual problems which inevitably turn up the moment Christians encounter a local variety of a world religion with which they are already in dialogue.

The present article describes and evaluates the different ways in which Surinamese Hinduism in the Netherlands can be approached within the framework of research on dialogue and syncretism. It is argued that in general the traditional 'oriental' approaches to Hinduism fail to contribute towards such research because they lack tools appropriate to making a usable analysis of a local variety of a world religion. It is therefore suggested that an approach which conceives of Surinamese Hinduism as the religion of an ethnic minority in the Netherlands could be more successful. This is because it takes into account two factors which are particularly important for the analysis of a minority religion. It sees culture (including religion) as a dynamic process, by relating religion to social and economic conditions, while on the other side, it acknowledges the inequality of power, linking the minority position of this ethnic group to the position of power on the part of the dominant culture. The paper concludes by noting that the latter approach could be a promising one for dialogical discourse, provided that due attention is drawn to the specific use of religion by a minority group in terms of survival strategies.

2. Surinamese Hinduism as 'Hinduism'

It is not too far-fetched to contend that the ways in which Hinduism is generally presented to Western Christianity have been strongly influenced by orientalist as well as by Hindu and Christian theological presuppositions which underpin various approaches to the study of this culture (cf. Jackson, 218).

This means, first of all, that there is a certain 'orientalist perception' of Hindu culture which determines to a large extent our overall picture of Hinduism. It is a biased perception of Indian civilization, which has grown historically and which has been too long dominated by the old colonial order (Burghart, 224ff.). It dates from the time in which colonial Britain needed clear-cut and intelligible conceptions of the civilizations it ruled. This perception has "above all led to a picture of Indian society as static, timeless, and spaceless, and dominated by the Brahmans as the

---

such questions may be, we cannot answer them until much more field research has been carried out.

guardians of the sacred order of society" (Cohn, 7). The same holds true for Indian religion; for example, the caste system —held to be the backbone of this religion— was presented as a static, ahistorical phenomenon by the Brahmanic ideology, since the castes were divinely ordained. It was furthermore supposed that Hinduism did not exist outside the caste system, let alone that it could survive without it.

From a holistic point of view, Hindu society through the ages is seen as essentially based on a system of ideas, values, and structuring principles pivoting around hierarchy and ritual purity by which all relations in the cosmos are regulated (Dumont 1972). The caste system is then the social elaboration of these principles. Its inherent inequality is explained religiously by the Brahman theologians, who made it socially acceptable by reference to their scriptures.

According to the same unitary Brahmanic world view, the confusing plurality of the Hindu religious reality should be reduced to the One Reality, the Primeval Principle to which everything owes its origin. Burghart rightly remarks that we should constantly be wary of the ideological significance of such essentialist notions (p. 246) which do not further the relationship with Hinduism and only confirm prejudices and misconceptions, running the risk of creating their own reality (Van der Veer 1987: 81).

A related controversial issue concerns the use of an ideological model of Hindu civilization, derived from the Indological interpretation of Sanskrit texts. On the basis of references to a selection from the textual tradition, which has been inspired by classical Brahmanic views, an abstract, timeless picture of Hindu culture is presented, with rather ideological overtones. Van der Veer is right in pointing out that such a method, if it were applied to European civilization, would meet much criticism and would be rejected as untenable (1986: 65). The major objections against such an approach is that it attaches too much importance to a specific class of religious literature. This literature is, historically speaking, not only too remote from contemporary reality but it also presents only a partial view of social cultural reality, while being of dubious social importance. Already in the sixties, the Indologist Van Buitenen observed that those who wished to understand modern Hinduism should take the study of much more recent texts as their starting point (Van der Veer 1987: 81). By this we wish to indicate that some of the most influential sociological and Indological approaches to Hinduism still accepted and widely followed in our time, are of litle help in analyzing a variety such as contemporary Surinamese Hinduism.

Since research on dialogue and syncretism falls more within the province of comparative religions, we next set our hopes on their approaches to the matter. These could be successful with respect to a minority religion provided that they are aware of modern developments in the scholarly approach to such a minority culture. Otherwise they run the risk of adhering too closely to the same preconceptions discussed above. This can be accounted for partly by the fact that scholars of comparative religion, like anthropologists (Van der Veer 1986: 66), generally borrow from Indologists, who for the most part are unsure about what material is relevant for contemporary Hindu believers. In this way, many of their findings could remain irrelevant to the study of dialogue with (contemporary followers of) Hinduism. In addition, not only anthropologists, but many scholars of comparative religion as well "seem to have adopted the *'emic'* view that there is an unchanging scriptural source for contemporary beliefs and practices. This view is fundamentally a theological one [Hindu or Christian, or both?] which is highly detrimental to anthropological research (and to comparative religious studies as well)" (Van der Veer 1986: 66).

Due to the important role which has been attributed to the textual tradition, a possible side effect of such unintentionally adopted misrepresentations might be the (wrong) impression that Hinduism puts as much emphasis on maintaining correct doctrine and faithfulness to the scriptures as certain forms of Christianity do.[2] The opposite is actually the case in this culture, where respect towards divine and worldly authority is considered far more valuable than abiding by doctrinal truth. Particularly in 'social,' i.e. *karmatic* Hinduism, 'orthopraxis' is regarded much more highly than orthodoxy. In this connection we would be hard put to find the *'sola fide'* of monotheistic Christianity —not to mention the *'sola scriptura'*— in a religion which is almost obscured among divergent ways of salvation, innumerable 'gods' and 'holy men,' as well as 'holy scriptures.' Instead, great significance is ascribed to worship in establishing group identity.

Taking all the factors mentioned above into consideration, it seems rather ironic that the variety of Hinduism which is the subject of our study not only lacks a caste system but also pays lip service to the textual tradition for want of a monastic organization. It would scarcely be entitled to the predicate 'Hindu' according to the criteria mentioned.

We will take up the issue of the caste system as an example of what we are trying to explain. The caste system is no doubt one of the most important features of Hindu society and religion. It divides the whole of society into a large number of hereditary groups which are hierarchically ranked according to the religious principle of purity derived from a holistic world view. We might call it a 'total' system, since it organizes almost all aspects of social life.

---

[2] In this connection it should be emphasized that syncretism should not be limited to religious doctrine or content alone. The term should also include the practices as well as the religious organization and the 'public face' of religion. (Cf. H. Vroom's Introduction to his article, p. 26)

Although Surinamese Hinduism originated in North Indian Hinduism, it differs significantly from it (Van der Burg and Van der Veer, 515ff.). North Indian Hinduism has a dual structure of meaning and organization, i.e. Brahmanism and sectarianism, each with its own relationship to the caste system. Surinamese Hinduism, on the other hand, lost this duality as well as its close relationship to the caste system, which could not be maintained after the labour migration to Suriname. A kind of Hinduism developed there which contained elements derived from both the previously mentioned forms of religion. As a consequence, the key notion of 'purity' underlying both society and religion has become a mere sentiment in Surinamese Hinduism, colouring but not determining religious practice and discourse.

In fact, a process of Brahmanization took place: after the period of indentured labour, the Brahmans not only resumed their position as religious specialists, but they were even able to extend their authority to areas hitherto closed to them. Within a few decades they managed to gain a monopoly position in an informally structured network of patron-client relationships concerned with officiating in rituals. Up to now, this informal network has been practically the sole form of organization in this kind of Hinduism, in Suriname as well as later in the Netherlands. This rise of a Brahmanic priestly hegemony is closely connected with the absence of the aforementioned sectarianism in Surinamese Hinduism, which basically involved ascetic monastic orders. These ascetic sectarian communities, as exponents of a philosophical attitude of world-renunciation, form a counterbalance to the worldly attachment of social Hinduism which is based on the caste system. For in Hinduism these ascetics are the ones who watch over the purity of doctrine and who provide it with a theological basis. The fact that such a sectarianism was absent deprived it of its most important religious spokesmen in Surinamese Hinduism. As a consequence, Surinamese Hinduism has enjoyed great doctrinal liberty for more than a century, hardly limited by the rather arbitrary doctrinal standards stressed by the Brahman priests, the only extant religious authorities.

There is no point in judging such a casteless Hinduism according to the sociological and Indological criteria mentioned. In that case, it would be measured by characteristics of an artificial academic construct of 'Hinduism,' leaving no scope for development in terms of reinterpretation and redefinition.

This is sufficient to indicate that the various ideologically inspired approaches to Hinduism —from the Hindu as well as the non-Hindu side— are unsuitable to adequately analyzing Surinamese Hinduism as a specific variety of Hinduism. They fail to draw the developments which Surinamese Hinduism has undergone into their analysis for at least two reasons. First, they stick to an incomplete and distorted picture of Hinduism as being a static, monolithic, and timeless culture. But religion should not be regarded as a cultural system of meaning divorced from social change. It is not 'given' or 'static,' but conditioned by changing social circumstances (Asad). Second, the power factor is insufficiently discerned as a factor, even though it plays a prominent role both with respect to those doing the describing and the descriptions themselves. Our concern is therefore to find an approach which is free of the drawbacks noted.

3. Surinamese Hinduism as a minority religion

It can be assumed that just as the kind of Hinduism formed in Suriname appears to be fundamentally different from the Hinduism of the native country after a 115 years, so the transition to the Netherlands should entail equally radical changes. The external and internal factors involved involved in these transitions appear to be only partially the same. The formation of the (religious) organization in the Netherlands which has resulted from a constant interaction between internal cohesion and external confrontation, must be analyzed from a perspective which focusses on the course of this process of change during the last 115 years in Suriname, as well as on the new possibilities and limitations which the Dutch situation presents.

On the one hand, the organization of Hindu religion in the Netherlands is conditioned by patterns which were already apparent in Suriname. The informal patron-client relationships between priests and laity are still the backbone of the religious organization. More formal organizations had established themselves with time in Suriname, in which the laity had also acquired a voice, in addition to the priests. Such formal religious organization in the Netherlands, however, has actually been deformalized, despite semblances to the contrary, as evidenced by the existence of numerous foundations (Van der Burg and Van der Veer, 523). This is because the laymen seem to have much less control over the entrepreneurial activities of the priests than in Suriname. On the other hand, the welfare organizations appear to be pursuing religious aims, along with their efforts to perpetuate their ethnic identity. The political lobby for the subsidized building of temples, for example, points in that direction. The influence of government policy upon the religious organization of Hinduism cannot be underestimated in this respect, and this deserves analysis as well. In addition, the effects on religion of the policy of de-concentration —which was launched in the seventies in order to distribute ethnic groups evenly throughout the population— as well as the effects of sharing in government funds through the mediation of welfare organizations and local authorities demand scholarly attention in this connection.

In giving a succinct outline of Surinamese Hinduism in the former section, we have already omitted a number of characteristic elements which in Western scholarly circles are regarded as being 'received standard Hindu.' In like manner, the Dutch variety confronts us, as we have tried to show, with problems of continuity and change under the influence of varying social conditions which could not have been solved by the conventional approaches mentioned earlier.

In order to arrive at an analysis of Surinamese Hinduism which is better suited to our purposes, in terms of studying its dialogical and syncretic capacities, and in order to do greater justice to its development into a 'Hinduism in its own right' —a part of whose characteristics we have already seen— we must resort to a less traditional approach.

Our suggestion is that we would obtain a much clearer understanding of Surinamese Hinduism if we were to approach it first of all in its capacity as the religion of an ethnic group in the Netherlands and only secondly as a part of universal Hinduism. Only then can we pose relevant questions to it, so that its characteristics are better manifested. With regard to research, we should begin with a set of analytical instruments different from those discussed above. Such analytical instruments are sooner to be found in the social Sciences, which are also capable of providing us with a conceptual framework suitable to our analysis.

As an ethnic group, then, the Hindustani minority can be viewed as a social entity which stands out from others by virtue of common cultural characteristics such as origin, history, language, or religion, that function as symbols and definitions of the specific nature of that entity. Thus, the identity of this group is based on cultural data, of which religion is one of the most important. In many cases such an 'ethnic' religion (see also Burghart, 232) is subordinated to the aspirations of such a minority group. In other words, it can be used as an instrument to maintain the group, to sustain its 'difference,' or even, if required, to improve its position.

An important advantage of opting for such a 'minority approach' to Surinamese Hinduism, is that we will be able to see such religion from the perspective of its 'being different,' or from the perspective of the group improving its position. Such a religion can be made into a serviceable vehicle for almost any aspiration of the group. That is to say, it can only be serviceable when it is flexible. And this is precisely one of the chief traits of a minority ethnic group's position, namely, that its culture, and by implication, its religion, have an inborn dynamism and flexibility, maybe more than the culture of a majority group or a group which is settled in its own cultural environment. This is the reason why the cultural data of such a group are constantly being redefined in the light of the variable power structures and clashes of interest which the group is subject to.

We are now in a position to see the relationship between the two religions involved in its true proportions, that is between a dominant official religion and a dominated one. That such a relationship is unequal is something which needs no argument.[3] Such an unequal relationship is by definition based on power. As Droogers correctly observes in his Introduction (p. 16), "When the social context involves cultural plurality, the power struggle may be not just between clergy and laity, or higher and lower clergy, but between different cultures. Official religion, whether imported or indigenous, almost always acts as a dominant cultural factor." In our case, this means that Surinamese Hinduism will constantly be subject to divergent intentions and aims from both within and without. A power dimension in religious contacts could lie end to end with the dynamics of a minority culture, in our opinion: because of the dominant culture's power, the minority culture has to be dynamic in order to have at least some freedom of action.

What are the implications of such an unequal relationship?

First, this means that the dominant culture will generally be in a position to remodel the minority culture because it controls the relationship between the two. Minority religions are thus more and more transformed within the context of the dominant culture, in spite of the minorities' attempts to preserve their culture and vernacular language (Burghart, 250; Pocock). Differences in circumstances and in the conception of religion lead to divergent reactions at this point, as the following shows. In an article on the religious life of Hindu immigrants in England, Pocock tells us how the Pramukh Swami, spiritual head of a certain Gujarati *sanstha* (religious society), advised the devotees resident in the United Kingdom to 'emulate the Jews' in making their adjustment to British society. "Simple and sensible as this advice may seem at first blush," Pocock remarks, "it encapsulates a host of problems." Although he can well imagine that "the Jews in Great Britain today provide an attractive model for any immigrant community who at the same time have strong religious convictions," Pocock is right in recalling that the Jews have been subject to a continuous process of adaptation, conscious debate, and examination of what was essential to their religious identity, in order to preserve their religion in an alien environment, ever since the time of the Babylonian captivity. When a Hindu leader in England takes the Jews as an example for believers in 1975, he can only be alluding to the result of an arduous, centuries-long process of adaptation —the emergence of distinctive religious culture capable of co-existing with a secular one. Curiously enough, it is

[3] Inequality of power is normal in any relationship. Equality is exceptional. So, analyzing the inequality of a given religious encounter is much more rewarding than merely stating that the encounter is unequal in terms of power. (Cf. Droogers in the Introduction to his article, p. 8.) This is something he himself readily agrees with, a little further on.)

precisely such a distinction between religion and society (or culture), between the sacred and the secular, which is contrary to the reports of what 'eternal Hinduism' has always advocated to the faithful. This leader of a British minority religion apparently saw the separation of religion and society (or culture) as the only possibility to survive.

This conception is in sharp contrast to what spokesmen of Surinamese Hindus in the Netherlands advocate to their fellow believers. These authorities do their utmost to maintain that such a separation of 'Church' and 'State' or between religion and culture is thoroughly inappropriate in Hinduism's case. Worse yet, it would deal it a fatal blow. Hinduism, they claim, is not a religion in the Western sense, but is a 'way of life,' characterized by a total integration of the various sectors of life. These Dutch Hindu leaders are quite apparently far from 'emulating the Jews' as yet, far from adapting or even examining what is essential to their religious identity. The problem is that if they do not exert themselves in making decisions on these issues, the society encompassing them definitely will, and has in fact already done so, since Surinamese Hinduism has already undergone a first adaptive phase. Already in Suriname, Hinduism was transformed from a culture enmeshed with its own society to an ethnic religion amidst other religions. Or would the ideology of 'being a Hindu' perhaps have a better chance of being accepted by the Surinamese in the Netherlands due to their lack of knowledge of Hinduism? Or is Surinamese Hindu culture perhaps as useful as it is in forming a political ideology aimed at improving the group's position in the encompassing society precisely because of its vagueness? (cf. Jayawardena). In the latter case the notion of the inseparability of 'religion' and 'culture' would fit well in this ideological perspective.

Second, this inequality of power implies that minority religions are sometimes forced by the dominant culture to behave and to organize themselves in this instance like Christian churches in order to survive or at least to be accepted. Thus, a certain pressure can be observed on Surinamese Hinduism from the side of the dominant culture to develop from a family and home religion to a congregational religion with a clear organization and structure and publicly recognized representatives and spokesmen.

Furthermore, these Hindus are increasingly assessed by criteria which are set by the dominant culture, so that in reaction they begin to see their religion and themselves through foreign eyes (Burghart, 243). Thus, as adherents of a minority religion, they are forced to make choices vis à vis the encompassing world in terms of a religious stance, and to make clear pronouncements about the meaning of their religious practices and the validity of religions conceptions, something which they have not been accustomed to as adherents of a minority religion in India or Suriname. The tendency by the encompassing society to see in every Surinamese

Hindu a fully versed and authentic exponent of the totality of his religion also contributes to this effect even though knowledge of one's own religion is not equally divided among Hindus either. The point here is not that one does not take the other seriously as a mature believer, nor that one shows less esteem for the religion of the common man, but that more is ascribed to him/her than can be reasonably expected. And it is the nature of Surinamese Hinduism to evoke this expectation often, in view of the absence of theological experts and the greater doctrinal freedom which has ensued. Such an approach often does little justice to the religion at issue, being informed by the aforementioned notion, which assumes that cultures (including religions) are timeless, static, and water tight compartments, separated from each other. Terms are then used such as "*coherent* religion pattern" (Pye), "*autonomy* of components" (Colpe), and "religions as (symbolic) *systems*" (Berner; see Droogers' article, p. 11-12). To be able to analyze Hinduism with greater success, however, as a minority religion forced to reinterpretation at numerous points in the light of its new context, an approach informed by the concept of culture as a process is to be preferred, all the more since such a conception averts more or less normative statements about other religions.

Lastly, in respect of the minority culture this means that we have to grow accustomed to the notion that such a religion —due to the role which religion plays in a strategy of survival and identity formation— is more flexible, innovative, and creative, but also more internally contradictory and, particularly, more difficult to grasp within our frame of reference than we are inclined to expect of a 'world religion' as we know it from books. This is one of the reasons why the "clerical perspective," a perspective of the "doctrinal and the official" —one adopted by many students of religion (Droogers, p. 15)— is inadequate for scholarly investigation and analysis of minority religions. The interest of scholars of religion in minority religions has accordingly been rather casual for a long time. Such religions hold little appeal for them since they have no link to established knowledge. Surinamese religion in particular is typically vague in respect of doctrine and organization, its history showing many deviations from 'doctrinal' and 'official' Hinduism, rendering it rather unrewarding to traditional scholarly inquiry.

4. Conclusion

Saying that Surinamese Hinduism in the Netherlands should be studied as a minority religion will hardly evoke surprise. Still, this suggestion does hold advantages for our knowledge of and relation to Surinamese Hinduism, and, accordingly, for our dialogue with it.

This opens the possibility of paying more attention particularly to the strategic importance of Surinamese Hinduism, to its strategic utility and its effectiveness, both with respect to its substance as well as its form. Not only can we square accounts with the old stereotypes concerning Hinduism, for they will no longer serve, but this enables us to take into account power as a factor in the encounter between Christianity and Hinduism. We are now perhaps better capable of seeing that syncretism can be the by-product of a minority situation, elicited, as it were, by the dominant culture, without either party being conscious of this.

Likewise we would then be in a position to reflect further on the notion of culture as a dynamic process. Apart from the theoretical question of whether culture should always be conceived of as dynamic or not, it will be clear that there is a world of difference in this regard between the interpretation of culture (including religious culture) in the conventional approach mentioned above, and the understanding of culture in 'minority' theories.[4]

As an ethnic group, the Hindustani community can no longer be considered a monolithic entity with one ambition and one aim. There are distinct religious traditions, factions and interest-groups. Their religious culture has therefore been made subservient to a multiplicity of intentions and objects. Consequently, it will continue to be subject to reinterpretation and re-use with regard to its form, content, and function, under the impact of changes in power-relationships and clashes of interest taking place within the group itself as well as in the encompassing society.

It is for this reason, particularly in view of the conceptual difficulties inherent to issues of dialogue and syncretism with respect to a minority religion, that we opt for an approach which is open-minded enough to take all these circumstances into consideration.

---

[4] One further remark about describing other religions, as an aside. It is said that "ideally, religious scholarship interprets and describes another religion in such a way that a believer would recognize himself." This is certainly a worthy aspiration in view of dialogical encounter, but it is not the premier task of religious studies. Just as do other areas of scholarly inquiry which deal with religion, religious studies should provide scholarly and tenable descriptions and interpretations of religious phenomena, even if the adherent of a religion does not always recognize himself in them. For such an adherent, even if a scholar himself, generally does not use a Western scholarly instrumentarium and Western scholarly categories to describe her faith. This circumstance alone renders recognition of his faith in what Western scholars write concerning it quite unlikely. So-called description of another religion 'from the inside out' is therefore not only an extraneous objective, but also unattainable for Western religious studies.

Bibliography

Asad, T. "Anthropological Conceptions of Religion: Reflections on Geertz." *Man (NS)* 18 (1983): 237-59.

Burg, Cors van der and Peter van der Veer. "Pandits, Power and Profit: Religious Organization and the Construction of Identity among Surinamese Hindus." *Ethnic and Racial Studies* 8 (1986): 514-28.

Burghart, Richard, ed. *Hinduism in Great Britain: The Perpetuation of Religion in an Alien Cultural Milieu.* London, 1987.

Cohn, B. S. "Notes on the History of the Study of Indian Society and Culture." In *Structure and Change in Indian Society.* Eds. M. Singer and B. S. Cohn. Chicago, 1968, pp. 3-28.

Dumont, L. *Homo Hierarchicus.* London, 1972.

Jackson, Robert. "Changing Conceptions of Hinduism in 'Timetabled Religion.'" In *Hinduism in Great Britain: The Perpetuation of Religion in an Alien Cultural Milieu.* Ed. Richard Burghart. London, 1987.

Jayawardena, Chandra. "Culture and Ethnicity in Guyana and Fiji." *Man (NS)* 15 (1980):430-450.

Peacock, D. F. "Preservation of the Religious Life: Hindu Immigrants in England: A Swami Narayan Sect in London." *Contributions to Indian Society (NS)* 10 (1976):341-365.

Veer, P. T. van der. *Gods on Earth: The Management of Religious Meaning and Identity in a North Indian Pilgrimage Centre.* Thesis, Utrecht, 1986. An English edn. is forthcoming.

——. 1987. "De Illusie van een Oude Beschaving." *Sociologisch Tijdschrift* 14, 62-83.

PART III

RECAPITULATION

Chapter 17

Dialogue and Syncretism: Some Concluding Observations

Dirk C. Mulder

Dialogue and syncretism is the overarching theme of this publication and of the symposium in which these articles were presented. The purpose of this final article is not to try and summarize the contents of the earlier articles or of the discussion during the symposium, nor to point out similarities and tensions between the different views of those who have contributed to the symposium and to this volume, but rather to make some concluding observations and if possible, to lend clarity to some of the problems discussed. Interreligious dialogue was our main concern, but our discussions on interreligious dialogue— on its possibilities, its rules, its risks, its limits, its goals— had a special twist: We discussed interfaith dialogue in relation to the issue of syncretism. That is why this final article is intended to deal first with syncretism, and then to make some observations concerning interreligious dialogue and its relation to syncretism.

1. On syncretism: The point of view of religious studies

"Syncretism is a tricky term." These are André Droogers' first words in the first article in this publication. I am afraid that the reader will not be under the impression that its trickiness has disappeared upon reading the articles. Let me have another go at it. I will start with some observations from the point of view of religious studies, sociology of religion, and religious anthropology, in short, from a non-theological, non-evaluative, let us say, neutral point of view, if such exist.

Let us begin by stating that in the course of human history religions, or religious currents, have met; or to phrase it more precisely, people of different religious traditions have met. Such encounters have taken place universally, even though their results have been different. There may have been rejection or indifference with respect to the other religion, but more common by far has been a process of interpenetration
adherents of one religion adopt and assimilate elements f

religious tradition. A similar process can also occur with respect to elements from another culture, or from social structures other than those in which a religious tradition originated.

When should we then speak of syncretism? If we use Droogers' definition (p. 20), syncretism includes an element of contest. Syncretism is *contested* interpenetration. This leads us to two points: a remark and a question.

The history of interreligious encounter and interpenetration provides ample evidence that 'foreign elements' (in the sense of elements from a different religious, or possibly cultural, provenance) are certainly not always incompatible. Many religious traditions have been very successful at taking over foreign elements and amalgamating them with their own original tradition, without causing any tensions, and it would appear that it is possible to do so both consciously and unconsciously. If we were to stick to the definition of syncretism as contested interpenetration, then such cases exhibit no signs of contest, and consequently no syncretism has occurred. For a particular religion, a student of religion could then establish in an objective, non-evaluative way which foreign elements have either penetrated and been accepted and/or which have been contested.

But then the question remains: contested by whom? The scholar of religion (as well as the historian, sociologist, and anthropologist) should restrain himself on this point. He is not the person to contend that a particular element is so foreign to a religion's original tradition that it is contestable, or should have been contested. As far as I can see, the student of religion can only observe, and state that a particular element has been contested or is contested —yes or no.

Let me give an example to clarify the point. Some Islamologists especially Western (Christian) Islamologists, think that the absolute distance between God and the believer is the central idea in Islam. The white-hot majesty of God makes impossible a relation of love between the Muslim and Allah. Islam allows only the relation of master and servant. How can one then explain *tasawwuf* (mysticism), which plays such a tremendous role in Islam and in which one does encounter a relation of love and intimacy between man and God quite clearly? These Islamicists would then reply that mysticism is a foreign element in Islam, and is incompatible with Islam's original traditions. This, however, is an assessment Islamicists have no right to make. Only Muslims themselves have the right to decide whether or not mysticism is incompatible with their own tradition. At most, Islamicists can explore whether mysticism has been contested by (some) Muslims, but they should refrain from stating that it is contestable or ought to be contested.

That brings us to the second point, a question: When a foreign element is contested (and of course that is often the case), by whom is it contested? Here the matter of power comes into play. Foreign elements are very often contested by those who are in power, by religious leaders, by theologians, etc. We should be aware of the fact that the same foreign elements contested by some, may be accepted by others. It is not uncommon that they are accepted by the mass of believers though contested by the religious leaders. Occasionally the opposite situation occurs. Religious leaders and thinkers accept foreign elements, but the grass roots-believer rejects them. Such would seem to have been the case with nineteenth century Protestantism in its relation to modern culture. In any case, the student of religion can and should examine only the factual situation. It might be wise to use the term interpenetration, in order subsequently to investigate whether this interpenetration has been contested and, if so, by whom. The neutral term interpenetration is to be preferred to the term syncretism because it would appear almost impossible to rid the latter of it pejorative connotation. That is why it would seem better to use syncretism in religious studies only to describe those occasions when it is observed that some religious people consider certain foreign elements incompatible with their religious tradition and, as a result, dub acceptance of such elements syncretism.

2. On syncretism: Theological considerations

Theological points of view did surface during the workshop on dialogue and syncretism, and properly so, in my opinion. A theological reflection on syncretism has validity in its own right. Lest we cause great confusion, however, the religious studies approach and the theological approach should be kept separate, at least at the initial stages. (They can be consolidated and engaged in dialogue with one another later.) We should also keep in mind that there are many theologies (or philosophies) of religion. Not only do we distinguish between Jewish, Christian, Muslim, Hindu, and Buddhist theology or philosophy of religion, but even within Christian (or Jewish, Muslim, etc.) theology, there may be several variations. I must limit myself to a few observations, mainly about Christian theological reflection on religion(s).

In the first place, there are many theologians, past and present, who have a negative view of syncretism: they belong to the contestors. Syncretism to them is an attempt to integrate foreign elements into the religious tradition which conflict with the original content of that tradition. To put it differently, such an effort is branded as syncretism, and syncretism has a clearly pejorative connotation here. Hendrik Kraemer, who left his mark on the Protestant discussion of syncretism in our century during decades, can serve as an example. His views can be summarized as follows. Religions can be divided into two categories. On the one hand, there are naturalistic, monistic religions aiming to attain self-realization; on the other, the prophetic religions in possession of divine revelation — Judaism, Christianity, and Islam to a certain extent. Syncretism is characteristic of the naturalistic religions, whereas the prophetic religion of biblical realism fails to exhibit such syncretistic tendencies, but tends rather to adopt an exclusivist attitude (Kraemer 1938: 210). Syncretism is a perennial threat to the distinctive character of the Christian message's truth.

Linked to this and to related opinions —and this is my second observation— there is a tendency by Western theologians and missiologists to warn the so-called 'younger churches' in the Eastern/Southern hemisphere against this threat of syncretism. This warning is frequently directed against interreligious dialogue as well. I noticed this tendency very clearly at the fifth Assembly of the World Council of Churches in Nairobi in 1975. A report had been submitted on the still pristine efforts of the WCC's subunit on dialogue, which recommended engaging people of other living faiths in dialogue. It was subjected to severe attack by some theologians and church leaders from the Northern/Western hemisphere. They were afraid that the purity of the Christian faith would be eaten away by syncretistic elements. This led to great irritation, particularly among Indian and Asian representatives for whom dialogue is a matter of life and death. Their reaction was to state that Western Christian religion is not all that pure either, and that it was totally valid to absorb valuable elements from non-Christian religions into the Christian faith. M. M. Thomas, the well-known Indian Christian thinker, ventured to speak of Christ-centered syncretism (this time using the term in a positive sense!).

The discussion is still raging. There are still many Christians, particularly of the evangelical brand, who are convinced that their faith is pure, untainted, and non-syncretic. But more and more Christian theologians are having second thoughts about syncretism, theologians from the Western world, as well as from the East and the South. They discern an opportunity to learn from other cultures, and possibly to rid Christianity of its all too Western features. They are taking the opportunity to introduce and assimilate elements from other religions in their own Christian reflections seriously. They generally prefer not to use the word syncretism in such cases, however, because it would appear very difficult to rid it of its pejorative connotation. If we were again to use Droogers' definition here, we would conclude that there is no contest and hence, the term syncretism is inapplicable.

It can hardly be denied, at any rate, that this issue will figure prominently in future discussion in missiology, theology of religion(s), and systematic theology in general.

To wrap up this first part of my paper, I suggest that use of the term syncretism be limited to contested religious interpenetration. That means employing the word in religious studies only in such cases where religious interpenetration appears indeed to be contested. We then could then ask: By whom and for what reason? I would give (Christian) theologians the advice to recall that the Christian faith has undergone and assimilated interpenetration by elements from foreign cultures and non-Christian religions and philosophies since its inception, and to ponder that this process is bound to continue. It is up to them to decide where and when this process may be accepted, and when it should be repudiated. (Subsequently they may, if they so desire, call it syncretism.)

3. On interreligious dialogue and 'syncretism'

The question is frequently posed whether the willingness to engage in interreligious dialogue presupposes the readiness to accept syncretism, and more often whether such dialogue does not inevitably lead to syncretism. However, in order to remain consistent with the first part of this paper and its suggestions concerning the use of the word syncretism, it would appear to be necessary to reformulate the questions.

The first question can be put in the following way: Does interreligious dialogue presuppose willingness on the part of the partners-in-dialogue to accept 'interpenetration,' to accept the possibility of being influenced by elements of truth in the other's religion, and of having to accept them. To put it in another way: does it presuppose the willingness to temper the claims to truth on the part of one's own religious tradition?

On the basis of my own experience I am inclined to say that this is not the case. I have attended many dialogues between convinced Jews, Christians, Muslims, Buddhists, etc., where willingness to accept the other religions' claims to truth was not a prerequisite. There are, of course, certain prerequisites for real dialogue. To mention an obvious one: the prerequisite of willingness to respect the other's faith. But to respect does not mean to accept. There is an opportunity for mutual witness in interreligious dialogue; there is a meeting of commitments, to use an expression coined by Dr. Samartha, former director of the World Council of Churches' dialogue program. We ought to listen to the witness of our committed counterparts with an open and respectful mind: we should likewise bring our own witness in a spirit of openness; but we do cannot demand in advance that the partners-in-dialogue temper their beliefs and convictions, or show a willingness to accept the other's point of view.

What then is the basis for interreligious dialogue? As far as I can see, it cannot be something akin to the lowest common denominator. I can recall a multilateral dialogue in Colombo in 1974, attended by Hindus, Buddhists, Jews, Christians, and Muslims, where there was little we could agree upon: not on the existence of God, nor on transcendence or the absolute, nor on a common spirituality or faith. But we did agree on the following points:

- the belief in the basic oneness of mankind, in the brotherhood of man, in the responsibility of man to man;
- the conviction of the inherent inviolate dignity of the person, a dignity conditional neither on his or her adherence to specific convictions or doctrines, nor on his or her sharing in specific insight or revelations;
- the demand for dedication to the promotion of peace and of social and economic justice, and to the struggle against social, economic, racial, and religious discrimination.

And so our co-humanity, our being human together, created the basis for interreligious dialogue.

In 1983 the World Council of Churches' subunit on dialogue convened a second multi-faith consultation, this time on the island of Mauritius. It was held in preparation of the WCC's Assembly in Vancouver and its theme was "The Meaning of Life." The final message, unanimously approved, reads:

> In our dialogue we spoke from the standpoint of our religious and cultural traditions, and we listened carefully to one another. We came to understand more clearly where we differ. But also we discovered where we converge and can affirm basic values and hopes together as religious people, not at the 'lowest common denominator,' but at the very heart of our deepest commitments and convictions.
>
> We share an affirmation of the fullness and the deep inter-relatedness of all life — human life to life, human life to the life of the world of nature, and all life to its divine source.

Now this is a beautiful example of what can happen in an interreligious dialogue. In Mauritius we did not engage in dialogue with a relativistic attitude; each embarked with his or her own deep commitments and convictions. But during the course of our discussions we discovered a certain amount of convergence, certain common values and hopes concerning life and its meaning. We all also accepted a common responsibility to pursue justice, not only on behalf of those of our own religious community, but for all people, and to oppose the tremendous threats that endanger the future of life in our world today.

That brings us to the second question: Does interreligious dialogue necessarily lead to interpenetration (some theologians would say: to syncretism)? Perhaps the word 'necessarily' is too strong. I know of many dialogical encounters which resulted in a better mutual understanding, a deeper mutual respect, a greater readiness to cooperate in the field of social justice, but not necessarily in a tendency to accept 'foreign elements' by integrating them into one's own religious tradition. On the other hand, there are a growing number of theologians or religious thinkers —mostly of Christian persuasion— whose theology has been considerably changed by the experience of dialogue with a different religious tradition. Some are trying to develop a 'theology of world religions.' Since the history of inter-faith dialogue is still very young, we will have to wait and see how things develop. But I have the strong impression that this venture will have deep effects on the future of religious experience and religious thought. Very few partners-in-dialogue will retain their original convictions unaltered. Most probably the results will be comparable to the intra-religious dialogue by the (Christian) ecumenical movement, with its growing convergence of denominational traditions and its growing inter-denominational cooperation, but also to its backlashes and tensions.

4. Some concluding remarks on interreligious dialogue

Two questions always crop up in the discussion about inter-faith dialogue, especially within circles of Christian theology and missiology: the question of truth and the question of salvation. Although it is impossible to deal with these questions adequately within the framework of this article, I will venture to make some observations because these questions were also touched upon during the discussions of the Amsterdam symposium.

To use Friedmans' expression: In dialogue there is an encounter between "touchstones of reality" (Friedman, p. 78). This means that people using different touchstones of reality meet in inter-faith dialogue, if I understand him well. Assuming that they are committed people —a meeting of commitments!— they can be expected to adhere to these touchstones, to the criteria of true insight into the fundamental problems of God or no God, of life and death, of man and the cosmos, as these themes have been developed within their respective religious traditions.

The question is, whether a criterion to decide between these different touchstones of reality exists, a kind of meta-touchstone. As far as I can tell, the possibilities of a rational scientific answer to these problems is limited, as are the possibilities for verifying or refuting these insights. I am inclined to put it this way: The most fundamental problems of human existence, such as,

- Is there a God?
- What is the meaning of life?
- What is the position of humankind within the totality of the cosmos?

cannot be solved by ratiocination, by human reason and rationality, or on the basis of scientific criteria. They can only be answered by convictions, be they religious or 'weltanschaulich,' which lie beyond all reasoning. If this is correct, then the importance of interreligious dialogue is not to reach common convictions on the basis of meta-religious criteria, but to achieve an attitude of mutual respect, of mutual willingness to listen and to learn, of mutual readiness to cooperate for the well-being of all humankind in spite of our differences on the touchstones of reality.

To make a short digression, I foresee a growing problem for Christian systematic theology since some theologians are in deep and serious dialogue with Buddhists, others with Hindus, others again with Muslims, and not a few with Jews. All of them attempt to introduce values of these religions into their own Christian thought. They pass over and come back, to use John B. Cobb's beautiful expression. But in the long run, systematic theology cannot be content with all these different 'dialogical theologies' existing side by side. It will have to try and integrate them. Will that be possible? A tremendous task still lies ahead in this regard, to be sure. It might even become one of Christian theology's greatest challenges in the near future.

I will conclude with an observation concerning the issue of salvation. Hans Küng has reproached the Protestant theology of religion for side-stepping the question of salvation in non-Christian religions (Küng 1987: 218). To a certain extent he is right. Roman Catholic theology has grappled much more seriously with this question, and some Roman Catholic thinkers have contended that all religions are ways of salvation in a certain sense. I can only make a few very short notes.

1) We should be aware of the fact that salvation —in the sense of *Heil,* harmony and wholeness, as opposed to *Unheil,* disharmony and brokenness— is not an unambiguous idea. All people would appear to pursue *Heil* and to avert or overcome *Unheil.* Yet religions (religious currents, and even religious individuals) would appear to differ severely concerning what exactly *Heil* and *Unheil* entail.

2) History teaches us that many religions (including Christianity!) have been and still are responsible for a tremendous amount of disharmony, harm, and suffering. Countless people have suffered and continue to suffer the effects of persecution, strife, and war. That is why I hesitate to view religions per se as so many ways of salvation. Their role has often been too negative to deserve such a positive appraisal.

3) The problem of salvation is not identical to the problem of truth. It is not necessary to have a full understanding of the truth in order to be on the way to salvation. For those who are convinced that salvation —final salvation— comes from the beyond, that is, from God, it is fully possible to allow the possibility that God may open the way to salvation for people in spite of their lacking or limited insight.

God loves humankind and wants it to be saved. That is a statement of faith, of course, theological for that matter, and not scientific. But this conviction can certainly be an incentive towards dialogue, and it can create an openness for listening to and learning from people of other faiths —God's people!— without the fear of 'syncretism.'

Bibliography

Kraemer, H. *The Christian Message in a Non-Christian World.* London/Edinburgh, 1938.

Küng, H. *Theologie im Aufbruch.* Munich, 1987.

INDEX OF NAMES AND AUTHORS

GENERAL INDEX OF SUBJECTS

generated aselectively by computer search facility

CONTRIBUTORS

CORSTIAN J. G. VAN DEN BURG, Indology, Institute for the Study of Religion (ISR), Free University: Amsterdam.

HANS DAIBER, Arabic Studies, Faculty of Semitic Languages, Free University: Amsterdam.

ANDRÉ DROOGERS, Cultural Anthropology, Faculty of Social-Cultural Studies, Free University: Amsterdam.

REIN FERNHOUT, Religious Studies, Faculty of Theology, Free University: Amsterdam.

MAURICE FRIEDMAN, Religious Studies, Philosophy, & Comparative Literature, San Diego State University: California.

JERALD D. GORT, Missiology and Evangelism, Faculty of Theology, Free University: Amsterdam.

JACQUES H. KAMSTRA, Comparative Religion and the History and Phenomenology of non-Christian Religions, Faculty of Theology, University of Amsterdam.

REENDER KRANENBORG, New Religious Movements, Institute for the Study of Religion (ISR), Free University: Amsterdam.

DAVID J. KRIEGER, Evangelische Studiengemeinschaft for Inter-religious Relations: Zürich.

DIRK C. MULDER, History and Phenomenology of non-Christian Religions, Faculty of Theology, Free University: Amsterdam.

MATTHEW SCHOFFELEERS, Religious Anthropology, Faculty of Social-Cultural Studies, Free University: Amsterdam.

RICHARD DE SMET, Hindu Philosophy, Jñānadeepor Vidyāpeeth, De Nobili College: Poona.

WALTER STROLZ, Religious Studies, Former Moderator of the Publications Program on Interrreligious Encounter for Herder Verlag: Innsbruck.

HAROLD W. TURNER, Former Director of the Centre for New Religious Movements, Selly Oak Colleges: Birmingham.

TILMANN VETTER, Buddhist Studies, Faculty of Letters, Rijksuniversiteit: Leiden.

HENDRIK M. VROOM, Philosophy of Religion, Faculty of Theology, Free University: Amsterdam.

ANTON WESSELS, History of Religions and Missiology, Faculty of Theology, Free University: Amsterdam.